# BETTER
# OR WORSE?

# BETTER OR WORSE?

## HAS LABOUR DELIVERED?

POLLY TOYNBEE
AND
DAVID WALKER

BLOOMSBURY

First published 2005

Copyright © 2005 by Polly Toynbee and David Walker

The moral right of the authors has been asserted

Bloomsbury Publishing Plc, 38 Soho Square, London W1D 3HB

A CIP catalogue record for this book
is available from the British Library

ISBN 0 7475 7982 2

Typeset by Hewer Text Ltd, Edinburgh
Printed by Clays Ltd, St Ives plc

All papers used by Bloomsbury Publishing are natural,
recyclable products made from wood grown in well-managed
forests. The manufacturing processes conform to the
environmental regulations of the country of origin.

# Contents

# Introduction

'The Work Goes On' was all the red campaign mug said. It was an unelectrifying message for a low-wattage campaign. Don't expect much, was what Labour ministers and candidates seemed to say as they went uninspired through the motions of an election that was no contest.

Flying back from Sedgefield to London on 8 June 2001, Tony Blair's entourage noted his melancholy air. A mighty victory, a never-before second Labour landslide, but where was the glory? The lowest turnout since universal suffrage had scuffed the shine. Labour had been allowed to win an excessive landslide on the votes of just a quarter of electors. Labour won fewer votes than when Neil Kinnock was defeated by John Major in 1992.

Elections to the House of Commons were unreformed – as much because of the Labour Party's conservatism as its leader's. As its first term ended, making representation fairer was not even on the back burner; electoral reform and proportional representation was at the back of the deep freeze and was going to stay there.

Excuses abounded. People don't vote when they are broadly content. Give them a second chance – the mood seemed to say – let's see if they can deliver this time. Anyway, why bother to vote when the result was certain? Psephologists were not panicked by the apathy: voters would be back whenever there was next a hot contest, they said.

Those election months had been ill-starred. Lingering anxiety about foot and mouth disease on the farms delayed polling for weeks. By night the television news showed Homeric hecatombs, with pyres of cattle, hooves pointing skywards in acrid smoke. It was as if some foul miasma had wafted off the land. But the media exaggerated and misreported, seizing on an event as if deliberately to wound the incumbent government. Foot and mouth was a mere blip in agricultural incomes and the reaction of farmers had alerted some country-dwellers to the economic facts of life – walkers and tourists were far more important to the rural economy than Old Macdonald and his rusting tin eyesores.

The election campaign had stretched the little the government had to say into tedium. Labour's manifesto was a sorry document, its signposts pointing backwards and forwards. Modernisation with conservatism, progress yet stability, wealth for the few alongside equality for the many. Triangulations designed to deflect Tories and their press assassins served also to sour loyalty and sap enthusiasm.

The parties, some jaded commentators said, had inched so close you could not stick a parliamentary order paper between them. But it was a lazy lie that voters had no choice. Labour pledged to spend more than ever before on health and education. Tory leader William Hague, who had shrivelled over the months into a petty Poujadist, sported a 'Save the Pound' lapel badge and promised to cut tax, which meant cutting spending. There was an ocean of blue water between them.

## A Quarter Bottle of Champagne – and Back to Work

At Millbank, Labour's soon-to-be-vacated headquarters, there were no hubristic celebrations. Campaign commanders kept the party modest: a quarter bottle of champagne each. In truth there was not much exuberance to cork. Tony Blair had nothing memorable to say to the party faithful: they heard a weary re-run of his stump speech before they went off to bed. Next day, the Work Went On.

Except it didn't. Where, asked the new Leader of the Commons plaintively, was the pipeline of new legislation? The cabinet had failed to stock the cupboard with new ideas and it was bare. What puzzled onlookers in the summer of 2001 was the absence of a flight path.

New Labour had been the wonder of Whitehall when it arrived in 1997, as they hit the runway with armfuls of precise plans, Brown especially. In a flash the Bank of England was set free. Devolution was enacted, referenda held. The minimum wage was established, hereditary peers all but banished and a score of other promises made flesh. By contrast they ambled into their second term with no more sense of renewal than schoolchildren back from a brief half-term break.

Wait for the second coming, Blair had said to visitors to his Downing Street study. His next term would be the time to define him and New Labour, he said. Just as Thatcherism was not invented as a doctrine until well after her second election victory when she discovered privatisation, so Blair would unveil his true self.

It made sense. After all, Labour had taken office in 1997 constrained by its promise to stick to Tory spending plans. Public spending actually fell as a proportion of national output in those two years. Hindsight says the hair shirt could have been thrown off much earlier, but the pledge did not just clinch public trust in Labour's fiscal discipline, it reassured the holders of capital that socialism really was a dead duck.

## A Slow Start

That two-year freeze meant that by 2001 the great spend was hardly under way. The vehicle of state took time to grind through the rusty gears into hiring staff and expanding programmes, more used to cuts than expansion. There were no reservoirs of talent and experience, no ready-trained staff to manage growth in everything from urban regeneration to the newly minted primary care trusts.

Now here was Blair, an election-winner beyond Labour's historical dreams, waiting to carve his legacy on the stones of history. He didn't. In the weeks after the election he created, in a confusing welter at the centre of the state, a Delivery Unit, an Office of Public Services Reform and a Strategy Unit – but delivery, reform and strategy had to wait for almost a year. Nothing much happened until Gordon Brown's budget in 2002 cascaded cash and programmes.

## European Ambitions

But by then the world had spun on an 'axis of evil'. Blair had discovered a mission far more compelling than anything the domestic scene could offer. Yet whatever it was Tony Blair had wanted to be known for, it could not have been Iraq. During the first term his attention was captured by foreign affairs; in their turn, sooner or later, every occupant of Number Ten is bedazzled by the ambassadorial cables and the transcripts marked Top Secret. Those seducers from the Joint Intelligence Committee turned up in his study with their charts and presentations for his eyes only. Saddam had caught his attention, but Iraq was nowhere near the top of the foreign affairs in-tray. It was the papers on Europe that Blair had ringed in felt tip. The European Union was both his greatest opportunity and his greatest political risk. In those days he would tell all-comers of an historic mission. The UK would head for the heart of Europe and lead in Europe, no less. It never happened.

As he slipped back into Downing Street that June morning, with none of the razzmatazz and cheering of four years previously, Blair had already been stymied by Brown's refusal to prepare for sterling joining the single currency. Outside the Eurozone the UK would slip to the margins of the European enterprise, along with Sweden and Denmark, small countries and the only other refuseniks. But Brown was now in control of the UK's European destiny. He had been allowed to set and assess the five tests for euro entry before deciding when – if ever – the time was right, and so had acquired the one policy Blair saw as his claim on history.

Circumstances were also unhelpful: the stability pact depressed growth in the Eurozone; the German giant had still not digested the East; Europe lacked an appetite for military spending to make active global diplomacy credible. The great British public and the great British press were hostile, clinging to incoherent Eurosceptic notions of their place in the world.

## Saving the Welfare State

Europe might be Blair's mission, but if you asked Labour MPs or ministers, their first priority was the welfare state. In 1997 it had been under threat. Thatcherites, economists and City slickers said it could not survive: it was too expensive, needed radical reform and besides the era of what they derided as 'monolithic' state-provided services was over. A wealthier population no longer needed collective provision, they claimed. Look how many employers now offered private health insurance. An individualised, atomised, consumerist society would inevitably abandon it. The belief proved remarkably durable, even surfacing in 2004 as Liberal Democrat thinkers strove to give their party 'radical' credibility.

Although the Conservatives had made little progress in dismantling the welfare state in their eighteen years, it was prudent to fear for its future. After so many low-spending years, a tipping point could come when under-investment would turn the tide of opinion. In 1997 public services looked worn and shabby, private affluence, public squalor indeed. It was Labour's mission to prove that money could bind the welfare state into the twenty-first-century future. The first term had been talk; now Labour must – the word was everywhere – deliver.

## The Big Spend

The cash was committed. When Tony Blair had suddenly promised that UK health spending would rise to match European Union average levels within five years, it had sounded preposterous. In other circumstances the fact such a stupendous promise was realised would have guaranteed a quick answer to the question which gives this book its title – better. England was likely to hit the EU average in 2005, Scotland had the year before.

The promises were breathtaking and the public was heartily in favour. In schools as well as the NHS, people wanted rapid improvement and the wind was in the sails of a government pledged to spend, spend, spend. Labour think-tankers and ministers in their private moments felt this was the welfare state's last chance. It would be the end of the road if a government with a vast majority and a fat Treasury could not secure services of which the country could be proud. So could they deliver?

In the second term disagreement within the Labour Party about how best to operate the state grew wider. The self-appointed modernisers wanted the state to be a purchaser on the citizens' behalf, striking the best deal from the best providers, public or private. It didn't matter which. On the other side were those who insisted that public services provided by public servants had a special ethos, irreplaceable qualities among which was equity. The citizen was not a customer, but a partner in a great collective endeavour.

## Social Justice

However, both sides were Labour politicians who, mostly, had entered public life in order to change the social landscape. They had already pledged in their first term to abolish poverty and prise open new paths to upward mobility for those left behind in the last decades.

But social justice had barely been mentioned at election time, for fear of alarming middle England. Labour had to keep the taxpaying classes happy while redistributing some of their money to the disadvantaged. People were partly aware of this sleight of hand. The polls showed ambivalence: over 80 per cent said Britain was too unequal yet they were equivocal about paying to make it fairer. But then they rarely heard the case for greater equality put by anyone in power.

## The Decline of Trust

One reason for writing this book is the dismaying gap between what happened during the past four years – as measured by figures, charts, laws passed, pounds spent, results achieved – and people's perceptions of public services. The public barely gave what the Labour government did a grudging shrug. Why were ordinary people so suspicious of statistics, wary of enthusiasm and more inclined to believe the cynicism of the press than the evidence of their own eyes? In the rough and tumble of parliamentary democracy politicians might expect little gratitude – or not until they are safely long gone and remembered with nostalgia. But Labour struggled – and fights still – against a cultural handicap in a climate of curmudgeonly disbelief that anything ever gets better.

Labour helped create it, over-claiming with figures semi-cooked as ministers pretended they were spending more than they were at first. 'Spin' was the word that stuck. Alastair

Campbell and Peter Mandelson, brilliant architects of New Labour, became mythic boiler-room stokers of factoids. Yet spin was a compound, a reaction against the prejudicial culture of British journalism, distinct press partisanship, cynicism among Labour's press advisers with poisonous rivalry between Number Ten and Number Eleven partly to blame.

In the second term, trying to banish the spin accusation, tough targets were set to cover everything that moved and breathed. Some, as we will see more than once in this book, were ludicrously over-precise. But this, surely, was an approach to honest government. Look, see, here are the results, Labour said, opening the books. But what good were the numbers to journalists who could not tell their median from their mean and a public with a limited grasp of quantity or probability? Maths was a poor substitute for conviction, and Labour leaders never offered quite enough of that.

## Political Reporting

Despite the number of newspaper titles, despite ostensible competition between the printed and broadcast press, political reporting ceased to be pluralist and its style, honesty and seriousness of intent changed. The right-wing biases in the newspaper press were not matched by biases in support of the government. There were left-wing biases too, in the *Guardian*, and in the *Mirror* and the *Independent*, which both struck out wildly to the left in an attempt to arrest circulation decline. But a bias in favour of this Labour government was nowhere to be seen.

The near mortal row that exploded between Downing Street and the *Today* programme on Radio Four sprang from a long grievance that BBC news programmes had adopted the sneeringly hostile tones of the raucous aggression in the press. Some individual journalists attempted to stem the tide of unreasoning bullying: John Lloyd tried to instigate a debate on standards; Peter Riddell, the *Times* columnist, despaired about coverage of the diplomacy prior to the Iraq war: too much of it was 'ill informed and superficial'. It reflected all too well 'the debasement of journalism in Britain'. There was sometimes less mission to explain than to attack. Political reporting turned into a sport, with politicians the butt of contempt and ridicule. Visitors to the UK were often aghast at the incessant crudity of the press in its assault on the political class. At times the media seemed to make the country almost ungovernable.

So the art of surviving the media became the principal skill and prerequisite for success in politics. Journalists cried crocodile tears when Estelle Morris resigned as Education Secretary in 2002: it was they and their antics she was escaping.

## Perception and Reality

Ministers were frequently demoralised to the point of despair by the growing gap between reality and popular perception. But consider the plight of the citizen who needs to know how well it is governed. Hardly surprising that poll after poll reflected precisely this popular perplexity.

Asked how the NHS or education or crime was faring, they said things were worse or much the same. But asked how they saw their own local school, GP or neighbourhood policing and they expressed rising satisfaction. They noticed the extra teachers, new buildings and clinics. They appreciated the footfall of more police on their streets and, despite the weekly crime horror stories in their local papers, they told pollsters they felt crime had fallen in their area. But they all thought their patch was the lucky exception to a state of the nation that they viewed through the dark glass of the media where everything was always going from bad to worse. So loud and certain was the media's blast, so graphic their anecdotes of a medical disaster or a violent crime, so eager were hostile commentators to use these as exemplars for sonorous condemnations that people felt forced to believe what they read or saw on television before they trusted the evidence of their own eyes.

## What was Labour for?

This is not a book about personalities or Westminster man-oeuvrings, up or down, in or out. It is not much about political ideologies, right versus left. We have tried to keep our eyes on actual outcomes so far: what was promised, what happened, what worked and what didn't. What, we asked at the end of *Did Things Get Better?*, did New Labour really want to accomplish in office? In that book, published ahead of the 2001 general election, we said Blair's historic achievement had been to make Labour electable again. But what, as the twenty-first century began, was New Labour *for*?

In the chapters that follow, we attempt to be fair adjudicators of what Labour did next, what successes Labour can claim and what might have happened anyway. Did things get better by 2001? We answered with a qualified affirmative. By 2005? Across Blair's second term falls the shadow of Iraq and for some its darkness occludes everything. Blair, they say, does not deserve light to be shone on his domestic dealings. The war and its aftermath did not, however, loom large in the daily lives of the majority; the condition of surgeries and schools mattered more, and personal bank balances flashing up at the cash dispenser most of all. Did things get better? This book is our answer.

## CHAPTER ONE

# Healthier?

On June 23rd 2004 Michael Howard blundered at prime minister's questions and inadvertently tugged on the tiller that was slowly turning the great liner of public perception about the NHS under Labour. Public opinion lagged far behind reality and it was taking years to persuade people that the NHS really was improving.

He did what the public tended to do when they assessed changes in health and relied on an anecdote. That morning in the Commons Mr Howard turned to his own troops with a look of glee. He taunted the Prime Minister with the tale of a woman (never named) in his Folkestone constituency who had been told she had to wait twenty months for radiotherapy for breast cancer. 'Why can't she get choice?' he demanded. Blair was flustered.

Except the constituent did not exist. Howard's staff had relied on rumour. No one was waiting twenty months in Folkestone or anywhere else in England. The most anyone had waited of late was fourteen weeks and that was for low-risk cancers where it was clinically safe to delay radiotherapy as a follow-up to other treatments. Labour's record was far from perfect, but no shrouds could convincingly be waved.

Labour had at last done it, immunised itself from the charge that there was nothing to show for the big increases in spending. Whether it had *enough* to show was to become its bugbear in the latter part of the second term. But for the moment the government could boast that nearly all – 99 per cent – of patients a GP suspected might have cancer were seeing a specialist within a fortnight.

## Waiting Lists

The day after that Commons episode was when Health Secretary John Reid was due to update Labour's ten-year strategy for health, which had been published in July 2000. In its place came a new five-year plan. The maximum wait for an operation would now be just eighteen weeks – the target to be reached by 2008. More important, the average wait would be only nine or ten weeks. This surely was further evidence of 'delivery' and tangible results from the spending boom. Between 1997 and 2005 cash spent on the NHS doubled. In spring and summer 2004 the money was cascading in and – provided Labour stayed around to realise its promise – annual real terms increases of over 7 per cent would continue at least until 2008.

So Reid invited the public to compare the new promise that no one would wait more than eighteen *weeks* with the eighteen-*month* maximum Labour had inherited in 1997. Even that figure had been something of an economy with the truth as the Major government had only started the clock from the day a consultant put someone on a waiting list. There were long waits to see a consultant and after that further waits for tests and their results. Some consultants even kept an unofficial waiting list for access to the waiting lists by delaying appointments.

Labour had abolished these hidden waits. The clock was now to start on the day a GP first referred a patient to the hospital to the day the consultant wielded the scalpel. If soon it was going to be only a matter of weeks between a worried visit to a GP, through outpatient appointment, tests and scans till surgery itself, this was an earth-shaking change. Since 1948 the NHS had subsisted on long lists. They held costs down, rationing by delay. An NHS without a slow shuffle along a queue was unimaginable. But in Labour's second term it was happening. Complaints abounded, about nursing, cleanliness, equality, community care, chronic conditions, mental health and nursing homes. But waiting had been the single most complained-about feature of the NHS since the days of Nye Bevan and now it was ending. American doctors who wanted an example of 'socialised' medicine and why the United States should never have a national health scheme always pointed to NHS waiting lists. No longer. Perhaps it was time for those highly paid American physicians to start attending to lack of access to care for forty million under-insured and completely uninsured people among their fellow citizens; to start explaining geographical and racial discrimination in care across the United States and the explosion of dead-weight costs associated with private health insurance bureaucracy, lawyer-proof testing and surgery that did nothing to reduce illness or enhance life expectancy.

## Does the NHS Produce Health?

Once balm had been applied to the sore of waiting lists, what next? In the second term Labour nipped and tucked across the face of the NHS, while pumping anaesthetising money in – the commissioning scheme, hospitals' identities, contracting arrangements were all changed. But Labour chose not to ask penetrating questions. What did NHS spending buy in health *outcomes*, how long we lived or the likelihood of contracting cancer or diabetes? Deaths from circulatory diseases (heart and stroke) – the most common cause of mortality – had been tumbling for two decades, the most striking annual drops coinciding with the years the Tories had spent least on the

NHS. Cancer deaths and mortality due to respiratory disease were on the decline too, though less dramatically. 'It is not clear,' the Office of National Statistics (ONS) said drily, 'how far the NHS has contributed to each of these improved outcomes, and how far they are due to higher incomes, better housing and other changes.'

## Money

Labour was following a trend across the advanced countries where health spending as a proportion of national income, stable in the 1990s, had been rising. In the United States during the period Blair was in office, health spending grew over twice as fast as the economy at large. In many countries, the Organisation for Economic Cooperation and Development (OECD) said, costs were pushed up by advances in medical technology, buoyant public expectations and the needs of ageing populations. In the UK it was a deliberate policy because the government 'realised that cost containment during the 1990s had strained their systems'.

The strain had indeed shown. In the first term, the famous television doctor and Labour peer, Robert Winston, said the health service was worse than Poland's. Anxious, in 2000 Blair made his promise to raise UK health spending as a proportion of GDP to the EU average. Soon after the 2001 election, Gordon Brown laid his plans by commissioning Derek Wanless, formerly of NatWest, to review the long-term needs of the NHS.

In time for Brown's three-year forward spending plan in 2002 Wanless delivered a devastating analysis and justification for huge extra spending. This, late in the day, was what Labour might have done first thing: open the books, throw up their hands in horror and make an intellectually robust case for spending more. This was Brown at his best. The case made, he pegged an increase of 1p in National Insurance (NI) to NHS needs. There was even a stab at fairness since at the same time he lifted the NI ceiling, making the better off pay proportionately more.

So it was only in the second term that NHS spending, £67.4bn in 2004–05, geared up. There was so little dissent that the Conservatives were soon obliged to promise that they too would match the largesse. In 2000, when Blair made his famous pledge, UK health was 6.8 per cent of GDP and the EU average was then 8 per cent. Blair had said the UK would get there by 2006. Parts of it were there in 2004. Scottish NHS spending was £1,593 per head compared with £1,396 in England and it hit the EU average a year early. England would realise Blair's promise in the year he stipulated, 2006 (or sooner if average EU GDP fell or desperate French and German efforts to cut their health spending were successful).

Under Gordon Brown's three-year spending plan from 2005 UK health spending was to rise to over £100bn a year or some 9 per cent of GDP – the bulk of it NHS. Superlatives were in order. But Derek Wanless had warned that the rate of growth of NHS spending was above what 'could sensibly be spent'. Making good use of the extra money was – he said euphemistically – a considerable management challenge. Richard Douglas, the NHS finance chief, started warning what would inevitably follow once the rate of increase tailed off after 2008. Some managers of this largesse were fearful. If they did not deliver, could the NHS survive? Wouldn't the anti-welfare-state voices call for it to be broken up and resort to private insurance (despite its profound problems, as the Germans and French were discovering)?

Extra money had taken the waiting out of wanting to be treated. By March 2004 there were only forty-eight people in the whole of England who had been waiting longer than nine months for an operation. The total number of people on any waiting list was the lowest for fifteen years, while the number of hospital admissions had risen by 22 per cent. The winter of 2003/04 had admittedly been mild but Sir George Alberti, the emergency care chieftain, had pronounced it the best ever. Flu jabs had been carried out on demand and unknown thousands of older people given some respite from infection. Despite a large increase in numbers of patients seen during the winter, waits in accident and emergency had been cut, 96 per cent of patients seen within four hours. Waiting on trolleys for admission was rare – always more likely to be the result of some local concatenation of circumstances than system failure. Was this freak or harbinger?

Even more impressive than recruitment were the figures for enrolments on clinical training courses, up 61 per cent for doctors, 53 per cent for nurses. Soon England's relative low ratio of clinicians to patients would approach Scotland's, then other European countries'. And test results would come through quicker as the NHS had expanded numbers of scientific and technical staff by 27 per cent.

Everyday treatments were getting easier to access. Some forty-three walk-in centres had been opened since 1997, near to where people worked, compensating for the lack of instant access to GPs' surgeries. If they did want to see their GP, patients were promised they would get access to see a nurse within twenty-four hours and a doctor within forty-eight hours – targets that were 97 per cent met by March 2004. NHS Direct took 6.4m telephone calls a year and NHS Online, the website, 6.5m hits a year. Ambulance response times were slowly improving, 75 per cent of life-threatening emergencies reached within eight minutes.

As well as new hospitals, there were twenty-six new NHS Treatment Centres offering fast-track cold surgery on joints and eyes, with another twenty in development plus thirty-two such centres operated by private companies. There were to be eighty by the end of 2005 supplying a quarter of a million operations a year, a means of keeping waiting lists permanently low. As well as the programme for revamping GPs' health centres, some 286 primary care centres were in construction, bringing primary care and community services into one-stop shops.

This exhausting list is far from exhaustive. The number of patients referred to hospitals remained satisfactorily static, as more GP surgeries offered minor tests and treatments. That was one reason the number of prescriptions rose, as did the cost of drugs, which went up by 25 per cent. One reason for the increased cost was expansion in the number of those given high-cost treatments, for example statins prescribed to all those at risk of heart failure.

People took the benefits for granted but statins were an example of UK practice being as good as, if not better than in most other advanced countries. As a new drug, strictly trialled, statins had been approved and rolled out under the watchful eye of the National Institute for Clinical Excellence through the agency of local doctors who by and large could be trusted to prescribe in the interests of their patients, not because they had been seduced by pharmaceutical company advertising or because they had been ordered to do so by central authority.

## Reform

Other intractable questions loomed. What did the conventional indices of patient activity and consultants' workload really measure? Did numbers waiting – or numbers treated – say much about the effectiveness of treatment? Medical inputs were not at all the same as people feeling better. The NHS was wrongly named, said pundits, as it is really a sickness service, patching up and making good. Numbers of operations and hospital bed allocation are poor measurements of citizens' true state of health. Besides, hospitals account for only 10 per cent of what the NHS does: most health work takes place in GP surgeries and in people's homes.

Those were questions for analysts. Labour had pledged itself to upfront delivery so that became the be-all and end-all of Blair's second term in health. But Labour convinced itself – though not clinicians or NHS managers – that a precondition for delivery was structural reform. In the past, reform had been a substitute for spending, squeezing more out of a cash-starved service. Now reform was for reassurance. But was there any causal connection between tinkering with the structure and improvements in patient care? Experts looked at the NHS since 1948, 'reformed' on average every six or seven years since its start, and they registered their scepticism. Ministers always arrive thinking they are in command of a PT boat when really they are on the bridge of an aircraft carrier and, besides, had got their gold braid because they were the prime minister's pet not because they had any experience in running a mega-organisation. Then they depart, long before the ship has half-completed its manoeuvre. Hierarchies shift, name plates change, regions, areas and districts are shuffled like cards, while precious time and energy is wasted on people re-applying for jobs under newly configured authorities and in reinventing the wheels on the hospital beds. The one thing the NHS begs incoming governments not to do is 'reorganise' but they always do. Both the Liberal Democrats and the Conservatives had their own brand new grand reorganisations ready and waiting in 2005. It's what politicians do.

## The Internal Market – Yet Again

In 1997 Labour had castigated the Tory 'internal market' as privatisation. Once in office they kept the motor of that market with GPs pretending to purchase care from hospitals and Labour re-badged it. The point was to establish what hospital procedures cost; it was known to vary giddily. Labour junked district health authorities and brought GPs into entities at first called primary care groups; they were later amalgamated and redesigned as primary care trusts (PCTs). GPs and not managers would be in the driving seat, which sounded politically appealing. They would even get notional 'budgets' to spend. The hope was that by letting them keep half of any savings for their own surgeries, they would provide scans and X-rays in their clinics and save the expense of sending people to hospital as outpatients.

If so, this reform would look remarkably like the GP 'fund-holder' model promoted by Tory Health Secretary Kenneth Clarke in the late 1980s. Now there was a fixed tariff for treatments with no competition between hospitals on price, only on speed and quality. The tariff was first worked out for a limited group of conditions, but by 2008 every problem diagnosed by a GP would have a price. The trouble was, PCTs had fixed budgets. What if the tariffs did not allow hospitals to recoup the actual cost of care? This was already causing some hospitals acute anxiety, as we shall see below.

## Primary Care

Some 75 per cent of the money allocated to the NHS budget would be controlled by PCTs but first there had to be a shakeout, as health authority staff re-applied for positions in the PCTs. The plan demanded more finance staff, and capacity constraints showed. By 2004 one third of PCTs still had no finance directors and the NHS Confederation was damning in its assessment of the competence of PCTs to do the business. In the brave new world of Blair's NHS that meant a market opportunity: maybe private companies could do the commissioning on contract? Simon Stevens, the Prime Minister's special adviser on health, resigned from Number Ten to become president of the European arm of an American company planning to do precisely that.

This move caused a stink made all the riper by the decision of the highly respected editor of the *British Medical Journal*, Richard Smith, to join the same outfit as chief executive. Cabinet secretary Sir Andrew Turnbull stepped in, extending the period before Stevens could lobby the government. His company, United Health, turned over £15.5bn a year and saw the NHS as a fertile field. Might it, for example, contract with the NHS to supply the 'community matrons' the government envisaged helping maintain the aged and those with chronic conditions at home?

Clinicians' lives improved in Labour's second term because their contracts were renegotiated at a generous rate and their hours cut. Hard to evaluate but important was the growth of NHS Direct and NHS Online which together with the new walk-in centres gave the public speedy and direct access to advice and offered hospitals a sort of triage service. After dropping in 2001, the number of patients seen by GPs picked up – though not at night. Under a new contract, which came into force in December 2004, GPs could choose to opt out of providing a 24-hour service – and lose £6,000 a year. Some nine out of ten looked likely to. PCTs scrambled to provide new out-of-hours services. Might NHS Direct coordinate it? The rate at which GPs prescribed drugs and treatments grew fast, too. Labour chose not to address upfront the various anomalies of general practice. GPs remained for the most part small businesses. Little was done to push more primary care doctors into salaried status, which might have delivered a more rational and more equitable distribution of them and their time.

## Foundation Hospitals

In the first term Labour had created regional hubs where specialist medicine would be practised and to which outlying district hospitals would refer their hard cases. All the evidence showed that general surgeons killed people with cancer and heart disease in droves; specialists were better. But this widely welcomed plan was blown apart when Alan Milburn arrived as Secretary of State for Health in 1999, full of the reformist talk that so infuriates health professionals. He called it a monolithic, old-style, one-size-fits-all, take-it-or-leave-it service and played no small part in making 'choice' and 'personalisation' watchwords of Labour's second term. The rational distribution of resources and specialisms was a secondary consideration.

Labour had calmed the fiercest aspects of the Tory 'internal market', where hospitals had outbid one another to offer lower prices to health authorities and fund-holding GPs. But in the second term competition between hospitals sharpened again.

New Labour think-tanks and policy advisers such as Paul Corrigan, at Milburn's side, advocated non-profit trusts in health and social services. They would be more responsive to local needs and provide much needed competition to councils and the NHS. As 'foundation' trusts a certain number of hospitals would be beacons, showing what clinicians and entrepreneurial managers could do once cut free from red tape.

## The Row

So foundations would be 'independent'. But the suggestion that they would be outside the NHS caused one of the loudest shouts of dissent heard from the Labour Party during the second term. But if the protests showed Blair the limits of his embrace of a 'mixed economy' in the supply of public services, it did not stop him trying to demolish other customs posts on the boundaries between public and private sectors. In his vision the NHS would remain as a funding body but a colourful cast of non-profit and for-profit organisations underneath it would provide the service.

Foundation hospitals would float free, set their own pay scales, sell their land and buildings and borrow money in the City. This would make them autonomous not-for-profit companies, no longer legally a part of the NHS or under the control of a secretary of state. Gordon Brown objected strongly. Part of his reasoning was Treasury prudence. Bodies allowed to borrow might someday need to be bailed out. But Brown also envisaged a single, Labour NHS. He had spent political capital in building a consensus about its spending and raising taxes for it. The row ignited the tinder of the Blair–Brown rivalry.

Labour MPs took sides. Old Labour, led by former Health Secretary Frank Dobson, thought the NHS as a political brand depended on its integrity. It was also about equity. Rich and powerful hospitals would flourish while the others went to the wall, regardless of local need. The unions opposed foundations: they would do away with national pay scales. The noes had it. By the time it came to a vote in the House of Commons, the protesters had already forced Number Ten and the Health Department to retreat on the more contentious issues. Alan Milburn had resigned – a puzzling episode in a political career that was then resumed, amid further controversy, in September 2004 – and the subtle and emollient John Reid took over at the Department of Health.

To wide confusion, Blair announced that all hospitals could become foundations and maybe even PCTs, too, and another regulator was promised to keep foundations in order. (Within a year, Blair was bemoaning the proliferation of regulators and trying to cut their number.) Foundations became encrusted with weird and wonderful ornaments, including a voting mechanism allowing separate colleges of staff, patients and the public to vote for their governing bodies, which would then (weakly) supervise their managers.

This was ad hoc policymaking at its worst. Blair was spending his time and energy at the wrong end of the pipe. If PCTs run by GPs were the prime movers, driving and commissioning for their patients in this new market-oriented NHS, then it was surely they who should have public elections and the appurtenances of local accountability. As things stood, foundations could be more 'legitimate' than the organisations on which they depended for their revenues.

On the eve of a crucial Commons vote on 19 November 2003, John Reid was obliged to promise no foundations would be created beyond the first wave of twenty-five already announced, at least until progress had been independently reviewed. The vote came at a bad time for Blair. George Bush was arriving for a state visit the next morning when he would be given the highest ceremonial honours, not calculated to please angry backbenchers. But the whips went into over-drive and, in the event, a government with a majority of 167 squeaked by with just seventeen votes, the lowest since New Labour came to power.

At first it looked like a victory for Brown since the foundations were no freer than under the Tory reforms of the previous decade. Reid decided to press ahead with a second wave but his plans unravelled. First, the Healthcare Commission got involved. The Commission was an inspectorate which started life under Labour as the Commission for Healthcare Audit and Inspection (CHAI), which itself was the successor to a somewhat weaker Commission on Health Improvement. It awarded stars to hospitals and PCTs on the basis of their performance and drew up league tables for the Sunday papers to reproduce.

Problem one, where did the stars leave local decision making and what was the point of voting in elections for the board of a foundation hospital if it was still bound by national targets? Problem two, what if the Commission's estimate of foundations differed from that of their own regulator, which was rechristened Monitor? In summer 2004 the regulators did publicly disagree in their judgements.

Then, despite the regulator, one of the new foundations, Bradford Teaching Hospitals, got into financial difficulties, performing more operations than its PCTs said they had agreed to or were willing to pay for. Being Yorkshire, there were tales of macho men shouting at each other across committee-room tables. Rational and caring, it wasn't.

## Nice Work

Meanwhile from Milburn, back in harness as election strategist from September 2004, the mantra of 'choice' was being heard more loudly than ever. But how could patients choose while PCTs continue to be responsible for commissioning their care? And where did long-term planning enter in? Labour MPs feared that choice clashed with equity, as of course it would. Wouldn't the middle classes manipulate choice in their favour, leaving the less well-informed the worst hospitals and clinics?

By January 2005 all cataract patients were due to be

offered a choice of at least two 'providers' (clinics or hospitals, public or private). A similar arrangement would apply to heart disease. By December 2005 all patients would be given a selection of places to go for their treatment. The PCTs would face a tremendous logistical challenge, supplying patients with information then tracking their progress through the system.

For all that it was 'national', the NHS had never managed to even up access to care across the country. The postcode lottery alarmed the public and had caused Labour in its first term to set up the highly regarded National Institute for Clinical Excellence (NICE). Intellectually rigorous but willing to consult widely, NICE laid down guidelines on the effectiveness of drugs and treatments and their value for money. Standards were in theory equilibrated by the Healthcare Commission. You could just about see the logic of national bodies setting the standards for a mostly devolved system of care – at least until John Reid announced he was culling these quangos and Blair chipped in with his own scheme for rearranging the regulatory deckchairs, yet again.

## Public Health

One casualty of the quango cull had been the Health Development Agency, the specialist body for promoting public health. This sent a confusing signal on the eve of Labour's announcement of a new plan in November 2004.

Healthfulness embraced length of life, fit babies, fewer early deaths, fewer chronic conditions, less asthma, diabetes, obesity, alcoholism or heart conditions. A healthy society would not exhibit such sharp social class divides in illness, infant mortality or death rates. The incidence of obesity had grown 400 per cent during the past quarter of a century; two-thirds of the population of England were overweight.

Labour wrung its hands but public health was tricky. It might mean asking why tobacco executives should have privileged access to ministers and might mean forcing companies to stop saturating the food they sold with salt. Labour published papers. But its efforts seemed marginal, like an off-Broadway show when the spotlight is shining on the main house. Public health advocates demanded the government join things up: housing, income distribution, smoking, diet. But that was asking for active, collectivist-minded government. Is your agenda essentially left wing, we asked Professor Sian Griffiths, president of the Faculty of Public Health, and she had to answer yes. But as ever, Labour was circumspect, a little here, a little there, but nothing to frighten the City or the hypocrites in the press, one day condemning the nanny state, the next demanding intervention.

In a report on public health to complement his earlier study for the Chancellor on NHS spending, banker Derek Wanless had described how citizens engaged with their own wellbeing would, over the years, bring health costs down. Leaner, fitter people would simply need less care. But what ought government to do? A walking and cycling strategy did emerge, much delayed and under-financed from the Transport Department in 2004.

Did the public get value from the £138m its Food Standards Agency spent per year? Controlling campylobacter in chickens and sending out hygiene videos to 300,000 caterers was important, as was checking Chinese food imports containing dangerous residues of veterinary drugs. But was there enough of a focus on healthy eating and everyday nutrition?

## Poor Health

Labour acknowledged that poverty caused ill health. If the alleviation of poverty was a long-run ambition, during the second Labour term more health resources were focused on the poorest. Separate targets were set for cutting heart and cancer deaths in poor areas. Allocations to GPs were weighted according to indices of deprivation. In a more modern guise the old Resources Allocation Working Party (RAWP) formula, devised when Labour was last in power and a miraculous survivor of the Tory years, kept pumping marginally extra amounts to poorer regions – but not necessarily to poorer patients. The trouble was no one could demonstrate that more health spending produced more health. In Scotland, on the contrary, the evidence went the other way. With a third more nurses and a quarter more doctors per head, the health of Scotland's inhabitants was worse than England's.

North and south of the border, smoking had become a much more strongly class-biased killer: half the difference in longevity between the social classes was accounted for by the fact that lower social groups had a higher proportion of smokers. In 2002 the Tobacco Advertising and Promotion Act banned most tobacco ads and sponsorship; it brought UK law into alignment with a directive of the European Commission. Further restrictions on advertising were coming and in 2004 Liverpool introduced a local ban on smoking in public places. The proportion of eleven- to fifteen-year-olds who smoked fell from 11 per cent to 9 per cent but many still puffed. In 2003, 53.5bn cigarettes were sold in the UK, compared with 55bn three years earlier.

To the derision of right-wing columnists, but offering poor people a reduced chance of contracting lung cancer, smoking cessation programmes were established in disadvantaged areas. Targets for cutting smoking were incorporated into Sure Start, Labour's programme for catching children (and parents) young. Here was a classic example of the costs and benefits of government under Labour. Smoking cessation programmes run by health trusts or councils or partnerships recruited staff, some of whom were bureaucrats, sitting in offices, pushing paper. It was hard, perhaps impossible, to specify some ratio of administrative inputs to outputs in the real lives of local people. Critics focused on the upfront costs, which were substantial; they rarely praised the longer-term changes in health that might – repeat might – result from what amounted to a sort of behavioural inoculation.

Sure Start strove to integrate health, nutrition and parenting into its care and education programme. In poor areas, doctors were able to prescribe gyms for their patients. Baskets of fresh fruit were despatched to schools. Some of it rotted; at least one school resorted to a fruit fight to get rid of it, but maybe it added marginally to the prospects of some children breaking out of deprivation. Breakfast clubs opened in schools so more children might start the day fitter to learn.

Overall, Labour set itself a target to cut 300,000 needless untimely deaths due to everything from accidents and low birth weight to heart failure. But the public and its proxies in the media were uncertain about how much intervention they would tolerate. Conventional wisdom said government should maximise consumer information, as if people were capable, let alone willing, to invest time in reading the small print on packages. League tables showed inhabitants of the UK to be among the fattest in the West – some 22 per cent with a health-threatening body mass index, compared with 11 per cent in Germany. Despite pâté de foie gras and boeuf en croûte, the French had only 9 per cent of people classified as dangerously overweight. Public health doctors looked at the growth of weight-related conditions among children and warned that their generation might die before their parents. But obesity was a flurry, a fleeting concern.

## Health in the News

A King's Fund report looked at media coverage, seeking to explain why it was so hard to shift public attention to focus on the real risks and the true killers. The number and prominence of health stories were found to be in almost inverse ratio to their risk to the public health at large. On a 'deaths per story' index, dramas such as variant Creutzfeldt–Jakob Disease (vCJD) took up a vast amount of reporting, yet the risk of death was tiny compared with smoking, obesity, alcohol and poverty – the real mass killers.

The media warped not just public perceptions but official policymaking. The Food Standards Agency calculated that every life saved from vCJD – the condition associated with BSE in cattle – ended up costing £13bn of money that would have saved hundreds of thousands of lives if spent more wisely than on expensive beef regulations. MMR was another case study. In February 1998, the *Lancet* published a paper suggesting a possible link between bowel disorders in children and neuropsychiatric disfunction (autism) and – unwarranted by the science – a further possible link between the two of them and immunisation with MMR (the single measles, mumps and rubella vaccine). The press and the BBC gave the work of a maverick doctor, Andrew Wakefield, excessive attention, despite a tidal wave of informed rebuttal. In February 2004 the *Lancet* withdrew the original paper, citing Wakefield's failure to declare an interest. But by then the damage had been done. Vaccination rates had dropped to 80 per cent, low enough to create the conditions for a mass outbreak of measles.

## The NHS Buys in Private Health

An old welfare state worry had been that unless the middle classes were kept on board – in public hospitals and primary schools – they would withdraw their consent to the taxation needed to maintain a decent system for everyone, especially the poor. Labour thought it would get around that in health by bumping up spending and it worked, to the extent that private insurance schemes offering clients access to private hospitals got into difficulties. But it partly worked because the private sector had been brought into the NHS by the front door, as a growing supplier of clinical services.

To uncork the bottleneck in capacity, the government – without telling PCTs or even local hospitals – invited health companies (mostly from outside the UK, from the United States, Spain and South Africa) to offer cheap, production-line treatments. So these fast-track cold surgery Diagnostic and Treatment Centres (later called Treatment Centres) were slapped on as another flying buttress on the gothic architecture of the NHS. In fact, many turned out as new units inside the NHS using existing staff and clinics. The Blairite modernisers talked breezily of outsourcing radiology and more. How much more? John Reid said a 15 per cent limit should be applied to private provision within the NHS. But the special advisers said as long as the NHS remained true to its cardinal principle of not charging people for treatment when they needed it, did it matter who provided it?

Ministers, like the media to which they responded with Pavlovian devotion, thought of the NHS as hospitals. But most people's contact with the NHS is at home or in surgeries, through networks of staff offering hard to measure care to the chronically sick, the disabled and to old people with multiple needs. The private sector was already involved, of course, in providing nursing homes and, though many forgot this, in GP practices – most of which remained small businesses. But companies liked to cherry-pick and the prospect of their providing effective community health care remained remote.

## Private Medicine

In the 1940s Nye Bevan had tried to make hospital consultants full-time employees of the NHS but in the end he had to 'stuff their mouths with gold' to get them to join the NHS at all. That allowed them to treat patients in private hospitals or private NHS wings, which created something of an incentive for the unscrupulous to keep their NHS waiting lists artificially long to stoke up demand for private treatment. Here was a segment of the private sector that Barbara Castle and other Labour ministers had tussled with a generation ago. It was long an ideological abomination to Labour Party members. And now here was Blair, knowingly or otherwise, finally all but killing it off, mainly through NHS capacity improvement.

In Labour's second term, the private sector felt a chill wind blowing from improvements in the NHS. In July 2004 the chairman of the British Medical Association's private practice committee warned his members to prepare for 'more change in private practice in the next two years than in the previous two hundred'. In some parts of the country, he said, cardiac surgeons had already all but lost their private practice. Ophthalmic surgeons anywhere near the new fast-track Treatment Centres could expect to lose all their private work shortly.

In truth, the private sector had never grown as fast as predicted and it saw little benefit even from Labour's policy of offering heart patients who waited over six months the right to go private at the NHS's expense. Despite growing wealth over the decades, only 11 per cent of people were covered by private insurance, most as a perk from their employers. Now the relatively few who paid out of their own pockets were starting to give up: the drop in NHS waiting times was one factor, along with a rise in the cost of health insurance. The number of people who pay for one-off operations out of their own pockets fell even more dramatically. Fewer wanted to pay £5,000 or so for a new hip if they could get it free on the NHS within a reasonable time.

Two of the biggest companies, Bupa (a non-profit distributing provident company) and Capio, finding they had growing numbers of empty beds, started selling off some of their private hospitals. Another of the largest private providers, Nuffield, abandoned private patients and decided to devote itself entirely to treating NHS patients on NHS block contracts. The new waiting-list-busting Treatment Centres were only allowed to charge 15 per cent above NHS costs, far less than the traditional private sector. Now if private hospitals wanted to compete, they had to get their prices down. In West Yorkshire, for example, private clinics said there was no way they would do cataract operations for less than £2,500 each. Before long they were contracting with PCTs to do them at the NHS tariff rate of £757.

## Consultants

The government offered consultants a new NHS contract with financial incentives to do more NHS work, so more consultants now found doing their outside private work less worthwhile. The contract, at first rejected then finally welcomed, gave consultants more money but put them (in theory) under stricter control of managers who now drew up agreed work plans with them.

A BMA threat to sue the Department of Health came to nothing. It protested against the ban on allowing any doctors who had worked in the NHS during the last six months from taking jobs in the new private Treatment Centres. This move was aimed at ensuring that the new centres did genuinely provide extra capacity to the NHS, without merely poaching doctors from the health service.

As a result, the UK managed to suck in medical talent as doctors were recruited from abroad; some 15 per cent of consultants appointed in the three decades prior to the 1990s had been trained abroad and a quarter of all those appointed since.

## The Private Finance Initiative

The Private Finance Initiative (PFI) was a bastard child of a disreputable public sector desire to get capital spending 'off the books' and private firms with an appetite for easy profit with rock-solid revenue streams guaranteed by the tax-payer. During the 1980s Labour local authorities (some of their then leaders subsequent luminaries of Blair's government) attempted to sell their civic infrastructure to finance houses then lease them back, securing for the council a capital sum.

During the 1990s the PFI package was refined. In a typical PFI contract the NHS would promise to pay a consortium a sort of rent for thirty years in exchange for which the consortium would build a hospital and, in some instances, also maintain it. The PFI doctrine said the private companies were taking on a risk but in practice their lawyers always cleverly outwitted the civil service in sewing up loose ends in the contracts. Besides, no health trust was ever likely to walk away from a newly built hospital or go bankrupt.

In the second term a new element was added to the PFI package. Companies which had negotiated the initial deal went bust or were taken over or sold their stakes. Title in a project shifted. Suddenly it was becoming difficult to know who owned a building which looked to most people to be in the public sector but in fact was plumping up the balance sheet of a City financial institution in a lucrative secondary market.

Labour used PFI contracts extensively in hospital construction so that by 2004 nearly all the sixty-eight new hospitals being built – twenty-four already open – were PFI deals. A version of PFI was devised for the reconstruction of 2,200 GPs' surgeries and local clinics, the Local Improvement Finance Trust, different in that the NHS would usually remain a 50–50 participant in any profits that accrued from the deal.

NHS buildings had fallen into decrepitude because investment had been frozen too many times over the years. Now the gateways through which citizens passed for their first contact with the NHS were made newer, brighter and more welcoming. The aim was to make the distinction between glitzy private clinics and the barrack-like old NHS hospitals less stark. The intention was laudable but PFI built in rigidities. Once designed and built a PFI hospital could not be altered, even if health demand changed.

In the financial circumstances of the first Blair government PFI could be said to be a necessary, if high, price to pay for getting building fast. But after 2001, as Treasury rules changed and PFI spending was largely brought back on the official books, it became less clear why a peculiar form of financing should be so prevalent in one sector, health, when other sectors such as schools or road building were much more eclectic in the methods used to lay bricks or Tarmac.

## Social Care

It was a perennial problem that more hospital beds would be available if old people too frail to go home could be cared for elsewhere; they needed care but not the intensive care of hospitals. Labour's reflex was to blame councils for not giving priority to community care. Councils in turn complained about inadequate grants and penalties if they chose to raise their own local tax.

In January 2004 the government started giving councils an extra £100m a year to help discharge patients, but threatened to fine them for every extra day they caused an NHS bed to be blocked. Councils were resentful. No fines were levied but the threat succeeded. In 2001 over 7,000 beds were blocked, but only 3,000 were by May 2004. Those 4,000 beds saved were the equivalent of adding another eight hospitals to the NHS.

The Institute of Public Policy Research said another 'Wanless' was needed, a major independent review of care offered to elderly people and those who relied on local councils for help. Somehow, Labour's generosity towards patients did not extend to the same people before or after they went into hospital. Part of the problem was the complexity of council finance. Money for social services went into one end of a machine in Whitehall but whether it bought home helps and day centres at the other depended on a host of intermediate decisions. The total sum for personal social services – £10.6bn in 2005 – though rising, was not matching the needs of an ageing society. Councils were short of staff – one in ten social care jobs was unfilled in 2003.

Squeezed between central spending targets and councils with other things to spend available money on (or palliate council tax payers by cutting spending) social services departments were often the losers. Unlike the NHS there were no promises from prime ministers sitting on sofas in television studios, no golden commitments from the Treasury. Personal social services spending was rising and Labour could boast that 14 per cent more hours of domiciliary care were provided in the eight years from 1997, but that was grossly misleading. To save on the NHS bill, people were being discharged from hospital in worse physical condition and local social services had then to concentrate resources on the frailest. That meant the slightly less frail got less. The number of older people with council-provided home helps fell by 30 per cent, despite growth in the number of frail old as Britain aged.

Some new initiatives were made. Councils were to be aided to the tune of £80m to provide alarms to 160,000 older people 'to keep them safe and out of hospital'.

## The Czars

Two indicators of better care on which the government fixated were for cancer and heart disease. For each a 'czar' was appointed, and a national service framework drafted (a plan by another name). In cancer care 1,000 extra specialists ensured that 99 per cent of patients saw a consultant within two weeks, up from only 63 per cent in 1997. The National Institute for Clinical Excellence specified that cancer patients were all entitled to fifteen new drugs that had previously often been refused them as too expensive. The number of MRI and CT scanners doubled since 2000. The result? Cancer deaths fell and survival rates improved; but then the former had certainly been falling before 1997. In heart disease it was a similar story. Labour's measures may have augmented the long-run trend, but only slightly. More operations and drugs contributed to a steady reduction in deaths.

But health professionals had their doubts. Did such a focus on waiting times, cancer and heart deaths lead to neglect elsewhere, such as sexually-transmitted diseases? Mental health remained a Cinderella, despite having its own national service framework.

## Cleanliness

For all the increase in staff dedicated to NHS infrastructure, a national panic could get going about hospital cleanliness. Prominent journalists wrote of their harrowing time recovering from infections contracted while in hospital. Labour was clearly tempted to launch a war on the 'superbugs' but wisdom intervened. Cleanliness had to be a matter for local management.

## Where Did All the Money Go?

Meanwhile, in the hospitals themselves, what was all the new money buying? The government itself said that by 2004 the NHS had become bloated, at least to the extent that £6.5bn worth of efficiency gains could be squeezed out. John Reid nearly had an attack of apoplexy when, in October 2004, the statisticians said productivity in the NHS had been *falling* just as spending was rising every year. There were serious problems with measurement but the trend data suggested money (the bulk of NHS spending went on hospitals) was buying more staff and more operations but the output of staff was falling. The NHS was fatter.

Total NHS employment (in England) was up by over a fifth in 2003 compared with when Blair took office. That translated into 88,000 professionally qualified clinical staff (full-time equivalents) and 62,000 new clinical support staff. These were not, as ignorant opposition MPs like to cry, 'managers' – as if management were not a fundamental precondition of delivering any service. If anything management costs were falling as a proportion of total NHS spending, even though during 2003 health administrators had expanded by some 10,500, most of them handling the extra finance and personnel. Four out of five NHS staff were in the 'front line', a phrase much used during Blair's second term. Many of the rest were in pathology labs and IT suites doing essential medical work. Only 3 per cent of staff could by any stretch be called 'managers'.

In lean years dedicated nurses, managers and doctors had shown all too well that they could cope. Now, foot off the brake, money was being spent on more training courses for them and more downtime for junior doctors, but the statistics were too crude to say exactly what was happening. The Office of National Statistics admitted it knew nothing much about quality of care. It had no idea, for example, if more and better tests and scans were being carried out on patients. Patients did seem to be staying in hospital a bit longer, as average length of stay, which had been falling, ticked up. Since there had been rising complaints about frail old people turned out too soon, this may have been a sign of better quality.

Statistically it would reduce 'output', but it might mean more comfort for patients and a reduced risk of a rapid return to hospital, which, absurdly, would have counted as extra productivity. Indeed, deaths within thirty days of surgery *were* falling. But such things will always be hard to explain under opposition and press barrage of jeers about apparently lower 'productivity'. So the Tories could claim that Labour spent 40 per cent more on the NHS between 1998 and 2003 but inpatient activity increased by only 5 per cent, as measured in 'finished consultant episodes'.

The NHS was audited and reported to death but it was still hard to form a clear picture of efficacy. Procedures that used to count as 'consultant episodes' in a hospital had become 'lumps and bumps' surgery being performed better and faster in go-getting and often better equipped GP health centres, but now uncounted in the statistics. The figures did not, for example, measure how the expensive new statins reduced the number of times heart patients went to hospital, though medical research said they made a major improvement.

Then more money went in higher wages – which had fallen behind badly. Hiring and retaining large numbers of new staff in a tight employment market urgently required more pay, especially in the South East where the NHS was still badly strapped for nurses. Agenda for Change, a progressive and imaginative new pay structure that rewarded staff for acquiring higher skills, added initially to the pay bill as it was introduced in 2004. It was held up as a model for creating good career ladders. However, it also embodied a multi-year pay bill of a kind which the Treasury said helped to keep public sector pay rates down relative to private earnings.

A charge that sticks is that restructuring costs extra in jobs, reappointments and sheer disruption to the core business of the health service. Reorganisations always waste money. Converting health authorities into PCGs then PCTs and preparing hospitals for foundation status demanded time and managerial capacity, which was sometimes lacking. For all their protestations about saving money from administration, neither the Tories nor the Liberal Democrats seemed to have learned that lesson: their own reorganisation schemes promised yet more episodes of redundancy, reappointment and disorientation.

Perhaps the future reorganisations that seem predestined whoever is in power might be easier if the NHS is connected electronically. Labour appointed a new information technology czar for the NHS and he set about letting mega contracts to secure a single network for the service along with readable and electronically storable patient records. The history of giant IT schemes – this one was to cost £6.5bn – is not propitious. One study said fewer than a third of them ever came out according to plan, in private as well as in public sectors. But the NHS had no choice but to upgrade its IT and seek to make its myriad systems communicate with one another. One prize would be an electronic system for appointments called 'choose and book' to be piloted in 2005. Health ministers were discomfited by stories in the computer press that the final cost of the NHS IT revolution was more likely to be five times the original estimate, or £30bn. But if it worked, a GP would be able to access the waiting lists and the quality of care of every consultant in the land, to choose the best for a patient.

## Scotland, Wales and Northern Ireland

Devolution was starting to provide a test bed for different approaches to the delivery of services, except no one in Whitehall seemed much interested in comparing and contrasting and making the results public.

English health ministers started gloating over worse waiting list results in both Scotland and Wales, Scotland having eschewed numerical targets. The Scots claimed they were losing money due to population loss, though they still spent more per capita. The so-called Barnett formula – which allocates Treasury funding to Scotland and Wales and Northern Ireland on a formula based on their relative population – had always been tweaked to favour Scotland. But now, a Scottish Chancellor notwithstanding, it was working and Scotland was having to make do with relatively less. (The Scots showed no sign of wanting to wield their tax raising powers.) The Welsh complaint was different. Barnett had never been allowed to deliver all they needed. The fact remained however that spending per head in both countries still exceeded England's.

Scotland, though keen enough on PFI deals, had marched the NHS administration back to pre-Thatcher days, unifying purchaser and provider again under local health boards. The Scottish executive purchased a privately owned hospital to bring it into NHS use. Both Scotland and Wales gave more prominence to health prevention. One striking difference was a vote by the Scottish Parliament to offer free care to all the elderly in personal care in residential and nursing homes, regardless of their incomes. (In England the state will only pay for the nursing element of the care of those who can afford to pay for their own personal care – a hotly disputed and unpopular policy.)

In Wales the main divergence was the offer to restore free eye tests and prescriptions to all by 2007. How these are to be paid for remains in dispute. Derek Wanless, in a later 2003 report, was critical and strongly urged the Welsh Assembly to stop their hospitals going into deficit. He suggested the Welsh health service was falling behind on several measures, but mostly waiting times. Some observers suggest the advantage of devolution – bringing government closer to the people it serves – also makes it far harder for devolved ministers to make tough spending decisions or face unpleasant options.

Scotland and Wales might reasonably reply that it is not they who have diverged radically, but the Blair government, especially in its second term. By starting to use the private sector, by sharpening up competition within the internal market, by introducing patient choice that undermines local planning, it was Blair who was changing the NHS radically, and they who were retaining it as it was. Over the years, this divergence within the UK would help test the relative values and weaknesses of a unified service cooperating at every level versus a competing service where the weak go to the wall. Or at least *could*, if anyone at the centre collated the figures and compared and contrasted across the devolved administrations. There was little sign of it.

## What the People Thought: Polls and the Press

What mattered most to ministers was sentiment – how people felt about their NHS. Things might be getting better on paper, but if too few people *believed*, what use were the graphs and Powerpoint presentation slides? Labour was running up a down escalator powered by a predominantly hostile press that relished scare and scandal regardless of whether any incident were true, fair or representative of the NHS as a whole. With over one million people receiving treatment of some kind every day, there would never be a shortage of stories that might or might not reflect how things were generally.

The British Social Attitudes survey showed 'satisfaction' drifting downwards over the years. But it was the same story in other countries. Across the West, there had been some loss of faith in health services – which caused an epidemic of reform as governments strove for better quality and more patient satisfaction while struggling to contain costs. The UK, insular and uninterested, always imagined it was alone in its social policy dilemmas.

What did polls signify? After treatment, some 95 per cent of patients rated their care good, very good or excellent. On the other hand a Eurobarometer survey found British patient satisfaction just under average in the EU. Asked about the state of the NHS, people were negative. But asked about their own experience in the clinic or surgery, they responded positively. GPs won high approval ratings, followed by hospital inpatient services. The old were more satisfied than the young. Those with recent experience of using the NHS were more satisfied than those without. Those who used private services were less satisfied with the NHS, and inhabitants of the South East of England were less satisfied than others.

MORI thought it found a tipping point during 2004 as slightly more people became optimistic that the NHS would improve compared with those who believed it would get worse. Attitudes (informed or plain ignorant?) shuttlecocked about. Optimism was highest just after Gordon Brown announced the extra National Insurance pledged for the NHS. But people seemed to expect an overnight miracle and when they didn't get it, turned pessimistic again.

Perception of public services had much to do with how those polled felt about Labour's general standing. So Tory voters refused ever to believe any good of the NHS, while committed Labour voters were deeply positive. Why were people not more impressed with the sharpest ever falls in waiting times? Because those grumbling on waiting lists of six months were not on the far longer waiting lists five years previously. Not until the first lucky people experienced a wait of only around one month did they begin to express their appreciation for speedy treatment. So if waiting times do keep falling fast then by 2008 people really might notice.

Faced with this ingratitude of the voters ministers ground their teeth. What role, they wondered, did venomous newspapers and tendentious broadcasts play? Still, there was doubt – which they shared – whether the NHS was good enough yet. In the unmeasurable domains of kindness, cleanliness and politeness, genuine care was too often missing from people's everyday experience of irritable GP receptionists, bad nursing on wards or dirty hospital toilets. Why were nurses grouped around the desk while an old woman in the corner desperately needed help? Why did no one supervise what that confused old man was or wasn't eating at meal times? Why did pain relief come too late for someone suffering agonies after an operation? Simply to dismiss public scepticism as misinformation would be a mistake. The next great leap forward after waiting lists has to be improving the personal experience of each patient. Any public relations adviser would say that a little more tender loving care counts far more than any number of good statistics.

## Conclusion

Despite Iraq, Blair's reputation was always going to stand or fall on whether huge amounts of extra health spending secured improved care. It did. By 2005, Labour's success was palpable, measured by waiting times, cancer and heart results or staff numbers. But the public's perceptions of improvement lagged behind. It relied on anecdote or press reports rather than official statistics. Cinderella services remained, such as mental health. Improvement was not uniform across the United Kingdom and sharp questions were hard to answer about precise value for the additional billions. But at its simplest, Labour did what people had been asking for. By devoting a higher fraction of national resources than ever before to health, the UK drew level with those Europeans the public otherwise did not want to get any closer to.

# Patients Waiting Over Six Months for Operations

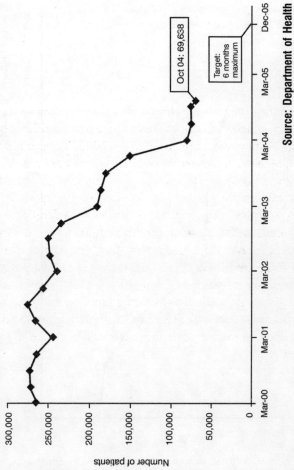

Oct 04: 69,658

Target: 6 months maximum

Number of patients

**Source: Department of Health**

Target: None waiting over six months by December 2005

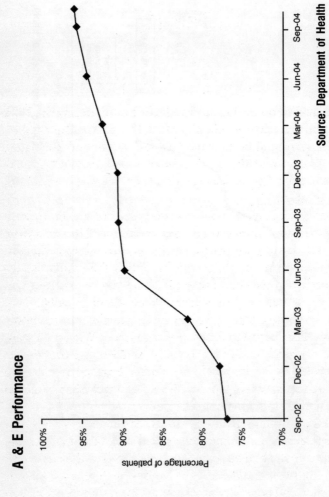

## A & E Performance

Percentage of people seen and treated or admitted in under 4 hours

**Source: Department of Health**

# CHAPTER TWO

# Fairer?

Emblazoned on the hustings and battle buses during the 2001 election were More Schools, More Hospitals, More Police. These were middle England's issues, so Labour calculated. The posters and the party political broadcasts did not say More Social Justice, Fewer Poor People or, heaven forbid, More Equality.

Yet if you asked Labour ministers and MPs why they were in politics and in power, they answered 'social justice'. More equality, fewer poor people – these were the slogans that got them up in the morning and on which they would judge themselves at the end of their political lives. But fairness was not what they or their leaders talked about in public very often. The first Blair government had turned out to be the most redistributive in decades; it ran Harold Wilson's 1960s' government close. But it was social justice on tiptoe, fairness by stealth, as if ministers hoped middle England would sleep through those bits of Gordon Brown's budgets that sought to redirect slabs of money to the poor.

Tony Blair himself had said that if he did not leave behind a fairer Britain, he would have failed. He talked of putting wealth, power and opportunity in the hands of those who did not have them and the tools to hand were Sure Start, schools spending and inner city programmes. He didn't mention cash transfers, or bringing them and their soaraway rich fellow citizens any closer together in income.

But then in the middle of that first term he had made an extraordinary promise to abolish child poverty by 2020. 'Our historic aim is that ours is the first generation to end child poverty for ever . . . It's a twenty-year mission but I believe it can be done.' It invited hubris – no government could or perhaps should imply it would hold power through such a length of time. But what a slogan. What a plank on which to fight successive general elections. That revolution-ary ambition might have become Labour's defining character from then on.

In Blair's second term Labour might have branded itself with that mission to end poverty in less than a generation. Here was radicalism, here was clear red water between Labour and the other parties, and if they felt obliged to match the pledge, then Labour would indeed have achieved its stated ambition of redefining consensus for a political generation.

Yet Labour did not choose to make child poverty its badge. The pledge remained, but it was approached softly, softly. Perhaps it was cold feet, perhaps misunderstanding of what the pledge entailed. Anyone who spent time on the nation's housing estates or in hard-pressed schools or overcrowded prisons must have wondered if the government understood the gargantuan task it had set itself. In only fifteen years from now the detritus of disadvantage and despair was to be swept away so that children were never again to be born into a life of poverty and failure? And who was to pay? The public at large conceived of poverty as lack of goods, perhaps to be remedied by (marginally) bigger benefits, though they were hardly popular. Ministers knew better. Poverty was a relative condition. You could end child poverty overnight by reshap-ing the distribution of post-tax incomes, but that required going back on another great pledge of the Blair era, not to raise income tax rates.

If there was no road map, there were street signs. In the first term, Labour had planted a host of schemes, programmes, targets, zones, initiatives, new deals – many of them under the 'community' rubric – all designed to micro-manage away particular aspects of poverty. The preferred phrase was social exclusion, less threatening and wider in meaning than poverty. These programmes continued after 2001, with some fine-tuned and tweaked, some schemes wound up, new ones created.

Fairness was not just for children. Pensioners, women, ethnic minorities, disabled people, the mentally ill were all, more or less, included in Labour's own moral self-assessment. The public – at least the 70 per cent doing well – might judge the Labour government by its grip on the economy, growth, jobs, wealth and mainstream public services. But Labour itself never felt they were doing enough as long as poverty persisted. Did social justice get any better?

## Progress

The Institute of Fiscal Studies, resolutely impartial, said Labour's decision to focus on benefits rather than taxes did work. The system as a whole was more progressive than it had been since Labour was in power in the 1960s. The income of the top 10 per cent was fifteen times that of people in the bottom fifth, but after taxes and benefit payments they were only four times better off. However, the forces in the economy pushing up higher earnings were strong and the question for Blair's second term was what, if anything, Labour would do to mitigate them, in order to prevent the distribution of incomes getting yet more skewed.

The answer was: at best, Labour stopped inequality in the UK getting worse. Its programme of benefits and credits was egalitarian and 'redistributive'. But it served, in the IFS phrase, 'just about to halt' growing inequality, not to cut it.

Labour's approach to unequal Britain was not taxation but an attempt to improve the lives of poorer people and pull them up towards the middle. The effect of Labour's many programmes will be unknowable for a long time. Perhaps it will be impossible to disentangle the results of one from another, as they crisscrossed. The same families, the same estates were targeted in separate efforts to improve health, education, community, estates, employment and crime – including credits that put extra cash into their pockets. What worked? Results were far from certain, but the lamps flickered green.

## The State of Inequality

Income inequality rose in the 1980s, was fairly steady at a high level in the 1990s and looks to have peaked in 2000. It did not get worse in Labour's second term; if it got better, the change was only marginal. Robert Chote, director of the Institute of Fiscal Studies, concluded 'income inequality in Britain is still higher than at any time in the previous eighteen years of Conservative rule and probably for at least twenty years before'.

If everyone got more, the better off got a bigger share of it. At the end of the 1970s, the tenth of the population best off had 21 per cent of disposable income. By 2003 they had even more, 29 per cent. But the first five years of the twenty-first century may come to be distinguished in the eyes of economic historians by the explosion of top incomes. On Blair's watch a relatively small number of people got grotesquely richer.

That was income, money coming in as pay, bonuses and the like. Wealth, what people owned by way of assets (and in their pension pots) became more unequally distributed as well. After the mid-1990s the share of wealth owned by those at the top of the distribution range increased.

But did these trends in the distribution of money matter? If the top echelons managed to get their hands on a freakishly disproportionate share did that affect people's experience of life? Labour tried to pretend that extreme wealth and income were not oppressive. Abandon the old politics of envy, they said. Yet four out of five thought the gap between rich and poor was too great, Britain too unequal.

Nor was the explosion of inequality, as ministers sometimes liked to imply, a force of nature, an aspect of inexorable globalisation. It was a phenomenon confined to the United States and the UK while other Western countries took action to avoid anything like it. The UK's income distribution was ranked fourth most unequal in the European Union in 2001 – above Spain, Greece and Portugal. (No European country had anything like the distribution of income of the United States.) Though inequality had been rising in a number of advanced countries, among those which bucked the trend – Denmark, Canada, France and Germany – several also did well on growth and trade. Market forces were not unstoppable: they did not dictate distribution of income. More importantly, economic success did not correlate with maldistribution of income: some of the fairest societies had some of the most successful economies. Political choices over taxation, pay and social spending could be made and sustained – if the people willed it.

## What is Poverty?

To be poor was to live at a point below incomes at large. The benchmark could not be average income. As the statisticians quipped, were Bill Gates and his dad to come and live in the UK average income would rise, though no one would be better off. A superior measure was median income, the midway point above which half the population earned more and below which half earned less. To be officially poor was to live on less than 60 per cent of median income. The Department of Work and Pensions calculated the poverty threshold was £94 a week for a single person, £172 for a couple, and £175 for a single person with two children – this the cash they had to live on in 2004, after housing costs had been paid. The child poverty target implied households with children would have to receive a lot more money from higher wages or the state.

The median income measure of poverty would shift as incomes in general rose and Labour, never quite making its intentions clear, suggested other measures to run alongside it. In the second term they began to include measures that asked whether a family had essentials of a decent life, coats for kids, a second pair of shoes. When the general population is asked about what they consider as necessities, they tend to add in extra items as the years go by, pushing up the level at which a family would be defined as poor. A holiday for children once a year had joined the list. Was protection from fire an essential? Labour thought so, and planned to offer more than one million poor homes a free smoke alarm.

Labour said it wasn't trying to duck the internationally agreed 60 per cent definition. Others were: at their 2004 conference the Tories said definitions had become so confusing they would abandon any targets for poverty reduction. But they had never claimed to be much concerned with income distribution. Was Labour? Poverty was a gauge of how people related to one another and whether, as society as a whole became better off, the gaps widened. Would Labour ever be prepared to use government power – tax – to check the flight of the bonus-takers and the share option winners into the upper realms of opulence?

## Children and Poverty

Politically it was always going to be easier and safer to operate at the other end and try to channel more money to poor families. Labour did precisely that in its second term. Defying gloomy early expectations it succeeded in reducing the number of households in which children lived in poverty by a quarter. In the circumstances it was a remarkable achievement.

Back in 1968, only 10 per cent of children were poor. By 1997 a third of children lived in homes which got by on weekly cash sums that better-off homes could blow in a single visit to Tesco. When Labour came to power, the UK had the highest rates of child poverty in Europe, ranking fifteen out of the then fifteen EU member states. A third of all the children in the EU classified as poor were born in the UK, a national shame.

Under Labour the UK overtook Italy, Spain and Portugal, rising to eleventh place in the child poverty league table. There were 4.4m poor children when Labour came to power and by 2005 there were 1.1m fewer. On the back of 1997's slender manifesto promises it was extraordinary. It had not been advertised much in 2001 either, and Labour's social justice ambitions remained well hidden from view.

The better off were sometimes cynical about cash benefits for the poor – wouldn't they spend it on booze, fags and trashy toys? But the Policy Studies Institute tracked spending and found that virtually all the new money paid into mothers' pockets was spent on essentials for their children. The proportion of poor parents who said they never had enough money for necessities by the end of the week dropped from over 40 per cent to 17 per cent. All the same, 23 per cent of all children continued to live in households where money was desperately scarce and the things most of the rest of Britain took for granted for decent living were absent. That compared with an EU average of 18 per cent (the original fifteen states), while in Denmark it was just 5 per cent.

It wasn't just cash. Poor children suffered every kind of disadvantage. In 2003 the child of a father in the lowest social classes was twice as likely to die within a year of birth, five times more likely to die in a traffic accident and fifteen times more likely to die in a house fire than those in the highest social class.

## Child Trust Fund

Progress was made by a combination of labour market policies and benefits, and occasionally brilliant shafts of policymaking, offering a glimpse of what Labour was capable of. One was the baby bond. Every child born since September 2002 qualified for a state endowment worth £250; about a third of infants, those from low-income families, would qualify for £500. The idea was that the money would be put in special savings accounts, to come on stream in 2005, to be held tax free to the age of eighteen, while parents could add up to £1,000. At the age of seven, the grant would be doubled. Initially, the money was to be reserved for education or a deposit on a first home. But no restrictions were imposed and young people would be allowed to choose how they wanted to spend the proceeds of the bond, which could be worth thousands of pounds. The endowment could have been bigger, could still be bigger, but it was pardonable exaggeration for the Institute of Public Policy Research, claiming credit for inventing the bond, to say that it would give the poor some of the financial buffering middle-class families can offer their offspring.

## Work

Unearned income from the state was, however, not going to be Labour's way. 'Work is the best welfare' was an early New Labour mantra and employment was the single most important factor in lifting families out of poverty. Over the two Blair terms, nearly two million more people took jobs as unemployment rates fell. The first Blair government added incentives to work through the increasingly generous Working Families Tax Credit; this was basically a state subsidy to low-paid jobs. Another substantial Labour first-term achievement, the National Minimum Wage (NMW), rose from £4.20 to £4.85 an hour during the second term. This was above inflation, but still not nearly enough for a family to survive on. The government preferred to use tax credits to raise low family incomes rather than resolve underlying injustices in pay and the labour market.

## Child Tax Credit

By 2005 all the benefits targeted on children through tax credits, Child Benefit and Income Support had risen by 72 per cent in real terms since 1997. There had never been a redistribution like it. No previous Labour government had done as much. The crank that turned the engine and pushed the living standards of families some way up the hill was Child Tax Credit. This was introduced in 2003 to replace the Children's Tax Credit and the Working Families Tax Credit. Confused? So was everyone. Gordon Brown's regime was fiendishly hard to comprehend and it changed in fundamental ways three times after its introduction.

At first the money was given to fathers (or mothers in working lone-parent families) through their pay packets. Why it was called a credit and paid by the Inland Revenue and not through the benefits system was to impart an added sense that work really was worthwhile. This was not welfare but something earned. But employers protested at the extra paperwork. Women's groups argued that money destined for children was more likely to reach children if paid to mothers, not fathers. Eventually the system bedded down and the bulk of the cash for families was shifted to the mother. Fathers got the same small Working Tax Credit (a maximum of around £400 a year) that went to all the low paid, with children or without.

The Child Tax Credit was now available to all families. It tapered off as incomes rose, but households with joint incomes of as much as £58,000 could claim. It was worth £3,000 a year for the first child in families earning less than £13,000 a year. This was almost the same system as the Child Benefit still paid universally to all families. Nine out of ten families got the Child Tax Credit, but what they received depended on their total income. It was, in other words, means tested, to allow most cash to be directed to the poorest.

By 2005 a typical family with two children would have seen an 11 per cent real increase in their tax credits since 2001. This has been the lift carrying a quarter of children out of poverty to date – and by increasing it each year a progressive-minded chancellor could continue to shift ever more children above the poverty line. Would that fundamental political choice be put to the voters at the end of the term?

Child Benefit, paid to all families regardless of their means, remained. The Child Tax Credit was paid to families whether breadwinners were in or out of work, so children without working parents do not lose out; it was not a disincentive to parents to take jobs. For those who worried that Labour put too much pressure on mothers to work and leave young children in day care, Child Tax Credit was a good answer: it was paid out neutrally, whether a mother worked or not.

## Childcare Credit

Labour provided money for working parents to help defray the costs of childcare. Although more generous than anything offered before, many fewer claimed the support than expected. This was because Labour offered help in the form of vouchers, exchangeable against nursery places or registered child minders, which the government envisaged the private sector would rush to provide. But the voucher would cover only up to 70 per cent of what the Treasury calculated as the average cost of a place: Gordon Brown promised to raise this to 80 per cent by April 2006. There were problems of supply and demand. Even where nursery places were available, many families found they could not afford the remaining proportion. Private nurseries did not set up in poorer areas, so there was little childcare to buy. There was growing pressure by the end of the second term for the state to become more active in providing childcare itself, for example through new children's centres with parents contributing to the cost on a means-tested basis. (See the section on childcare in chapter nine).

## Single Parents

Ministers were largely unconcerned with the moral status of lone parents; they were targeted because, out of work, they were poor and their children suffered. A target was set to get 70 per cent of lone parents into work by 2008 since research consistently showed that the only long-term route out of poverty was through the labour market. Children did better in households where someone had a job than where money only arrived as a benefit cheque. Women who stayed out of the labour market for more than three or four years were likely never to work again. Deskilled, they lost their nerve.

Yet when single parents did take a job, a high proportion of them left work within their first year, unable to juggle their difficult lives. Unsurprisingly, the best off – those who were homeowners, who owned cars and who received maintenance from their child's father – were most likely to manage to stay in employment.

By 2004, Labour had increased the numbers of working lone parents by 9 per cent. But still only 54 per cent worked, a rate of progress which made the 70 per cent target look unreachable. Giant assumptions were made about the future course of the economy, witness the pledge to reduce the number of children in workless households by 5 per cent between 2005 and 2008.

Most single mothers – except those with very young children – said they wanted to work. Most did take jobs if they could find affordable childcare and work that paid at least a little more than life on benefits, with hours they could manage. But those were big ifs. The jump from benefit to work was difficult, although the system tried to adapt by letting mothers who had been out of work for six months keep their benefits for a while until they had settled into their job and received their first pay cheque. In November 2004 Gordon Brown announced that they would get £40 a week extra for their first year in work. Lack of flexible, trustworthy and above all affordable childcare was a key reason fewer lone mothers worked compared with mothers in couples. (The irony was that the women who were now 'housewives' at home were the ones who were not married.)

## Teenage Pregnancy

Young motherhood was both a result of poverty and a cause of deprivation in children. Teen mothers were concentrated in the poorest places. In families where children fail at school, boys risk turning to crime while girls risk getting pregnant. Labour fixed a target to halve conceptions in the under-eighteens by 2010. Sure Start Plus programmes were set up in the thirty-five areas with the highest number of young mothers, to support them, offer childcare and encourage them back into education. Results were unimpressive. By 2005 there had been a 9.4 per cent reduction in under-eighteen conceptions – nowhere near the rate needed to reach the target: it should have been cut by 25 per cent.

Could enough be done to promote sex and relationship education in schools while ministers bowed in fear of hypocritical ranters in the *Daily Mail*? It was even harder to ensure that every girl was guaranteed swift access to the morning-after pill, contraception and strictly confidential advice from a trusted school nurse.

## Child Support Agency

The ill-fated Child Support Agency (CSA) was a decade old in 2003. Had either the Conservatives who set it up or subsequently Labour managed to make it work, its mechanisms for recovering money could have transformed the lives of many lone-mother families. If even relatively small sums could be cajoled or strong-armed from children's fathers, mothers found it easier to buy childcare and go out to work. But the CSA's record barely improved.

In 2000, Labour had made the bold decision to sweep away a complex formula for assessing absent fathers' contributions. Instead the CSA asked for less money on a simpler basis, hoping to increase the total. Staff could be shifted from making difficult (and mostly wrong) calculations to collecting smaller simpler sums. It didn't happen. As so often, a computer system failed. Although the CSA had powers to seize non-paying fathers' assets, very little extra was handed over.

By the end of 2004, only 54 per cent of cases were processed with fathers paying the full amount due. Better than nothing, but it left £783m still owing to mothers in 'recoverable' child maintenance. Other untold debts had long been abandoned over the ten years. So shaky was the whole outfit that no target was set to reduce this debt. The CSA's humble target was to increase to 60 per cent the number of parents caring for children and receiving benefit who do get maintenance.

Astoundingly, the CSA was required to shed 2,600 staff posts as part of the Treasury's July 2004 efficiency drive. This was not efficient. A large increase in staff might have helped the CSA finally deliver. If it ever were to work, it could make a satisfying dent in child poverty.

## New Deals

Labour's New Deals were outstanding successes, attracting admiring visitors from countries wherever long-term unemployment was a problem. Labour claimed that since its New Deal for Young People began in 1998, followed by a New Deal for over-twenty-fives, they had 'resulted in the virtual eradication of youth long-term unemployment and the reduction in adult long-term unemployment by around three-quarters'.

Researchers were less breathless. The New Deals were closely monitored, but how many of their graduates would have gone back to work anyway, attracted back into the labour market as the economy prospered and more posts were advertised? What impressed the foreign visitors was that Labour had managed to change the social climate. Unemployed people felt differently. What worked was a clever mixture of carrots and sticks, personal advisers for each jobseeker and, above all, a clarion call of 'no fourth option' for those who refused to work, train or study.

Department of Work and Pensions staff, who never got much credit from their political masters, prodded and encouraged people into work. They did more than crudely threaten, but they served to remind those out of work that times had changed and there really were jobs out there.

Second term, the New Deals were refined. One was established for disabled people and another for the over-fifties. They, no more than lone parents, were not being compelled to work, but they were obliged to attend an interview and hear what help was on offer. Under New Deal 50 Plus some 110,000 older people returned to the labour market. Over the six years to 2004 260,000 lone parents were found jobs, 178,000 over-twenty-fives, and 35,000 from under the New Deal for the Disabled.

Star performer was the New Deal for Young People at 490,000. But not all jobs lasted. Two out of five of those who got a job through New Deal for Young People and New Deal 50 Plus were back on the dole (jobseeker's allowance) within six months. Also puzzling were the sixteen- to twenty-one-year-olds who were not in school or college or training schemes and were not claiming benefits. The numbers of the disappeared were estimated to have risen from 6 per cent to 7 per cent between 2001 and 2004 – an indicator, perhaps, of the growth of the 'grey' or informal economy. Some academics argued that up to 15 per cent of GDP turned over unofficially, outside the official statistics. If even remotely true this would mean that gibes about the 'burden' of taxation and the scale of government spending were misplaced: the weight of government was a lot less than conventional wisdom said.

Building on the ethos of the New Deals, JobCentre Plus was launched in 2001. This was a programme to combine and reconcile the pursuit of work and claims for benefit. Applicants were allocated a personal adviser. New open-plan offices were plush, with carpets and soft furnishings. A greeter at the door welcomed people in and ushered them to the right place. Gone were the old battered Perspex screens and plastic chairs nailed to a lino floor. The changes brought one civil service union out briefly on strike, afraid that without the screens their members would be at risk. But the strike was thinly supported as staff saw the calming and civilising effect on both clients and staff of an environment smarter than most high street banks. Now Department of Work and Pensions managers were to be given some autonomy and encouraged to spend their money more imaginatively on ways to help people over the barriers to work. They could buy in training specific to local labour markets, or even help a claimant acquire a car. But the 'Plus' bit was not universal; many jobcentres remained as they were and only 200 of the new models opened. It was a hallmark of too many Labour programmes: a good idea too thinly spread. DWP promised JobCentre Plus would go nationwide by 2006.

## Pay

Before Labour's 2004 conference, with Blair keen to please the unions as Iraq took its toll, a pledge was wrung out of him to end the 'two-tier' labour force in the public sector. He guaranteed that the staff of contractors in schools, hospitals and all government offices would be no worse off than public sector staff directly employed. It would improve the lot of low-paid manual workers and cleaners working for contracted-out services – but it had taken seven years for Labour to finally offer what the unions said was merely a restoration of a pre-Thatcher status quo.

But criticising – let alone intervening in – the operations of the labour markets was not for Labour. Tax credits were in effect a subsidy to employers who could not or would not pay more than a poverty wage. The number of low-paid jobs grew. Tax credits even allowed employers to pay low wages in the overheated South East where there were labour shortages. Labour had, however, nailed its flag to the mast of flexibility and Gordon Brown liked to mount the pulpit to preach to the UK's European neighbours on its success at creating (lower-paid) jobs. One result was that under Labour the biggest group of the poor was no longer either the unemployed nor the pensioners but those in low-paid work.

## Pensioners

In 2002 Gordon Brown had said Labour's aim was to end poverty among pensioners but no specific targets or dates were set. Progress was made. The number of pensioner households living in poverty fell by a fifth by 2005, although two million old people still lived below the poverty line.

State pensions were more generous, rising faster than under any other government ever – both the basic state pension and the new pension supplement (the Pension Credit), a means-tested top-up introduced in 2003. A new State Second Pension was begun in 2002, to give extra entitlement to carers, disabled people and the low paid who had failed to accrue pension rights, potentially helping about twenty million people. Climate change may have made Labour winters generally milder but the special fuel payment for pensioners was doubled to £200. The over-eighties received an extra £100. Then the payment was raised by a further £100 in 2004, the government panicking in the face of protests from some pensioners about increases in their council tax bills.

Labour spent most on the Pension Credit, which replaced the previous top-up, the Minimum Income Guarantee (MIG). The state pension had risen in line with earnings until the Thatcher government broke the link. Old Labour promised to restore it; New Labour retreated but spent more. Restoring the link would have cost £6bn, and the money would have been thinly spread to all, including richer pensioners who didn't need it. Instead, Labour spent £10bn on its Credit and put all the extra into the hands of those who needed it most.

By 2004 the poorest third of pensioners were £1,750 a year (£33 a week) better off than under the system as it used to be. In comparison with what had gone before, Brown's was a bold and generous scheme, a ready instrument for abolishing pensioner poverty. By 2004 the Pension Credit guaranteed no pensioner would fall below £105 a week, which was £5 above the poverty threshold set by Age Concern.

The Credit, unlike the basic state pension, was linked to earnings, so poor pensioners ought never to fall behind again. But it also made government assistance with retirement more complicated than ever. Pensioners with their own savings or small occupational pensions saw fellow pensioners drawing the same sums, even if they had never saved a penny in their lives. Resentment stirred. So a new Savings Credit was introduced that disregarded a proportion of pensioners' private income so allowing them to receive extra, to take their lifetime savings into account.

The basic state pension continued to be linked to prices, which would ensure that its value relative to the economy would fall over time (since earnings would continue to rise more than prices). But Brown was blown along by gusts of political wind. Pensioners were a potent lobby as he had discovered in 2000 when he put it up by just 75p, to their outrage. Against his instincts Brown intervened, budget by budget, to push up the real value of the basic pension by 7 per cent from 2000 to 2004, from £62 to £79.60.

But Brown's system for making sure the poorest got most had many enemies, some in his own party. One of the problems with the Pension Credit was complexity. It lacked political recognition. So people quoted the basic pension rate as if that were all pensioner households were living on. But no one had ever been expected to survive on just the basic pension. Since it was introduced by Beveridge it had always been topped up by means-tested National Assistance.

The central – and possibly lethal – problem with the Pension Credit was that a third of pensioners entitled to it had failed to claim. Contrary to myth, ignorance not pride was the reason. The state already paid pensioners a weekly basic, so it knew who they were and where they lived and yet the Department of Work and Pensions seemed unable to knock on every pensioner's door and help them fill out a simple form to make the claim. It pledged to raise the number receiving the credit to 3.2m by 2008.

But the fact a third of poor pensioners had not been reached undermined the case for means testing. The Liberal Democrats and the Tories wanted to put the money into a bigger basic pension for all – far more politically seductive. This would mean redistributing from poorer to richer, but it would please the majority of pensioner voters.

Meanwhile insurers and pension companies saw Pension Credit becoming more generous and claimed it would provide a disincentive to today's workforce to save for old age. Given almost total ignorance about pensions, let alone estimates of what some state payout might be in thirty or more years time, this was unlikely. In any case, the people poor enough to qualify for the Pension Credit – two-thirds of them low-paid women – would never earn enough in their working lives to be able to save anyway.

The Pensions Commission chaired by former CBI director Adair Turner gave an interim report in October 2004 offering a list of solutions as to how the rising numbers of pensioners could have their incomes maintained. One option was to raise the retirement age to seventy. But that would be hard on manual workers for whom retirement was blessed release. There was a marked social class difference in life expectancy. Many working-class men had only a few years of life left after they retired at sixty-five while middle and upper classes lived much longer. It meant that Labour's decision to offer free television licences to pensioners over seventy-five cost less than expected: few working-class men lived long enough to qualify.

## Other Benefits

Labour pledged in November 2001 to end fuel poverty within fifteen years and within nine years – by 2010 – eliminate fuel poverty in households deemed vulnerable, that's to say those where elderly or disabled people or where children lived. A fuel-poor household was defined as one which needed to spend more than 10 per cent of its income on fuel, in heating the dwelling to an adequate standard of warmth. One way was to cut energy costs. A new programme of grants for cavity wall and loft insulation and for draught proofing was launched, with 800,000 homes the target. Some 670,000 took up the scheme. As a result of various measures, fuel-poor households were said to have fallen from five million in 1996 to 2.5m in 2003.

Adjustments were made in other benefits. Families were allowed to earn a little more before housing benefit was cut and the benefit was raised for families where the breadwinner worked part time – incentives to work. Two million pensioners were offered automatic help with their council tax bills, worth £400 each, but large numbers did not claim this benefit, saving the government £1bn a year. Information technology made it simple – in theory – to ensure entitlements were fully met.

Labour's record on benefits, taken in the round, was 'unprecedented', with 3.7 per cent real terms growth each year in the three years to 2005.

## The Childless Poor

One group fell down into deeper relative poverty under Labour, and it happened intentionally. While pensioners and households with children saw their incomes rise, it was adults of working age without children who were not in jobs who were left behind. Labour was ruthless. Able-bodied adults should take jobs and the jobs were available as the economy boomed. The public was profoundly suspicious of scroungers so being super-tough on this unpopular group made political sense. (Survey after survey, however, showed the public to be clueless about the most basic facts of the social security system.)

The result was an increase in the number of childless adults living below the poverty line – from 3.3m in 1995 to 3.8m by 2003. Benefit rates for this disfavoured group were linked to prices not earnings, so they kept falling behind relative to the economy at large.

Some lived in blighted areas from which heavy industry had fled, in the coalfields and the dead zones of the industrial revolution. Others were misfits, people marginally mentally ill or damaged young people brought up in care and cast out without qualifications or support. There were growing armies of ex-prisoners. The higher the prison population rises, the more ex-cons there are, finding it hard afterwards to get a job with a prison record. Finally, there were the single mothers who had never worked, who when their children reached sixteen found themselves cut off from child-related benefits but unable and ill-equipped to get a job. No doubt there were some workshy people too.

Many of these could be helped into work. But it would take great effort, training, support and personal care to nurture them into employability. Their benefits were pitiful: £55.65 a week for a single adult, £87.30 for a couple. Labour revamped the way housing and other grants were paid to one million people classed as vulnerable – women fleeing domestic violence, young people leaving care, people with disabilities and mental health problems. But the new scheme, called Supporting People, had a rocky start. The government applied an all-embracing formula that left some councils and social landlords – and the people who depended on them – short of money.

## Incapacity Benefit

The light of Labour's attention next fell on those registered as unable to work. Why were there so many of them? New Labour's fervent belief in salvation by work got caught up with anxiety about the amount of money involved in paying growing numbers Incapacity Benefit (IB). Claimant numbers had shot up in the late 1980s and early 1990s when unemployment was high but they crept up still under Labour. All the evidence suggested the population at large was getting healthier not sicker, yet by 2004 there were more incapacity claimants than unemployed people and lone parents put together, some 2.7m.

Once they had tended to be older men, close to retirement. Now younger people and women were claiming, many citing mental health problems. Towards the end of the second term Blair launched a new crusade. Money saved by getting IB claimants back to work would be spent on pensions. He and Brown showed little interest in research showing large regional disparities in IB claims – virtually none in Surrey but a quarter of the workforce in run-down Easington, County Durham. Shouldn't the government be getting the jobs to the depressed areas, some MPs asked, instead of goading the vulnerable? But interventions in the private economy was not New Labour's way. Instead, thirty pilot 'Pathways to Work' were started, offering £40 extra a week to IB claimants taking a job.

## Disability

To strengthen the rights of disabled people, clauses of the Disability Discrimination Act that came into force in October 2004 obliged civilian employers to take reasonable steps to ensure their workplaces were suitable for people with disabilities and to scrutinise how they advertised and recruited staff. These were rights that, as we have seen, came with responsibilities, especially to seek work. People in wheelchairs had chained themselves to Downing Street railings to protest at new benefit rules but Labour held firm: the employment rate of disabled people rose from 43 per cent to 50 per cent.

## Human Rights

High on Labour's own list of its achievements since 1997 came passing the Human Rights Act in 1998. On one level it was a tidying-up exercise, the importation into UK statute law of rights citizens already possessed under the treaty which gave them access to the European Court of Human Rights in Strasbourg. On another, Labour was empowering people as individuals, not in the traditional way of negotiated group rights by trade unions, or the state. The thrust of the human rights endeavour was against the state, and essentially anti-social democratic. It was ironic but not inconsistent that in autumn 2004 tobacco companies should pay an expensive QC to lead an action on their behalf citing their 'human right to free expression', asking a judge to strike down an effort by the Department of Health to minimise point-of-sale advertising of cigarettes.

Prompted by think-tanks, Labour published a white paper in 2004, *Fairness for All*, announcing a rights rationalisation. A single equality organisation – the Commission for Equality and Human Rights – would replace the three bodies already dealing with gender, race and disability. It made sense for employers to have one port of call, one set of regulations. From 2006, it would also take on the new rights territory of religion, sexual orientation and age discrimination. (A law against age discrimination would have to be introduced by 2006, to comply with a European directive.) A new law was to make it illegal to incite hatred on the grounds of religion.

## Gender

Girls might outshine boys in school exams, but not in life. Some 70 per cent of the low paid were women, clustered in catering, cleaning, caring, and behind cash registers – work undervalued largely because women did it. After seven years of Labour, most women still did not earn enough to become the breadwinner for their families; the majority of women, once they became mothers, were destined to rely on a partner or the state to provide a living income.

Even local authorities and public bodies dragged their feet over edicts to carry out pay reviews to make sure women's work was fairly valued. Very few private companies bothered. A pay gap was apparent at every level and stage in life. Even in their first jobs on leaving university, women were paid 15 per cent less than men (which perhaps meant they should pay correspondingly lower tuition fees).

The gap between women's and men's pay did slightly narrow under Labour, but by 2003 women still earned only 82 per cent of men's median hourly pay. That was an improvement of only 2.5 per cent since 1994. Some 43 per cent of women work part time and the gap between their pay rate per hour and full-time men's is 40 per cent, unchanged since the 1970s. Women's low earnings meant a pensionless old age. Their low pay meant women were the main winners from the minimum wage, over a million of them better off as it rose. Although research showed men were doing a bit more childcare, though not more housework, women still did most of it, even when they were in paid jobs. Half of all women have an independent income of less than £100 a week. Glass ceilings may have been broken, but progress is slow: only 2 per cent of FTSE 100 directors are women.

However, Labour did a great deal for mothers, against belligerent opposition from employers. Child Tax Credits were the biggest ever state boost to mothers' incomes. Labour hit its target of creating 1.6m new childcare places. Over 1.5m mothers rapidly made use of the new right brought in by Patricia Hewitt – who doubled up as trade secretary and minister for women – in 2003 to request flexible working hours from their employer. They got paid time off for family emergencies and three months parental leave. Maternity pay rose to £102.80 a week, up from eighteen to twenty-six weeks, with the right to unpaid leave for a further six months. Labour pledged to raise paid leave to nine months by 2007. New pension-sharing arrangements on divorce should see fewer women end up in old-age penury.

The House of Commons was still male, with women MPs forming only 18 per cent of the total. The Sex Discrimination (Election Candidates) Act 2002 allowed political parties to take positive measures to ensure a fairer gender balance in selections for candidates. Labour itself did not make sufficient use of it. The government did set a target of placing women in 45–50 per cent of public appointments by the end of 2005.

## Ethnic Minorities

During Labour's second term ethnic minorities remained worse off on almost every scale, but not all of them. A generalisation based on the experience of citizens of West

Indian descent, and those from the Punjab and Bengal, would miss the different experience of Indian Britons and those from West Africa. If race was a potent explanation of disadvantage, after 9/11 religion emerged as well as a cause and a consequence of separation and worrying differences.

Some minorities were desperately excluded. While 20 per cent of the white population was poor on official measures, it was 69 per cent for Pakistanis and Bangladeshis. The employment rate for non-whites remained markedly lower than for white people, despite growing job opportunities: only 58 per cent, which was some 17 per cent below the rate for the whole population. What explained the finding that 40 per cent of young whites left the New Deal to take a job compared with 31 per cent of non-whites? School students of Indian descent achieved well, beating the record of white pupils at GCSE. But students from Pakistani and Bangladeshi backgrounds fell far behind. But improvement was possible. Bangladeshi students moved up from bottom place over the last decade, overtaking both Pakistani and black children.

Disadvantage was reflected in where minorities lived. Three times more Pakistanis and Bangladeshis lived in unfit housing. Black students were three times more likely to be excluded from school. Some 16 per cent of African Caribbean men were in jail, when they formed only 2 per cent of the population. The Commission for Racial Equality found that white prisoners were far more likely than black to be let out early on tagging schemes.

Yet action by the Labour government was taken, both directly and indirectly. Because they were the poorest, ethnic minorities were often the focus of poverty and regeneration projects which ran the risk, said some MPs, of building resentment among residents in other areas who felt they were losing out. As the second term began, disturbances in Oldham, Burnley and Bradford showed how polarised life was in some areas of past migrant settlement. 'Community cohesion' became a Home Office theme. In 2004 the Audit Commission started assessing how well councils were performing under this rubric. Without specific targeting, it was often minorities who were among the principal beneficiaries of Sure Start and schemes that offered hope of improving life chances.

An Amendment to the Race Relations Act was introduced in 2003 as a result of an EU Directive that strengthened anti-discrimination law. The UK was far from alone among European countries in underachieving and discriminated-against ethnic groups. Across Europe race and religion were coalescing as themes in politics as fear of Islamic extremism and separation grew. Fundamentalist Muslims seemed to reject Western values – not just Western materialism, sex and greed, but core values of democracy and women's freedom. The liberal-minded found themselves in confusion. On the one hand, the British National Party attacked Muslims with naked race hate. On the other hand, some Muslims seemed to threaten the liberal values of British citizenship. Political alignments were hard to decipher. Elements of the left espoused Islam as a badge of their joint opposition to 'the West'. Liberals were alarmed at government appeasement of religious exclusivity as Blair encouraged the creation of more 'faith schools'. Confusion reigned as some argued that because Christian churches ran one third of all state-maintained schools, it was only fair the Muslims had their own. But single faith schools were not promoting 'social cohesion'. Instead they stood for 'multiculturalism', which was dangerously like separate development.

Trevor Phillips, chair of the Commission for Racial Equality, called multiculturalism lazy, arguing instead for 'an integrated society based on shared values and shared loyalties which allows for diversity and difference'. But what were these core values and what ought to be the fate of those who rejected them? Labour was as perplexed as its political opponents.

## Gay and Lesbian Rights

Labour did well on gay rights but on occasion it suited the Prime Minister and his colleagues to equivocate. The relatively little and eccentric opposition showed again how far the country had moved since Mrs Thatcher's day. In 2003 the hated Section 28 – of an obscure Thatcher local government act – was repealed. It was a largely unused and useless law brought in to prevent teachers and councillors 'promoting' homosexuality, which had deliberately caused deep offence and occasionally inhibited sex education.

In 2001 same-sex partners were given equal rights under the Criminal Injuries Compensation Scheme, after a bomb in a gay bar in Soho revealed that some of the victims were not eligible. The new equal age of consent at sixteen for gay sex became law in 2001. Immigration rules were changed to allow long-standing partners to stay together in Britain, in the same way that marriage to a British citizen bestows citizenship rights. A campaign against homophobic bullying in schools was launched in 2001, Don't Suffer in Silence.

But the most radical and, for gay couples, by far the most important legal change was the Civil Partnership Act of 2004 to give gay and lesbian couples the same tax and legal rights as married couples, without actually being married. They will be able to register their partnership in a registry office and acquire the same right to inherit one another's pension, pay no death duties on their shared home and enjoy the same inheritance rights. It will also reduce some entitlements. As a couple, not as two single people, they will also draw less in benefit and state pensions. The House of Lords tried to add wrecking amendments. It was another gnashing of the old teeth of the only half-reformed Upper House – but the law passed pretty much intact.

## Fairness: the Remarkable Top and Bottom One Per Cent

In the decade to 2005, average earnings rose by 45 per cent. But chief executives of the FTSE 100 companies enjoyed a rise of nearly 300 per cent. The picture was darker lower down the league. The bottom 1 per cent of earners saw their real incomes drop by 1.5 per cent between 1997 and 2001, despite the new tax credits. But, again, the fate of the bottom percentiles themselves distorted the picture. The bottom were not just poorer, they saw much lower increases than the average, so they kept falling behind year on year, while the top just carried on rising.

In our audit of Labour's first term we had a chart for the redistributive effect Labour's tax and benefit policies should have had across the spectrum. It showed the bottom 10 per cent should have gained most, while the top should have had their wings clipped a bit. But that was only a projection of the effect of government measures. Things did not work out that way, we now can see. Means-tested benefits such as tax credits were never claimed by a large slice of groups entitled to them, and some benefits for the childless fell behind.

When Labour left office in 1979, the top 1 per cent of income earners took 3.5 per cent of all income; by 2001 that had risen to 8 per cent. That top 1 per cent now earned over £107,100. Liberal Democrats urged that earnings over £100,000 should be taxed at 50 per cent: this would bring in another £5bn – enough for Labour to pay for universal children's centres to give all children a head start. But the Prime Minister went out of his way in the Commons to mock the idea and slap down any Labour minister who dared whisper support for this modest tax rise. Considering that Mrs Thatcher cut the top rate of income tax by 34 per cent, this seemed needless cowardice to many on Labour's side.

## Wealth

When the second term began, the top 1 per cent of the adult population owned 23 per cent of marketable wealth. The top 5 per cent owned 43 per cent. Imagine ten people waiting on a quayside for a consignment of ten Mercedes Benz saloons; one steps forward and claims five. The top half of the population owned 95 per cent of all the wealth. Those figures exaggerate the maldistribution slightly because they don't count in people's claim on state and occupational pensions. The point, however, is that we have no reason to believe the picture of inequality changed much between 2001 and 2005. The signs were that growing income difference converted itself into growing wealth inequality, as the rich invested in larger slices of property and shares. They had more to pass on to their children, cementing the wealth of those who came after them. Inheritance tax might stop the calcifying effect over the years but under Labour 95 per cent of estates paid none at all.

The pressing social disaster was the steep rise in property prices that would deepen the divide between the 70 per cent homeowners and the 30 per cent who owned nothing. The government did nothing.

## Fairness – Did Runaway Wealth Matter?

The government directed all its energies to pulling the poor over the poverty threshold. Was that not enough? Why are the rich in the upper stratosphere relevant to abolishing child poverty? New Labour forswore the politics of envy. The Prime Minister woos the rich and the Chancellor never rebukes them in his flattering speeches in the City. No one tells them of their rights *and* responsibilities.

It was as if Labour had bought the idea that having accepted capitalism, abandoned Clause Four and all that, you should never so much as raise an eyebrow about greed, excess and the sheer dysfunctionality of top pay. Directors of FTSE 100 companies took an average increase in salary of 17 per cent in 2002, and another 24 per cent in 2003 even as share prices tumbled, and 16 per cent in 2004, when the *Guardian*'s annual boardroom survey showed directors' pay soared at over three times the pace of average earnings. But still the Chancellor said nothing, not even about the lack of relationship between the noses in the troughs and their corporate performance. There was Sir Peter Davis, chairman of J Sainsbury plc. He walked away from a failing company, having wasted £3bn of shareholders' money on an IT system that did not work. His leaving package was corpulent, £2.6m in cash plus half a million in salary till his contract ran out plus pension contributions. Yet Davis could turn up at the Labour conference in Brighton in October 2004 to sit alongside ministers as if there was nothing wrong.

Poverty was bad from a UK plc point of view, forget social justice. The poor are poorly educated, they hold back aggregate wealth-creation, they lower productivity. All parties called for greater equality of opportunity, so that all children could become self-supporting, taxpaying citizens. New Labour has done much to further that aim, but had little or nothing to say about the damage done by inequality itself.

People did not like it. British Social Attitudes regularly reported that 82 per cent of people thought the gap between the rich and the poor too high. Poll after poll showed a strong, consistent belief that low earners deserved more, while top earners were paid too much. Professor Richard Layard showed how people draw a sense of their esteem and worth from their relative place in a nation's pecking order. Asked a hypothetical question, most say they would choose to have less money in a society where everyone had a fairer share, than more absolute wealth in a society where everyone else was far richer. It is recognition of this basic human instinct that fixed the international poverty measurement not as some absolute measure of need, but as a relative proportion of the wealth of the surrounding society.

The rich became increasingly isolated, ignorant of how ordinary people lived, let alone the poor. They did great damage, as their exorbitant pay began to persuade others that high earnings were normal. A salary of £100,000 became a benchmark in more spheres, although only 1 per cent of the population earned that much. Newspaper editors and BBC directors and everyone they knew in their hermetic worlds all earned many multiples of £100,000. In the media they controlled they reflected a world of privilege – so a threat to private school education or private health was wrongly described as an attack on 'middle England'. (Only 7 per cent of children went to fee-paying schools, only 11 per cent had any kind of private health policy.)

Other people's earnings were inflated. The median wage was only £21,000, the average only £26,000. But the privileged talked and wrote as if everyone earned at least twice as much. When we asked a merchant banker to guess the median salary he said £44,000 – more than double. That of course was a long way beneath what he could possibly think of living on; we dared not ask what he did earn.

## Social Mobility and Life Chances

Those who did well in an unequal society imagined they earned their place through merit. Justice, like history, gets written by the winners. Part of the prevailing mythology was that the structure of rewards was justified because everyone had, or could have, a chance to get to the top. We all approved of equal opportunity.

In 2002 Tony Blair had looked forward to the day when two babies born on the same day from different ends of the social scale would have the same chance of fulfilling their potential. Yet as Labour came to power, social mobility was slackening. In the postwar period, children had in large numbers moved up and away, ending up in a social position above their parents'. Despite its affluence and its job opportunities, Blair's Britain was seizing up slightly. People were staying up. A child born into a middle-class family was now fifteen times more likely to stay middle class than a working-class child was likely to enter that upper echelon. Children born in 1958 were far more likely to exceed their parents' social class and income than children born after 1970.

Of course the size of the social classes had changed. The middle or white-collar class was bigger. But in a genuinely open society, you could fall as easily as you could rise. The trouble was, middle-class children were being made fall proof as never before. They had money and power behind them. The expansion of universities benefited the not-so-clever better-off students before it did their contemporaries from lower-income homes. Even marriage and partnership was solidifying, as fewer young people 'married out'. Young people were marrying more rigidly into their own social class, further solidifying their status.

Things did not seem quite so rigid in other countries. France, Sweden and the Netherlands were more equal societies, and their education systems seemed better able to counteract their social divisions, though they, too, confronted ethnic and other divides. Estelle Morris pointed out that every year in school deepened rather than ameliorated class difference. Some 74 per cent of children in the highest social classes achieved five or more good GCSEs, twice as many as the children from the lowest social groups. Success in school itself depended on social programmes that relieved a family's poverty and helped a child to be ready to speak, think and learn when they go to nursery or primary school, so becoming fitter to fulfil their potential in junior school and in later life.

## Conclusion

In this chapter, 'better or worse?' translates into fairer or less just? Labour justly directed cash straight into the pockets of the poorest and as a result made large numbers significantly better off, including those not yet lifted over the threshold and out of officially defined poverty. Foundations were laid for a national network of children's centres that could, maybe, begin to re-equilibrate life opportunities, mitigating the effects of material deprivation. Great hopes were invested here, where children's prospects are first formed. This generation of politicians would be long retired before Labour's babies reached adulthood and the fruit of this great ambition could ripen – provided the paper plans were put into effect and the budgeted money spent. And provided the centres became a fixture of local life, high quality, never cut back and skimped, never turning into warehouses for young children.

Labour never got credit for monitoring, in the open, its own record on social justice. Every year a fat, well-presented document called *Opportunity for All* emerged from the Department of Work and Pensions with a detailed analysis of forty-two indicators of deprivation. It was remorselessly frank, its charts often depressing. It reminded us, for example, how far class determined success: 'The UK continues to have one of the widest socioeconomic gaps in educational attainment in Western Europe.' Although by 2005 most figures were moving in the right direction, how slowly they inched upwards. Some indicators remained inexplicably, obstinately flat.

Although this social Domesday Book was widely distributed, the media were never much interested. Slight monthly changes in house prices were eagerly reported, but deprivation indicators were not news. For yet more evidence, you could turn to *Breaking the Cycle – Taking Stock of Progress and Priorities for the Future*, from the Social Exclusion Unit. It told a grim tale of housing in Blair's Britain: both an example and a cause of widening wealth inequality. Some 70 per cent of people owned their own homes and they had seen their value double on Labour's watch.

Yet fewer homes were being built, both private and social, than for years. Not surprisingly, the number of families accepted by councils as homeless and in need of emergency accommodation more than doubled from 40,000 families in 1997 to 90,000 in 2004 – and these were only at the extremity of housing need. Spiralling house prices meant fewer people now moved out of the shrinking amount of council and social housing to make way for others because fewer of them could now afford to make the jump into buying their own homes. A growing number of first-time buyers now benefited from parents' or grandparents' assets cascading down to them, multiplying the distance between the property-owning families and families with no assets. The social divide between homeowning wealth-holders and those with no chance of getting a foot on the ladder now risked being set in concrete.

Paralysed by questions about the distribution of wealth, Labour stood by while the housing market drove divisions in wealth and social standing. For Labour continued to hope that it might be possible to create a fairer society – even a society with no poor children – by pulling them all up to somewhere nearer the middle, while doing nothing at all about the incomes and the accumulating wealth at the top. But fairness could not just be stopped at one point. It was symmetrical. How could you break a cycle where only 15 per cent of children of the unskilled go to university, compared with 79 per cent of children of professionals, without creating fewer differences between those two backgrounds? Over decades Nordic countries had flattened out wealth distribution and they still showed high growth and prosperity. In private Labour policymakers acknowledged it. In public they were dumb.

Small mercies. Labour came to power barely breathing a word about social justice and yet accomplished more than anyone expected. But if Labour remained in power, how much further could it travel along the path to fairness and opportunity for all without engaging the public and the well-off with the ideas of social justice?

# Child Poverty

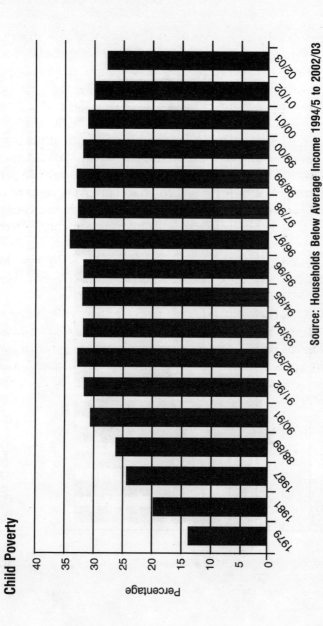

**Source: Households Below Average Income 1994/5 to 2002/03**

Children living below 60 per cent median income, after housing costs 1979–2003

**Pensioner Poverty**

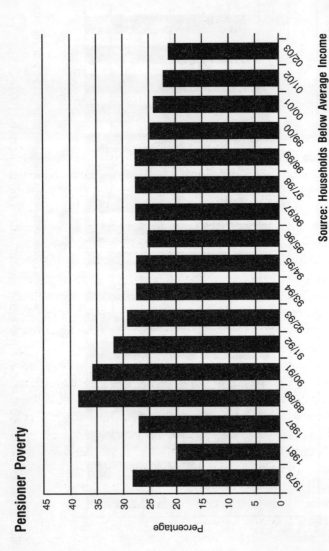

**Source: Households Below Average Income**

Pensioners living below 60 per cent median income after housing costs, 1979–2002/03

# CHAPTER THREE

# Wiser?

Towards the end of the second term . . . backlash. Labour's school results were called into question. Cultural conservatives attacked students' burgeoning success at GCSE and A-level. A real Conservative, Chris Patten, the chancellor of Oxford University, led a donnish charge against 'social engineering' in those injured tones reactionaries always use when bastions of privilege are opened up. He failed to explain why pursuing a national interest – Oxford as a premier research university – required more than half its undergraduates to come from private schools masquerading as charities while barring their classrooms to children unable to afford fees of £15,000 or more a year.

Of course exam standards had to be queried as results improved. But the critics never shared Labour's educational goals. They never saw the point of mass higher education, and feared only dilution of quality. Schools minister David Miliband said widening achievement challenged 'those who see danger in meritocracy, who see snakes and not just ladders in the educational rise of middle England'. His word 'revolution' was typically hyperbolic but his point about the defenders of the 'old order' was well made.

What was accomplished during the second Blair term was remarkable, and of course it was students not ministers passing the exams. Attainment, indeed annual increases in attainment, were the new norm. Parents, teachers and above all students shared a new mindset that defined schooling as progress. It was about burnishing the equipment young people would take with them into further education and careers. Miliband's ladders were now essential kit and they were expected to scale ever higher walls. Achieving schools were to drive the accelerating expansion of higher education that would fuel the 'knowledge economy' that had to be the UK's future.

But how inept ministers proved at convincing both their party colleagues and the arbiters of opinion of the need for change in student finances as a precondition of further growth in the universities. Vice-chancellors who stood to gain so much from this burst of expansion were struck dumb. They left the heavy lifting to often beleaguered Labour ministers.

However, higher numbers reaching university at the top were matched by continuing failures lower down, especially among those who left school as soon as they legally could. The UK had some seven million adults with 'inadequate' basic skills. The definition was not patronising: they could not read, do simple sums or understand enough to live the lives they might wish; they were barred from growing numbers of jobs. Although under Labour the UK moved up the league tables for attainment at fourteen, it remained rooted at the bottom for staying in education beyond the age of compulsory schooling. In its second term Labour struggled, like previous governments, to establish the connection between schooling, training and job performance. As ever, political sound and fury was vented on what affected the children of opinion-formers – A-levels and universities – and precious little public notice was paid to the vocational ladders up which the majority might scramble, improving themselves and improving the national skill set.

## Who and What was Education For?

Ministers extolled education as a personal acquisition and a collective benefit. Of course it was both, but they never quite got round to saying what proportion of each. To read Treasury papers was to see spending on education justified as an economic driver, deepening the UK's productive capacity: schooling was equated with skills that would increase output per head and make our goods and services more easily saleable abroad. Competitiveness was Gordon Brown's mantra, and it depended on human capital. Blair and Charles Clarke, Education Secretary after the departure of Estelle Morris, emphasised individual benefit and increased earning capacity.

The new student fees were justified because higher education was a personal asset designed to improve an individual's lifetime earnings. But Clarke then moved on effortlessly to discover the 'strategic' importance of chemistry and German for the nation's good, subjects in sad decline in universities. Yet, if Labour wanted it both ways no one else offered a model of how modern Britain should be educated and trained. Asked what they would do, practically, the educational reactionaries and the self-proclaimed opponents of dumbing down mumbled; they did not have the courage to face their own mean exclusivity. In East Asia, in North America, the doors of educational opportunity were swinging open and that was Labour's pivot too. Haltingly, Labour presented the country with the only credible version of its mental future.

## What's So Good About a Degree Anyway?

Out of the air Blair had plucked a target: Labour wanted 50 per cent of the eighteen to thirty age group to take degrees. Something of that order was a precondition of the knowledge economy. In the UK, said Brown, only 15 per cent of children from the poorest families went to university, compared with over 70 per cent from professional classes. Look abroad, to the United States, to Taiwan or Korea – they were moving towards 70 per cent of the entire population. Higher education was no luxury but a commercial imperative.

So far so good, but Labour rarely offered deeper thoughts about the purpose of education. Gradgrind target-chasing kept all eyes on the floor, not on the blue horizon. Ministers used the jobs argument exclusively in making the case for how to pay for expanding higher education. They might have cited evidence that people with degrees had more tolerant and civilised attitudes than those without. They were less likely to vote Conservative, so Conservatives might have been wiser than they knew in resisting the spread of high education.

Still, a less uplifting portrait of university life was painted by a survey in *The Times Higher Education Supplement* that found the typical early twenty-first-century undergraduate was 'likely to be a Liberal Democrat-voting, *Sun*-reading party animal who works part time in a shop and aspires to a career in advertising or the media'. As more graduates poured out of more universities, would there be cultural rewards – in the shape perhaps of a better-educated, less philistine, less loutish Britain? Would a graduate populace make other cultural choices in the television programmes watched, the newspapers read or even in the sophistication of its politics? Labour's utilitarian approach to education was in danger of washing away the faith that schooling was and should always be inherently civilising.

## Turning Around the Schools

Fruitful changes had been made under the Tories, but Tony Blair was entitled to highlight the transformation of schools as his big domestic legacy. Health care was something consumed when people needed it; but education was an investment, building muscle fibre. Not all schools, however, and not all students. Education was another sphere of Blairite social policy characterised by the gap – which may have grown – between the upper four-fifths and the bottom feeders, down in the darkness in terms of policy and public attention. Fewer than before, significant numbers (as many as a quarter of the school population) still left primary school not only underachieving but ceasing to care about achievement; children's attitudes meshed with their parents'.

David Miliband put up slides proving primaries in the poorest areas had improved faster than schools at large. But Labour failed to emancipate large numbers from a culture of failure and underperformance. By the end of the second term, Labour was forced to confront how very much harder it is to overcome generations of failure than had been blithely assumed in 1997. Radical steps were suggested. The Commons' Education and Skills committee proposed a crack squad of higher paid and specially trained teachers mobilised to be drafted in to work in the most difficult schools.

But Labour's persistence did win something that had been perilously close to collapse: a renewal of confidence by the public in schools based on a renaissance of teacher professionalism. Higher paid, better respected, more of them, better supported in the classroom, some 399,200 teachers were in service (on a full-time equivalent basis) in English schools in 1997. In 2004 that had risen to 427,800. The National Union of Teachers (NUT) carped as ever at conference time, though when its members had a choice they decided to replace the repetitively negative Doug MacAvoy as general secretary with a more positive voice.

## Blair's Children

No one had yet referred to 'Blair's children' but they were there, passing through the secondary schools. The age cohort that entered junior school in, say, 1998 should be doing better; research had shown the introduction of a literacy hour in primary education had lingering influence, even up to the age of fourteen. The grand plan had been: first, improve the primary schools, then attention would shift to the secondaries. But how sustainable were the gains made in the first term? After 1997, there had been a breakthrough in primary schooling, but it was far harder second time around to keep up that rate of progress. For results at seven, eleven and fourteen the metaphor during Blair's second term was plateau or flatlining, as Charles Clarke put it.

## Primary

Class sizes had been cut in primary schools as they refocused on basic literacy and numeracy. Targets had been reset on the assumption that rates of improvement would go on rising; they were mostly missed. Old, super-confident promises came back to haunt Labour ministers. When David Blunkett was Education Secretary in the first term, he had pledged that by 2002, 85 per cent of eleven-year-olds would reach the acceptable age-related standard in English. In fact, by 2003, only 75 per cent did. Similarly in maths there was what the Treasury delicately called 'slippage'. The target was reassigned first to 2004 then to 2006. Teachers, inspectors and (privately) ministers and officials said it would be hard going to achieve it by that date, too. This was the most important test of all: a child not reading on moving to secondary school was destined to flounder and drown.

At age seven, 84 per cent reached the expected level in

reading, 90 per cent in maths. Writing scores dropped in 2003, but the content of the tests had changed. A year later, when assessment based on teachers' reports had been added to the mix in some schools, there was little average change – 90 per cent in maths and 82 per cent in writing. Reading improved one point to 85 per cent.

At age eleven, the numbers leaving primary schools with the requisite level of written English for their age did rise slightly, to 77 per cent in 2004, while 83 per cent could read adequately. Maths was up to 74 per cent but science down a shade at 86 per cent. There was, of course, a steep social class gradient to attainment and failure. The number of low-performing schools fell, but in 2000 Labour had promised to cut to zero the number of local education areas where fewer than 78 per cent of pupils achieved the norm at age eleven; this target too was missed by a wide margin.

Labour's reputation with figures was poor. This was partly a successful piece of sabotage by the right-wing press, partly a self-inflicted wound. The great achievement had been to get three-quarters of eleven-year-olds up to the standard for the first time; the failure was the fate of the other quarter. David Miliband expressed the difference between that 75 per cent and the 85 per cent target in terms of real individuals: 'We are not willing to give up on those 60,000 young people,' he said. He did not elaborate what he thought about the rest, the 15 per cent of those passing from the primary schools as solid non-achievers.

Failure in whittling down these numbers meant another phalanx marching – stumbling – into secondary school class-rooms and then into adult life as chronic underachievers, relatively unproductive, relatively unfulfilled and likely in turn to produce underachieving children. However, Labour was never deterministic about these 'cycles of deprivation'. Even if helping these children later on in the system became ever harder, it was never impossible. What Labour saw in the research as associations between parents' level of education and children's was just that, a link, not an inevitable cause.

Still, it was dismaying how, after 2001, the plateau became a peak as even David Normington, the permanent secretary at the Department for Education and Skills, confessed 'the greatest difficulty moving it upwards'. His colleague, Peter Housden, director-general of schools, had rejected the 'plateau' figure of speech, saying success knew no limits. But where were the crampons and pickaxes with which to climb?

Primary schools were being 'targeted', with heads being offered packages of advice and support. More effort was made to track the progress of individual children, to catch those needing extra help. There were, in 2004, some signs that you could get improved figures from schools in deprived areas which had been made the focus of effort: these schools improved faster than the rest. But the reservoir of under-achievement was constantly refilled as children in the second term continued to enter first primary then secondary schools disposed to fail themselves.

## Catch-up – the Transition to Secondary School

Without reading and writing at the level of their age group children were predestined to keep on underachieving in secondary schools. Labour pumped new money, £670m, into the 'transition' but catch-up schemes for those entering comprehensives with poor maths had limited success.

Ministers had said they would move to target secondary schools. Indeed, the 2001 white paper *Schools: Achieving Success* talked 'transformation'. Variations in achievement between schools and areas were to be ironed out. Performance at fourteen was the new focus, what the education world called Key stage 3. The tools were more training for teachers and that concentrated attention by ministers and by inspectors that seemed to have produced results in the first term.

It did seem to work. The proportion of fourteen-year-old students reaching the norm (level 5 in the jargon) in English rose four points to 69 per cent between 2001 and 2003. Maths showed a five-point rise to 71 per cent. But this was improvement well short of the official targets, which said 75 per cent of fourteen-year-olds should reach the norm now and by 2007 it should be 85 per cent.

## Sport

If they could count, could they kick a ball or run a circuit? A new target was set: for three-quarters of schoolchildren to take part in a minimum of two hours of PE or sport each week, by 2006. By the autumn of 2004, only 61 per cent of children were putting on their kit and panting through their paces. Lottery money had been channelled into building and renovating sports halls and changing rooms. Labour said it had arrested the precipitate decline in school playing fields: schools were applying to sell them off at the rate of forty a month in the 1990s, now it was only seventeen in a year of which nine were approved. Playing fields were symbols rather than fields of Olympic prowess; when they were at their maximum acreage, medals were scarce. Some of the money won from selling what the sports minister Richard Caborn called soggy fields had been recycled into all-weather, floodlit pitches. Ministers talked of rehabilitating competitiveness. Out with the 'politically correct nonsense of the 1980s that competition damages children' (spouted by the selfsame ministers in their younger days). In with fat-busting, goal-scoring exercise. Labour's plan was 'partnership' between specialist sports colleges and other schools, plus a reserved fund to pay for professional sports coaches and trained PE teachers to go into schools with missionary zeal.

## GCSE

You didn't need a maths GCSE – or a good result at Key stage 3 for that matter – to wonder if, in this welter of numerical targets, Labour ministers ever thought through their ambitions. Let's assume that the content and difficulty of GCSE exams remained the same from year to year (which is official doctrine and is intended to be assured by the examining bodies' independent status). If the rate at which students secured top grades increased, within a comparatively few years everyone would get top grades, which would severely lessen the usefulness of the exams as indicators of attainment.

Yet this is what ministers did, setting as a target from 2002 onwards a 2 per cent annual rise in the proportion of sixteen-year-olds getting GCSE grades A* to C. The 2004 figure was 52.9 per cent across England, Wales and Northern Ireland, up 1.1 per cent on the preceding year. This could be hailed as solid, incremental achievement. Every year since 1997 (or 1987 for that matter) the proportion getting a decent GCSE grade had risen.

But you could state the converse. Two out of every five sixteen-year-olds are still passing through nine years of compulsory schooling with very little to show for it, not in terms of the certification on which modern employers judged potential and attitude. Proportionately more of them were male. Girls did better than boys by a full 5 per cent in getting GCSE A* to C grades. What seemed to have been happening in secondary schools was that strenuous efforts were being made between ages fourteen and sixteen to push students through GCSE. But it had the effect of marginalising (weeding out) those unlikely to pass. The result, nationally, has been more passes at the top grades but growth also in the proportion who failed altogether.

## The Rise and Fall of Subjects

On Labour's watch, the study of foreign languages in secondary schools became optional from age fourteen, leading to justified fears that fewer students would acquire any knowledge of non-English language and the 'difficult' languages (ie those other than French and Spanish) would be studied by tiny numbers. However about seven out of ten still studied a language at sixteen. The government asserted that measures to encourage language teaching in primaries would be more effective long term than 'force feeding' reluctant GCSE students. Languages were a falling subject in universities as well. Ofsted showed that the numbers doing a language were markedly fewer in schools with poorer pupils.

But there had been a rise in the numbers taking subjects such as maths, chemistry and physics. What was to be made of concurrent trends towards more entries in statistics, ICT, physical education and religious studies? Anxious about maths, the government commissioned a study and then appointed a maths czar, Professor Celia Hoyles of the London Institute of Education. Among likely moves forward were subject-specific in-service courses for teachers. Ofsted said schools did a good job in teaching music but feared poorer children missed out on learning to play an instrument even when fees were remitted. Here was a good example of how, despite the allegation of centralisation against Labour, vertiginous variation remained between areas. Some charged; some raised large sums from parents; some were enthusiastic – and some the contrary. The future cellists of the Birmingham Symphony Orchestra would be women and their trumpet players men. According to a survey gender differences were marked in choice of instrument at school. The saxophone was the one instrument played in equal numbers by young men and young women.

## Selective Schools

Most children at eleven went to comprehensives. But there were around 150,000 students in state grammar schools, compared with 112,000 in the early 1990s. This was about 4.6 of all secondary-age students, a number which, to Labour's embarrassment, actually rose slightly since 1997 as some schools expanded. The famous Blunkett compromise in the first term gave some parents an effective veto on changing local selective systems, whatever the genuine local sentiment about grammar schools (which was mainly against). The Blunkett local voting system was used only once, in Ripon, where a vote kept open a local grammar school. Unfairly, parents with children at the secondary moderns, which are the necessary unfortunate result of grammars, were given no such device to overturn the system that was so disadvantaging their children. Secondary moderns are among the lowest attaining of any secondary schools. Studies comparing comprehensive with selective systems have to contend with the differing social profiles of selective schools, but grammar school education authorities have done noticeably worse overall. However, Kent, finding itself falling ever further behind similar counties in educational results, began to dismember its grammar school system voluntarily, in order to improve all-round results. Using entitlement to free school meals as a guide to home circumstances, only about 2.7 per cent of grammar students are poor. The average for secondary schools across England and Wales is 17.1 per cent.

## Private Schools

Under Labour the smallish numbers of children in independent schools – that euphemism for parents paying fees – continued to rise slightly. Fees averaged just over £9,000 a year, £18,000 for boarding schools. Fees had also been rising sharply, by over 9 per cent in the year to 2004. Was it surprising, as with private health care, that more well-off families did not abandon state education? In 1972 6.1 per cent of children were in private schools, but this had only risen to 7.1 per cent by 2004. This was a low number – fee-paying schools educated some 6 per cent of pupils in egalitarian Sweden, admittedly on the basis of a state voucher scheme. It made the undue influence of this privileged sector on cultural life all the more astonishing. Ratios of public to private were abnormally high in certain London boroughs, 40 per cent of Kensington and Chelsea's children were in private schools. This had profound effects on local state schools and the dysfunctions of London education were allowed to colour and distort Westminster and Fleet Street opinion about the education system as a whole.

They certainly seemed to affect thinking inside Number Ten. Despite contrary evidence New Labour thinkers feared the flight of the middle classes from the welfare state. If the better off no longer benefited personally from the NHS or state schools, for how much longer would they pay taxes? In education, it became an unannounced policy to refashion secondary schools to make them more attractive to middle-class parents. Yet statistically there was no significant sign of middle-class flight – except when seen through the distorting prism of the London school system.

## Making All Schools Specialist

The subterranean theme was selection but the policy was 'specialisation'. At the same time as GCSE results were improving – a sure sign of the comprehensives' general success – Tony Blair personally ordained that they all change radically. Alastair Campbell, his press spokesman, pro-

nounced the end of the 'bog-standard comprehensive'.
Schools were to acquire a new identity expressed as a
particular strength. The theory was that they would still
be comprehensive, open to all, and offer general education,
but in addition specialist courses, in business studies, technology, arts and music; they would be allowed to select 10
per cent of students according to their 'aptitude', though it
was never explained how an eleven-year-old's aptitude for
business was to be spotted. The one proscribed specialisation
was 'academic' – it was fair suspicion that any test of
'aptitude' would predispose a school to select the more
academically successful. Yet it proved unfounded. By 2004
only 100 specialist comprehensives had used their 10 per cent
quota and Charles Clarke said it would be abolished.

The theory was that excellence in any one field was infectious and raised the sights of all the students and teachers and it
was not a new one. Already in 1997 one in twelve secondary
schools had a specialist focus. By 2004 Labour had increased
that to six out of ten and the government said these schools'
attainment levels as measured by GCSE results were higher: 10
per cent more of their sixteen-year-olds were getting a good
reasonable result than the average.

## 'Foundation' Schools

In 2004 the government unveiled a new five-year plan for
education. Much of it restated existing policy but it was put out
with those deferential nods towards middle England that had
become so characteristic. 'School uniforms and Hogwarts-
style school house systems belong in this category', noted the
BBC's education correspondent Mike Baker, observing there
would be no actual legislation to make them happen.

The plan was to move beyond specialisation into the education equivalent of 'foundation' status. (Education already

recognised the phrase; under the Tories, the word had been used for their efforts to move schools away from local authority control.) State-funded still, officially non-selective and required to teach the national curriculum, they would acquire new freedom to own their own land and buildings, employ staff and put some extra emphasis on business studies, foreign languages, arts or IT. Independent, yes, but the money for their buildings would still be doled out by councils. As in health, where 'choice' became a watchword in the latter half of Blair's second term, ministers did not pay much attention to the detailed ecologies of public institutions; how far in many areas could there be any more choice than the local school, regardless of its proclaimed specialisation? Sport was one of the new specialisms. By mid-2004 there were over 230 sports colleges, with 250,000 pupils. The government swore that students who preferred reading to rugby would not be penalised, but the right not to choose a particular specialist school was denied to swathes of families.

## City Academies

A variation was the 'city academy', newly built comprehensives in the poorest areas endowed with £2m of private capital provided by business or religious institutions. There were to be 200 of them by the end of the decade. Since they were all to be located where local schools had failed for years, the fears of defenders of the comprehensive principle seemed exaggerated. In 2004 one, the King's Academy in Middlesbrough, showed GCSE results better than the schools it replaced. There was a slight whiff of hypocrisy in the air. The King's Academy was supported by the Vardy Foundation. The Vardy family, who made their money from car dealing, were evangelical Christians. Richard Dawkins, the biologist, had described the teaching in another school supported by the family as educational debauchery, because it took a creationist line. But the very foundation of the 1944 educational settlement had been the admission of thousands of church schools into state support. Nuns and priests who might be tenacious followers of Vatican beliefs on homo-sexuality or single motherhood were paid by the state to teach in Roman Catholic schools. It was already a bizarre feature of this most secular land that one third of all its State schools were religious.

## Choice

Religious parents – that's to say Anglican, Catholic and to a limited extent Jewish parents – had a right to choose state-subsidised sectarian education. Amid declining church atten-dance the denominational Christian schools became even more anomalous. Catholic schools educated 720,000 young people in England and Wales, 10 per cent of the school population. Muslims were demanding the same and, under Labour, their claims were starting to be recognised. For the bulk of parents choice was usually exercised, if at all, within an ecology, a local pattern of primaries and secondaries. Only one in ten appealed against the secondary school to which their children were allocated (compared with one in thirty primary parents). The trouble with choice was that popular schools were often suspected of doing the choosing. Also it would always be the case that astute parents would be best at operating a choice system, but then they were equally adept at moving house to be close to better schools in a geographically based system or navigating any other device. Choosing the right combination of a specialisation, a single sex or co-ed school, and choosing or avoiding a religious school would need a sophisticated computer program to navigate, but it was largely an academic exercise. Within reasonable travel time of home, outside London and the inner cities, there was often only going to be one school – a community school in fact if rarely in name.

## Standards Rising or Slipping?

Labour had a go during the first term at refashioning the post-sixteen curriculum. Its efforts turned out to be both too much and insufficient. Curriculum 2000, as the plan was called, strove to widen the education of young people while satisfying the universities that highly specialised eighteen-plus qualifications were still there to fill their needs. But it led, inevitably some said, to an excess of exams; it was a missed opportunity to think about school-leaving qualifications in the round. This task was later handed to the former schools inspector Mike Tomlinson, but not until an ill-fated experiment in AS-levels had broken over the heads of the guinea-pig age cohort of sixteen-year-olds from 2000 through Labour's second term.

AS-levels were a clutch of examinations at seventeen, intended to broaden the first year of sixth form studies but still allow focus in the eighteen-plus exam. The original idea had been that students would pick an extra AS-level of the opposite discipline to their main one. The government bottled out since there were not enough maths and science teachers to force every arts A-level student to take a science, in the European mode, rendering the whole upheaval of dubious value.

## Truancy

Unexplained absence from school was an affliction of under-achievers, indeed truancy was a measure of educational potential: those not in a classroom would never pass a test.

In the second term truancy did not go up, but it did not go down, either. Over 1 per cent of half-days marked by secondary teachers in England in 2002–03 were missed by truants; that constitutes a vast number of hours of instruction, stimulation and preparation lost. That figure did not improve and is broadly the same as in 1997. In primary schools, where truanting is even more damaging, just over 0.4 per cent of all half-days were lost, slightly down on 1997's 0.5 per cent.

## A-Level

A-level results in August 2002, the first fruits of the new system, showed improvement but also produced complaints, inflamed (as ever) by press reporting. The allegation was that the examination boards (now semi-autonomous and supposedly 'business like' in their operations) had doctored the results to ensure comparability with the pre-AS era. In the panic, the chairman of the Qualifications and Curriculum Authority, Sir William Stubbs, refused to fall on his sword like an English gent.

An inquiry by Mike Tomlinson found nothing untoward in the way the exam boards adjusted marks. The Commons' education committee in its turn concluded that press reports about tens of thousands of students complaining were plain wrong – by no means the only example in Labour's second term of direct and damaging intervention by the newspaper press in social policy. While the A-level curriculum and methods of assessment were changing, the examination boards did a good job of ensuring year to year comparability.

The MPs gave Labour (and its Tory predecessors) a bouquet by declaring that the increased numbers passing A-level could be explained by, first, the changes in the exam since 1983, and by widespread improvement in teaching quality and resources over two decades. In August 2004 an unprecedented proportion of entrants passed their A-levels (96 per cent). Some 22.4 per cent got a top grade and 22,000 English students received straight As.

The results fuelled debate about post-sixteen education. In another report, Tomlinson proposed a single diploma covering work done after the age of fourteen. It would record work experience, which he said should be available for some pupils for two to three days a week. GCSE would transmute into an exam moderated by teachers themselves, which would mitigate the growing costs of external exams. A-levels would be kept and concessions made to the universities by offering new super grades and essays giving them clearer sight of top performers. But the thrust of the plan was to offer something more from school to the 60 per cent of the eighteen-year-old age group who did not sit A-levels. Labour might have seized on the bones of the plan, however much quibbling there would be on the details; here, potentially, was a way of tackling productivity deficits at the same time as bumping up opportunity for the many. Ministers were tepid. Employers, who had been calling for a new sixteen-plus scheme along Tomlinson lines, went limp, saying they feared the changes would be disruptive.

## School Budgets

There's a law in contemporary history that says second-term cabinets find tinkering with the machinery a lot easier than getting the vehicle going. Labour spent time altering the way schools were paid for, further diminishing the role of local education authorities. They no longer controlled school budgets but were left, as a kind of afterthought, with difficult things such as school transport and special educational needs. School heads were required to become super administrators as well as inspiring educationists, and school governors took on new responsibilities.

The Blairites harped on about schools' autonomy, only to be confronted halfway through the second term with demands for better integration of schools into their surrounding communities. Schools were suddenly destined to become the hub for all kinds of support for families and children, social services, health, arts and sport and for adult learning. But that was exactly the kind of local integration that local education authorities had been supposed to help engineer. (This mirrored the twin contradictory aims for foundation hospitals which were supposed to be in independent competition with each other, yet cooperate in an integrated hub-and-spokes operation.)

But for Number Ten and the Education Department, LEAs had disbarred themselves by failing to tackle failure or to respond to parents' demands over many years. Unlike LEAs, inherently variable in performance and spending, centralising educational administration produced guaranteed minimum budgets, allowing heads and governors the unwanted luxury of planning for three years ahead. But rhetoric from other ministers about the 'new localism' and promises to expand the autonomy of councils in order to revitalise local democracy ran directly counter to this centralising move which leapfrogged local council control.

## Targets

Labour did lighten the regulation burden on schools but only slightly. The targets applied since 1997 remained securely in place. Ministers and civil servants would think up numbers which schools, teachers and students would be asked/told to achieve. In education, as in health, the public heard the instructions being issued and assumed an instant response. People seemed to think education was command and control, edicts turned overnight into operations. They did not understand the disarticulation between ministers and the chalk face. Letters and instructions were sent out, inspectors called, payments adjusted, but improvement depended on councillors, local officials, heads, governors and teachers choosing to pull in the same direction. And even if they did, results depended on students and their families, peer pressures and money.

Schools minister Miliband said he got the message about over-specifying schools' performance. By 2005, all 24,000 English primary, secondary and special schools had been inspected at least twice since Labour came to power. Under Labour the budget of the Office of Standards in Education (Ofsted) nearly tripled, rising from £86m in 1998–99 to £208m in 2003–04. It was, MPs noted, 'the size of a small government department'. Was it time, the government wondered, to back off a bit? Inspectors were to turn up less frequently but without warning, making inspection less burdensome. Greater weight was to be given teachers' own assessments. The dread 'special measures' for failing schools remained. Ofsted, which now monitored pre-school children as well might, Blair said, usefully be amalgamated with other inspectorates dealing with children.

## Building Boom

During Labour's second term tracts of the public sector became a building site. A proxy index of what Labour's second term achieved is the share price of companies building and leasing cranes. They lifted and swung above thousands of hospital and school sites. Many heads, in addition to their educational worries, had to juggle dump trucks and temporary accommodation as a huge programme of physical improvement unfolded, with a tilt towards schools in economically deprived areas. In 2005–06 more than £5bn would be spent on school buildings, seven times the capital available in 2000. The plan, published in May 2003, was called *Building Schools for the Future*, but would have been more aptly entitled 'Coping with a great backlog of repairs and maintenance caused by stopping and starting and, for long years, freezing capital spending on the nation's infrastructure'.

This was the sheer unprecedented scale of it: overall capital investment in education in England was worth £1bn in 1997 and £6bn in 2005. Under Gordon Brown's plans it would rise to just over £8bn in 2008. That, Brown said, provided the wherewithal for transformation. It meant 'that for every constituency in the country by 2015 every secondary school can be refurbished or rebuilt with world-class technology'.

## IT

It was not just the buildings. Ofsted reported in 2004 that schools' information and communications technology (ICT) resources were 'at record levels'. But a laptop and a modem are so much scrap metal without someone to log pupils on. Ofsted also reported 'the competence of school staff in information and communications technology has risen dramatically since 1997'. In *ICT in Schools: the Impact of Government Initiatives Five Years On*, inspectors said nine out of ten teachers were competent users of ICT; six out of ten lessons in ICT were rated good or better.

Despite that, pupils' exposure to computers and the internet varied. In many schools chances to use the new technology on a daily basis were lost. Ofsted expressed its 'severe disappointment' at gaps in another essential part of the ICT revolution – updating and upgrading teachers' skills. Excellence in parts combined with some weakness and inconsistency.

## Libraries

Children found better services out of school, though local librarians complained about budgets. They were under pressure from the Department for Culture, Media and Sport to 'go far beyond their once traditional role of book loans to make substantial contributions in areas such as literacy, lifelong learning, community building, good citizenship and social inclusion'. By 2005 all public libraries were connected to the internet, with 89 per cent (2004's figure) offering broadband access.

## Museums and Galleries

Blair's children were spending more time in museums and galleries. Visits by children to museums and galleries in England increased 80 per cent in the four years to 2002. The national collections (Science Museum, National Maritime Museum, Walker art gallery and so on) recorded thirty-three million visits in 2003, up 40 per cent on 1998, after Labour had abolished entry charges; many of these new visitors were children.

## Pay, Conditions and Assistants

Classrooms were better stocked. Amid controversy at first with union claims of 'dilution' (extraordinary, since teacher numbers were shooting up), Labour's creation of a new sub-profession, the classroom assistant rapidly gained wide approval. By the end of Brown's spending period in 2008 there should be 80,000 of them in England.

In the second term the attractions of teaching in those classrooms also rose unmistakably. If not trendy, teaching became a much more popular option for graduates – a novelty in a time of high graduate employment. (It was a sign of the times that the denizens of the TV series *Teachers* were young, smart and sexy – Channel Four even found a way, in *Green Wing*, of making hospital managers a laugh a minute.) Initial teacher-training numbers rose from just under 30,000 a year in the year before the 2001 election to just over 40,000 in 2003–04. Even so, half of all teachers were aged over forty-five – which would pose the schools problems as they retired.

Yet the job again took on some of the trappings of a decent middle-class career with status, good pay and access to honours at the top end. The starting salary for teachers moved to £18,500 plus. Increases were not startling, 2.5 per cent in April 2004, with another 2.95 per cent the following year, but a new spine made progression easier. To make the career more attractive maths graduates were offered a golden hello worth up to £5,000; for them the salary scale was unplugged, allowing some to move beyond £50,000 a year after only five years' experience. Numbers entering initial training in science had fallen in Labour's first term, but now picked up. In 2003–04 2,500 graduates started training to teach maths, nearly 1,500 more than in 1998–99. But fewer than half those who began teacher training were still in the classroom five years later. Part of the problem was support and organisation in the early months of a teacher's career.

## The Status of Teaching

The lightening of the inspection regime for schools fell short of the NUT's demand for self-evaluation by teachers, subject to external validation. This was tantamount to saying, trust the professionals. But professionals, generally speaking, did not belong to trade unions. They expelled members whose standards fell short. So teaching hovered somewhere on the margins.

Labour had established the General Teaching Council which gave teachers some role in regulating admissions to their own ranks. Headteachers had rich autonomy. What told against professionalism was the dog-in-the-manger attitude of many teachers. Opinion surveys found extraordinary signs of alienation. Only a quarter of secondary school teachers – in a poll published in *The Times Educational Supplement* in January 2004 – agreed schools were better funded than in 2004. (Real funding per pupil had risen from £2,930 in England in 1996–97 to £3,660 in 2003.) Teachers complained about lower status and increased insecurity. Only four in ten accepted their pay had improved since Labour came to power – one in five even said it had fallen, in blatant disregard of the (average) truth.

Was it the pupils that were the problem? Indiscipline, violent behaviour and verbal abuse were cited by many for leaving or thinking of leaving the profession. Labour's initiatives on poor behaviour had to work. Yet the irony behind this psychic disorientation was that schooling – by all objective measures, especially the government's – was more effective than ever, at least in the basic sense of certifying students' progress. In one poll, working in education ranked third in students' top ten desired jobs, after advertising, public relations and the media. Whatever that says about the values emerging from Blair's second term, at least teaching had gained in glamour, respect and desirability.

## Mass Higher Education

The rapid increase in A-level passes made unassailable Tony Blair's determination to expand university places. Those who oppose expansion never said what they would do with disappointed successful A-level students denied the chance to progress.

Mass higher education realised Old Labour dreams of opportunity, opening up the Ali Baba's cave of campus and college to the many and no longer the privileged few. Blair could claim (though he never liked Old Labour analogies) he was realising the work started by Harold Wilson in the 1960s, when alongside the plate-glass institutions he opened the Open University. This was what Neil Kinnock had lunged towards in his speech in 1987 about being the first of a thousand generations of Kinnocks to get the chance of higher education. For any Labour government, this blend of individual opportunity for betterment and collective national benefit (the knowledge economy and all) should have been a heady mixture.

But if under Labour courses and colleges burgeoned, ministers proved curiously inept at firing popular imagination with its ambitions. Fees provoked placards and a parliamentary revolt. Ministers dithered, allowing the vice-chancellors to define too many terms. Further education colleges, a great, unsung archipelago of educational opportunity, vocational preparation and second chances remained curiously marginal in Labour's vision. They might have been and could still become the vector of expansion. But they would need to be recognised as degree-giving institutions and emancipated from dependency on universities.

Official numbers in higher education rose from 41 per cent in 1999 to 44 per cent in 2003; by 2010 50 per cent were to attend college. That American phrase 'college' was apt. Entry to higher education became the normal expectation of all middling households. Charles Clarke envisioned universities as hubs of regional economies, drawing private capital to the cities of the North while enriching their cultural lives. Yet he seemed unable to work out the nomenclature and dynamics of a system that could contain – as the American system does – elite research institutions at one end and jobs-market-attuned community colleges at another.

Indeed, Labour found the politics of this transformation hard going in a territory still ruled – literally and metaphorically – by graduates of ancient and exclusive universities. It was not just the problem of redistributing the costs and benefits of acquiring a degree but the government's ambiguity about one of the very purposes of education, especially at its upper end – to discriminate between the sheep and the goats, the alphas and the gammas, the internationally excellent and the locally adequate.

Top-up fees charged at variable rates only served to make steeper the existing hierarchy. Blair and Brown talked about world-beating universities to take on the Ivy League but never about the inevitable consequences – downgrading scores of lesser universities which had for years clung to the belief that they, too, could be the equals of Manchester, Nottingham and Cambridge. But the available public money had to be concentrated. Blair and Brown also talked about the universities' role in wealth-creation, which, they said, was not fully developed. Universities (thanks to state funding) were to become more active partners for profit-seeking companies. Some did; pharmaceuticals, biotechnology and aspects of IT benefited enormously from the academic connection. Suggestions for strengthening the university–business link came from a report commissioned in 2002 by Gordon Brown from the former editor of the *Financial Times*, Richard Lambert. As universities became more attuned to commerce they would become freer, thanks to new non-government streams of revenue.

But at the same time the government tinkered and twitched in the face of criticism. Dumbing down was a wounding charge and one minister made an unfortunate remark about 'Mickey Mouse degrees' to be had from the former polytechnics, which seemed to support Tory ideas that a degree in golf course management was a waste of time and money.

(The Americans found it perfectly possible to accommodate degrees in aromatherapy – a serviceable job training – alongside archaeology and astrophysics.)

Labour inaugurated new two-year 'foundation degrees' in more vocational subjects. The higher education opportunity, ministers seemed to realise, was financially feasible if larger numbers studied at the institutions offering a great array of non-traditional subjects. Companies in the private sector were crying out for the new qualifications, Charles Clarke said, but this turned out to be another example of Labour wishing the private sector were more farseeing than it is. Only about 25,000 students were taking foundation degrees in 2004, rising – the government hoped – to 50,000 by 2006.

## Universities Unwilling to Change

Student numbers had grown under the Tories but funding per student had fallen behind. Universities complained, but they seemed unwilling to ask some basic questions about their identity, and ministers neither. Some ancient traditions were too sacred to challenge, such as the cost of hundreds of thousands of eighteen-year-olds moving to expensive far-away student accommodation so that they had in effect two homes, while in other European countries with less state subsidy students attended universities nearby and lived at home. And why three relatively relaxed years and not two more intense? And why were so few academics properly trained, like schoolteachers, to impart knowledge? There were questions that should have been asked about the nature of degrees themselves, and the growing specialisation of academic knowledge and the uselessness of some of it, but that would be seen as political trampling in the sacred groves of academe.

The UK's economic success depended on the production of

new knowledge, but how much and at what cost? In conditions of austerity, it turned out UK science had done remarkably well. Chief scientist David King argued (in a paper in *Nature*) that the UK's share of world scientific publications in the four years to 2001 was disproportionately high. He said it might be explained by the spending levels in the fifteen years prior to the mid-1990s which 'encouraged a level of resourcefulness among researchers and approaches to industry that are now bearing fruit'.

## Who Should Pay and How?

In its first term Labour began to recalibrate the individual's and the collective costs and benefits of higher education. Most people accepted that, one way or another, students themselves should pay more, either upfront or on a deferred basis, with the money coming from the higher earnings commanded by graduates. The basic argument was that the general taxpayer – including the low-paid families who never went near a university – should not be made to pay for the privilege of those destined to earn the most.

But Labour's rethinking of student finance became a battleground between Number Ten and the Treasury. The fight was ostensibly over flat-rate top-up or variable fees and over a graduate tax versus loans. It was probably more about the signs and symbols of Blairism, New Labour and egalitarianism.

All universities charged, but what they charged fell short of the real cost of undergraduate education and was capped at a uniform level by the government. Even the richest families, the maximum fee-payers, contribute only 25 per cent of the cost of their offsprings' courses, with subjects such as medicine and engineering far more heavily subsidised.

## Top Up

Top-up fees had been sold to Blair through his special adviser Andrew Adonis. They reflected the interests of the 'Russell' or elite group of universities (their vice-chancellors used to meet in the Russell Hotel in Bloomsbury). These wanted state support but not state controls; they wanted the government to subsidise higher fees while they were allowed to charge their students extra for degrees the market would value more highly.

Labour had already started charging students a notional contribution towards the cost of university education; poorer students (family income less than £21,000 a year) were exempt. In the second term, Tony Blair moved to increase fees and adjust the loans scheme (which had hitherto covered accommodation and living costs) to pay for them.

The package which emerged in a white paper in January 2003 sought to balance Labour egalitarian worries about access for the poorest with Labour's elitist commitment to the top universities. From autumn term 2006, universities could charge fees up to £3,000 a year. Clarke, hubristically, promised that they would stay at this level for the duration of the next parliament following their introduction. (Where will he be then?) The non-repayable maintenance grant, abolished in Labour's first term, was reinstated, worth up to £2,700 for low-income students. Universities would have to top this up by £300 a year, giving a total of £3,000 in non-repayable support. Clarke, late in the day, worked out that a third of all full-time students would end up getting the new maintenance grant.

Tuition fees would be met by means of loans repayable after graduation. No real terms interest would be charged; repayments would only be inflation adjusted. Outstanding debts would be written off after twenty-five years and only ever be paid by people once they were earning more than £15,000 a year at the low rate of £5 a week. The irony was that in the end it was a more generous and attractive plan for low-income students than before. But it had only been arrived at in a panic by a government facing defeat in the Commons, the concessions drawn out one by one like dragon's teeth. As a result this generosity never got the public acclaim it deserved and many poorer school students pondering university may never have heard the good news.

## Fair Access

Scotland had gone down a different track, abandoning upfront payments altogether in favour of clawing back some of the cost of university education from graduates in paid employment. This was called an 'endowment' scheme, prompting the BBC's Mike Baker to observe that better choice of language could have saved Blair and Clarke a lot of grief. If they too had said contribution rather than fee, people might have concentrated on the way in England, as in Scotland, policy was shifting away from upfront payments (which were covered by loans) to postgraduate charges. Baker was right to observe that 'universities must accept some of the blame for failing to win public support for reforms which the majority of vice-chancellors believe are necessary'.

Past experience said graduates earned substantially more in their lifetime and could afford repayments, especially since Gordon Brown saw off proposals to charge commercial rates of interest on the loans which would have greatly expanded the flow of revenues from the scheme. Nicholas Barr of the London School of Economics said the repayments scheme was progressive, and light. It would be possible to pay off £10,000 of student debt in a decade by giving up a smoking habit of a pack of twenty a day.

The middle classes still did well though they never knew it: the perversity of providing interest-free capital to asset-rich graduates is underlined by the campaign by Further Education (FE) students for the right to subsidised loans. The majority of FE students are amongst those from the lowest income backgrounds who are most in need of access to capital to support their study.

In the event, much of the political trouble stirred up was unnecessary. The spending increases coming on stream during Labour's second term produced substantial improvements in university funding, especially through the science budget. In January 2004 Gordon Brown published a ten-year framework for science and innovation, promising to sustain increases in support for science through the research councils and a mechanism inherited by Labour from the Tories, the research assessment exercise. The Higher Education Funding Council graded university departments and channelled funds to the 'best'. Brown's definition of best veered towards how well they collaborated with firms in biotechnology and information technology. The academics who ran the show were not going to be tied to 'relevance'. They successfully resisted tilting it in the direction of applicability or utility.

## The Education Budget

This was not a government which spent much time extolling education for its own sake, although this chapter is entitled 'Wiser?' In truth, Labour saw education mechanistically – either as a tool for productivity or as an engine of social justice.

So, on the productivity score, how much extra capacity to produce goods and services did the increase in education spending under Labour bring about? Spending rose from £38bn in real terms in 1997 to £76bn by 2008. Education spending in England had risen only on average by 1.4 per cent a year in the eighteen years to 1997. But under Labour it rose on average by 4.4 per cent. By 2005 real resources allocated per pupil doubled from 1997's figure of £2,500. The figure to watch is proportion of GDP spent on education. If Brown's spending plans are realised, an extra 1 per cent of growing GDP will have been devoted to schools and colleges. In a 'knowledge economy' is that dramatic or, given the huge dimension of the failure of half of all children, is it dramatic enough yet to improve productivity?

We don't know: it's far too straightforward a question. Since 1997 output per worker in the UK rose faster than in France, Germany or the United States. By 2002 UK productivity was converging on German levels (themselves depressed by unification) and was a little more than 10 per cent below France's. That is still a big gap. It reflects the higher number of hours worked by British staff and the higher proportion of the working-age population that is employed – more people working longer hours but producing less. David Brent and *The Office* are part of Blair's Britain: workers spend a lot of time at work not working.

Productivity data are contested. But in recent times no challenge has been made to the idea that knowledge is the principal factor of production, so equipping people with it and the skills to acquire more of it is right. How far does a GCSE in geography or an undergraduate degree in business studies achieve in the end?

Again, the causality is not straight. What we know is that if GCSEs do add something, then under Labour there are more people with them. The signs are that UK productivity has been rising, yet no one can say definitively whether that had to do with education or vocational skills or the way work was organised and decisions made by employers. The UK has the fourth highest dropout rate after the age of sixteen among

countries in the Organisation for Economic Cooperation and
Development; the Treasury estimated that 20 per cent of the
productivity gap is caused by skills shortage.

How 'productive' were university degrees? During Labour's
second term enrolments on economics degrees rose by a few
hundred while those for media studies degrees increased by
over 2,000 a year to 5,000. This exceeded annual enrolments
to study physics by 2,000. Charles Clarke was wringing his
hands about subject choices, which was inconsistent with an
otherwise neoliberal approach. 'We are empowering students
but we are a bit queasy whether students will make the "right"
choices,' said Sir Howard Newby, the chief executive of the
Higher Education Funding Council for England.

## Training and Skills

As ever the Cinderella in Labour's education kitchen was the
same bedraggled creature who had sat by the ashes for
decades – skills for work. One job vacancy in five is thought
to go unfilled because the stipulated skills are in short supply.
The Trades Union Congress said one reason was that at any
given point in time four out of ten employers provided no
training for their staff at all. The *Skills Strategy*, published in
July 2003, struck at a number of targets, including both the
general improvement of skills for work and regional and
social class gaps. This was a pattern repeated over and over
during Blair's second term. Ministers tried to do two things at
once, by promising a universal service, but having the money
and motivation only for selective provision.

As we saw with the response to the Tomlinson report,
Labour ministers hesitated to identify themselves with parts
of the system providing skills training as opposed to higher
education. A separate quango, the Learning and Skills Council, channelled £8bn a year to local colleges that had once

been run by councils but were now freestanding and to sixth forms in schools. Its target for the sixteen- to eighteen-year-old cohort in 2004 was 80 per cent taking part in some kind of learning. It got there. The government wanted the further education colleges to be more demand led, meaning firms and people themselves specifying courses, and contributing towards their cost. Total budgets were rising but so were student numbers – over the decade 2000–10 the size of the cohort aged sixteen to eighteen increased by 10 per cent.

The pass rate on sixteen-plus vocational courses – at 91.5 per cent – was notably worse than for GCSE; which may reflect the relative balance of time and energy given them. Ministers talked up the 'modern apprenticeship', a structured sequence of work experience and training beginning in the late teens, but missed their own target. By 2004, 28 per cent of young people were to start a modern apprenticeship by the age of twenty-two; at the end of 2003, the figure was 23 per cent. Initiatives abounded. The Learning and Skills Council opened three learning centres in Sainsbury's stores where shoppers could take IT classes during opening hours; thousands of firms encouraged staff (50,000 by autumn 2004) to enrol on basic skills courses. Away from the theories about productivity, it was self-evident that the life chances of many adults would be expanded if they functioned better.

The Confederation of British Industry put a £10bn price tag on the economic effects of poor basic skills. Labour, target mad, translated that into a mission to reduce the number of adults in the workforce who lacked National Vocational Qualification Level 2 or equivalent (a pretty basic level). The number of adults lacking basic skills was to be cut by 1.5m between 2001 and 2007; by 2004 half that number had been rescued (except New Labour would never use such a pejorative word). Blair introduced grants to help adult learners and a new entitlement to free training for all at Level

2 and targeted support at Level 3. Employer Training Pilots are experimental schemes for low-skilled staff, some 14,000 of whom had signed up to improve their basic skills or move through Level 2. In his 2004 pre-budget report, Gordon Brown promised free training up to Level 2 to all employees.

## Paying Children to Stay on in School

In a commercial society, why not use money as an incentive to secure a social good? Educational maintenance allowances showed New Labour at its best. They were given a trial, starting in 1999 in poor areas. The results of the experiment collated, a full-blown scheme was then rolled out across the country. From the autumn term 2004, students were offered from £10 to £30 a week to stay in education or training after GCSE – provided their family's income fell below a threshold (below £19,000 qualified for the full £30 a week). Typically New Labour, too, the administration was outsourced to a private company, Capita, and there were teething troubles. Students who signed up for a second year of study could earn a cash bonus. The pilots showed the allowances did not increase numbers doing A-level but did – which was the purpose – keep some students in education to complete basic and vocational qualifications.

## Equality of Opportunity?

If education's other great purpose was to drive social justice, did Labour succeed in redistributing opportunity through school or college? Labour had picked up then dropped initiatives to try to focus money and attention on geographical areas where schools and students were underperforming. Education Action Zones gave way in the second term to a scheme for grants to 2,400 schools in fifty-eight deprived areas, Excellence in Cities.

The targeting – which paid for mentors for students and learning support units – seemed to work: the proportion of sixteen-year-olds getting five or more GCSE grades A* to C increased at twice the rate in schools with these programmes compared to others.

Research showed that the strength of the association between poor results and poverty grew during a student's school career. At the age of seven, 80 per cent of pupils on free school meals (the usual proxy for household income) achieved the expected level in maths. For the rest of their contemporaries, the figure was higher but not dramatically different, at 93 per cent. But seven years later, the gap between students had widened. Some 46 per cent of four-teen-year-old free meals students got the expected grade in the assessment tests compared to 75 per cent for others.

The simple conclusion was that poverty determines school outcomes and, some might add, that remains the case what-ever teachers do and however well endowed the schools might be. Labour could claim to be operating on both fronts, with its commitment to eliminate childhood poverty and a variety of programmes to boost the early educational chances of children from poor homes. The Department for Education and Skills managed slightly to boost the number of students coming forward for higher education from postcodes deemed to cover poor areas. It claimed its AimHigher programme increased applications to universities from target areas by 4.2 per cent between 2002 and 2003 compared with a 1.6 per cent rise elsewhere.

Was it 'positive discrimination' to force the universities to make renewed efforts to bump up the number of students from poorer backgrounds? Labour swore blind it was not setting quotas. Universities would merely have to exhibit new 'access plans', monitored by a new quango, the Office of Fair Access, in place for the academic year starting in autumn 2005.

Oxford did not like it. If forced to hold to a 'benchmark' of 77 per cent admissions from state schools, well up on its 2004 entry of 55 per cent, the quads threatened to go it alone. Oxford embarked on a fundraising drive, so that within fifteen years it could become an American-style Ivy League institution charging £10,000 a year.

In 1997 students from social classes III–V constituted a quarter of the student population. Since then the proportion of lower socioeconomic groups in higher education rose by less than 3.5 per cent. The top social class sent 80 per cent of its sons and daughters to university, while the bottom sent only 7 per cent. Some said uncertainty about the new means tests was a deterrent. The real barrier children had to cross was A-levels: virtually all those who get two A-levels do go on to university. Once over the A-level hurdle, the difference in the degree results between students from different social classes is nothing like as important as the gap between those who get A-levels and those who don't. For all the political, cultural and snobbish ferment over the quality of universities, the great educational struggle between will-haves and won't-haves happens at school – or before. Every penny spent on the under-fives yields far more future opportunity than money spent on those who have already made it to universities of any kind. The under-fives were where Labour in its second term began to invest most of its hope – a story we tell in chapter nine.

## Conclusion

During Labour's seven years there was steady improvement in equalising chances of succeeding at school. But Blair's children – those who started primary school in 1997 – are only just reaching secondary school. Even they are not the true measure of what difference Labour may yet have made.

Not until the first toddlers who come through Sure Start reach eighteen shall we see how Labour did or didn't improve the life chances of all its children.

Perhaps, in time, Sure Start and compensatory programmes in schools will boost the numbers of students from poorer homes acquiring the certificates needed for university study. An encouraging study showed that students from low-income homes who achieved the same GCSE grades in maths and English as their counterparts from more affluent backgrounds were equally likely to go on to university. Despite the creation of the Office of Fair Access, vice-chancellors can breathe easily for a while longer.

The message from research published in July 2004 by the Institute of Education and the London School of Economics was that educational opportunity was expanding; everybody was more likely to go into higher education. But the gap between rich and poor was also widening. 'People from wealthier neighbourhoods have benefited most from the expansion of higher education – they are the ones who are crowding into universities. People from poorer neighbourhoods are more likely to go than in the past, but not at the same rate.'

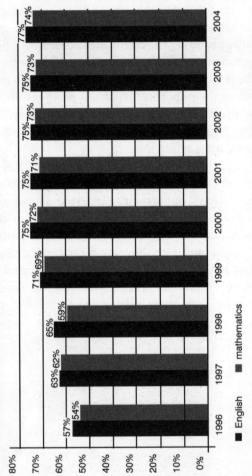

**Percentage of 11-year-olds Achieving Level 4 or Above in the Key Stage 2 Tests for English and Mathematics (England)**

| | 1996 | 1997 | 1998 | 1999 | 2000 | 2001 | 2002 | 2003 | 2004 |
|---|---|---|---|---|---|---|---|---|---|
| English | 57% | 63% | 65% | 71% | 75% | 75% | 75% | 75% | 77% |
| mathematics | 54% | 62% | 59% | 69% | 72% | 71% | 73% | 73% | 74% |

■ English  ■ mathematics

**Source: National Curriculum Assessments, key stage 2, Department for Education and Skills**

Target: To raise standards in English and Mathematics so that by 2006, 85 per cent of 11-year-olds achieve Level 4

**Percentage of 16-year-olds with at Least Five GCSEs at Grades A\*–C (England)**

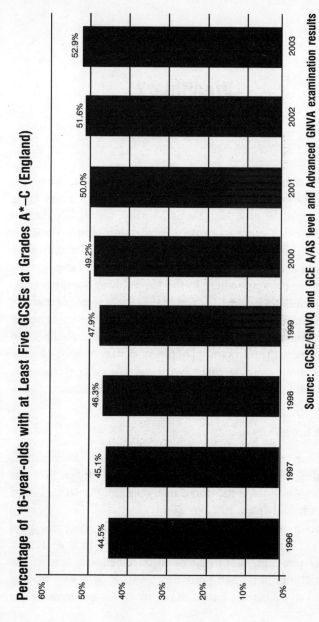

| Year | Percentage |
| --- | --- |
| 1996 | 44.5% |
| 1997 | 45.1% |
| 1998 | 46.3% |
| 1999 | 47.9% |
| 2000 | 49.2% |
| 2001 | 50.0% |
| 2002 | 51.6% |
| 2003 | 52.9% |

**Source: GCSE/GNVQ and GCE A/AS level and Advanced GNVA examination results**

Target: By 2008, 60 per cent of those aged 16 to achieve the equivalent of five GCSEs at grades A\*–C.

# CHAPTER FOUR

# Wealthier?

To commemorate ten years of relative peace in Northern Ireland, news bulletins in late August 2004 ran good news stories from the province. Denis Murray, the BBC's veteran reporter, did a piece to camera in the shopping precinct in Coleraine. His words were 'bustling', 'prosperous' and the like. The point of the story was that these were *normal* scenes: they could have been anywhere in the United Kingdom, north or south. Indeed they could. In camera shot was a staple of the high street, Clinton's the card shop. It's a chain the very existence of which demonstrated Blair's Britain was booming, the epitome of consumerism and a symbol of the modern economy – people making money selling things with no particular purpose to people with growing amounts of disposable income.

## Gordon Brown

Credit for the buoyant state of the economy was claimed, justifiably, by Blair's Chancellor and rival. Gordon Brown's Treasury dominated the domestic agenda of the second Blair term as it had from 1997 to 2001.

It was a growth era. In the 1990s the UK economy grew each year on average by 1.7 per cent. In the new century it was 2.7 per cent. A lot depended on when you started the clock ticking and when you stopped it: Brown was no less tempted to adjust the hands than any of his predecessors as chancellor except perhaps Gladstone, with whom Brown shared the classical belief that economic cycles were forces of nature not manmade. Funnily enough, during the Iraq war, Tony Blair was also compared with the Grand Old Man, who also oversaw morals-driven foreign military adventures.

Brown's supporters cut the government's achievements in twain. Progressive measures, the pursuit of social justice: these were down to Gordon. Blair did middle England, ensuring the electoral coalition Labour had built for 1997 prospered. But Labour's division of labour was nothing so simple. Brown had become a capitalist-fatalist. He believed that if the markets paid staff less than they could live on, if the markets showered not especially competent executives with gold and silver, a government's only duty was to compensate the losers not interfere with the sacred mechanics. Still, the Brownies had a point. From the thickets of tax and benefit details emerged a Chancellor intent on leaving poor people better off. And the rest of us too.

## Boom Time

The UK economy had kept growing during the global slow-down after the internet bubble burst in 2000; indeed shoppers in the high street and staff at work were hardly aware of a 'cycle' at all. Growth was combined with the lowest price inflation for three decades, the lowest interest rates for forty years and the highest levels of employment in recorded history (Brown loved repeating all this good news, and repeating it again). In 2004 claimant unemployment was 2.9 per cent, the lowest since Ted Heath was Prime Minister. In the three months after Brown's 2004 budget, earnings grew at an annual rate of 4.2 per cent, excluding bonuses. A lot of people were a lot better off.

The economy's 'relative performance over the past decade has been miraculous compared with its miserable former showing', said Brian Reading, director of Lombard Street Research, an unimpeachably non-New Labour source. True, he credited Thatcher-era supply-side reforms. But above all, it was Brown's prudence in cutting public debt, so giving the UK fiscal room for manoeuvre, and an inflation target for the Bank of England that had effectively become a growth target and had been delivered.

Economic growth in 2004 was twice the French rate of 1.7 per cent, with Germany struggling to get anywhere near that figure. No wonder Brown had begun his March 2004 budget speech exultant: it was the longest period of sustained economic growth for more than 200 years. And the reason, Brown said, was Labour policy – independence for the Bank of England, the New Deals to get unemployed people into work, Treasury fiscal rules and the reduction in national debt, now 34 per cent in the UK against 45 per cent in France. Unemployment was costing £3bn a year less than in 1997 and debt service £7bn less.

GDP was slated to grow during 2004 by 3.5 per cent but during the year the lights changed to amber and forecasters disputed the Treasury's optimistic 3 per cent plus for 2005. Public spending was exceeding revenues, for this was a boom based on consumption – high street sales in summer 2003 were well up on the previous year – and government spending. It was as if Brown was testing his own model, as the Bank of England, unquestionably independent, raised rates, five times since November 2003. How unusual, they said, to have a prolonged rise in rates in the run-up to the general election predicted for 2005, visibly slowing the economy. What faith the Chancellor must have in the Bank's ability to fine-tune.

## Lucky Gordon

But Brown had changed the rules. City slickers, ever carping, needed to be reminded that if it looked easy, why had none of Brown's predecessors seized their chance? Yet he was also lucky. No one seemed much concerned that sterling had risen or that the real exchange rate was higher than since the early 1980s. Sterling was worth a third more against the dollar than when Richard Nixon was in the White House, with more than half this appreciation taking place during Blair's second term.

Once the fate of a Labour government hung on trade figures. Now, the volume of exports having fallen since 2001, record trade deficits went unnoticed. Officially the current account deficit was 2 per cent of GDP but could be as high as 3 per cent. Oil prices rose. But the pundits said the UK was going to be the industrialised country least hurt, partly because of North Sea production (the Treasury looked like netting a £7.5bn windfall from extra tax proceeds), partly because the UK used a third less oil per unit of output than it had in twenty years previously. Policy, Labour policy, was also a factor: the economy was more resilient because the labour market was more flexible than elsewhere in Europe and, confronted by signs of slowdown, the Bank of England could act quickly.

And yet the house that Gordon built sat on those sandy British foundations of household debt and house price inflation. Rising interest rates in 2004 discouraged borrowing, but did not stop households taking on an extra £10.4bn worth of debt in the single month of July, pushing the total to over £1,000bn. But the fabled bust in the housing market had been predicted many times before; analysts were divided. Some pointed to the ratio between mortgage payments and household income and said the margin of safety was there still.

The 'British model for monetary and fiscal policy', the Chancellor said, meaning the Brown model, 'is locking in stability for the future with lower debt and lower deficits than our competitors'. That invited hubris. He was as guilty as Tory boom and bust merchant Nigel Lawson and chancellors before him of assuming that temporary circumstances were permanent, that deep-seated trends in productivity and trade balance had been redirected.

One commentator, frustrated by congestion on the road back from Heathrow airport, turned sour. 'Such experiences make statistics showing the UK's output per hour well below levels in the advanced continental countries more believable. Is it possible that even the UK's booming economy is a mirage?' The World Economic Forum agreed – in its competitiveness rankings – that UK infrastructure needed improvement but, giving Britain a tick for macroeconomic management and a 'good business environment', it pushed the UK up from fifteenth in 2003 to eleventh in 2004. If such surveys are any guide, social democracy works – four Nordic nations were among its top six for growth prospects.

In the UK, the gap in GDP growth between the regions of the UK grew to its widest for three years. No coincidence that the region doing worst in the growth stakes was the home of metal-based manufacturing, the West Midlands. In the midst of Labour's annual conference, the Chancellor had to promise the unions he would intercede with Ford over its decision to shut its Coventry factory making Jaguar cars. Within months, Rover – apparently 'rescued' – announced insolvency-threatening results and possible takeover by the Chinese. Old Labour, New Labour: some things never changed. Brown could do as little about the UK car industry or the decisions of multinationals as Denis Healey a generation before.

## Jobs

Whatever else Blair's Britain did, it worked. One reason asylum-seeking and migration became the issues they did was the availability of work in the UK. It was a magnet offering jobs with comparatively much less by way of form-filling and labour-market regulation.

From 2001 to 2005, some 1.5m jobs were created; a million or so disappeared. The net result was near full employment, even in the worst parts of the United Kingdom. In Northern Ireland, official unemployment in mid-2004 was just over 5 per cent. That still left a lot of people who might have worked – people classed as retired or disabled. But it also meant many families which had relied on intermittent employment or benefits now had more regular incomes, which was reflected in the high streets. As we looked around at Labour's annual conference in Brighton in autumn 2004, delegates had a lot to be unhappy about. But most of them weren't because their leaders had delivered something precious to them and their neighbourhoods, work and prosperity. Employment had risen by 1.7m since Labour came to power, with three-quarters of people of working age in a job, the highest ratio in the seven leading economies (though the employment rate had dipped slightly) and up by five whole percentage points since 1992.

Measured by those getting income support because officials accepted they could not find work, unemployment was 2.7 per cent. Measured by the number saying they would like a job but couldn't find one, unemployment was higher, at 4.7 per cent. These were historically low figures. They still left millions who were not in a job, looking after children full time or in full-time education and training. The number claiming sickness and disability benefits hit a record 3.1m in the second quarter of 2004, up from 2.8m. Many were de facto unemployed. Indeed the number of adults registered as economically inactive rose to eight million in 2004, up 124,000 on the previous year. Among them were over a million aged under twenty-five – a huge and dismaying waste of potential.

The National Audit Office (NAO) calculated that among people over fifty lack of employment cost between £19bn and £31bn, measured in lost output, unpaid taxes and welfare payments. In areas where jobs were traditionally scarce, the system left them to rot. The auditors criticised lack of training and staff turnover at jobcentres.

## Galloping Consumption

As for the types of work available, it was not for politicans to choose between stacking shelves in Tesco or assembling washing machines. Brown marvelled at the pace of economic change in China and India and how, inevitably, they would challenge not just UK manufacturing but services, too. What had been touted as a boom industry of the new Labour era, call centres, proved exportable to Bangalore. (Though in fact more call-centre jobs started up in the UK than were lost abroad during the second term.) What was left at home?

In the second term, as before, the UK prospered on the back of household consumption. Think Manolos and Diesel jeans. Textile, clothing and footwear sales climbed 26 per cent in the three years from 2000; in the same period engineering lost 10 per cent on the Office of National Statistics production index. But in 2003–04 the textile in-dustry lost 19,000 jobs, part of a total loss of 102,000 manufacturing jobs, according to the unions. What could not be exported were jobs in restaurants and DIY stores; it would be hard for Beijing television studios to make

*Changing Rooms* or other programmes celebrating homes and making them over.

## Savings and Debt

Private households owed £1,000bn, or the equivalent of 102 per cent of GDP, more than at the peak of the Lawson boom in the late 1980s. But it seemed they could afford it, thanks to low interest charges. The proportion of household income spent on debt did not change much. Consumption rose as savings fell. In 2003 savings were 4.8 per cent of household disposable income, half the mid-1990s level; for every pound of GDP just 14p was saved, compared with 20p in the Eurozone.

Individual savings accounts, introduced in 1999, remained popular, with fifteen million people subscribing some £130bn, on the back of £1.6bn worth of tax relief. Brown said he wanted to promote saving. A suite of new 'stake-holder' products, simple, low cost, risk controlled, were to be available from April 2005. But surely he was ambivalent. While the Germans and Japanese were trying to kick-start their economies by getting people to save less, the UK was kept buoyant by consumption. The confidence to spend came from feeling wealthier.

## The House Price Boom

Labour did not encourage housing speculation but it stood by, let it happen, and reaped the feel-good gains. Then, timidly, the Treasury started talking about the hollow foundations of the boom – the failure of housing supply to respond to the rise in prices.

The price of an average home doubled between the 2001 election and 2004, injecting phenomenal wealth into the accounts of the 70 per cent who owned their homes or were borrowing to acquire them. Average house prices rose to 5.5 times average earnings, higher than during the Lawson boom. Yet – thanks to low interest rates – payments stayed manageable expressed as a proportion of household income. Under Blair, the cliff separating the haves, the owner-occupiers, and the have-not renters grew to Beachy Head proportions.

## Changing Rooms

The puzzling fact was that the UK was short of housing. Brown commissioned a report from economist Kate Barker, a member of the Bank's Monetary Policy Committee; it will rank as one of the principal state papers of the Blair era. Barker showed that for all the money flying about to *buy* homes, less was *invested* in bricks and mortar in the UK than elsewhere. These were paper transactions, paying for land not buildings. For all the television programmes and make-over mania, insufficient was being spent on the fabric of dwellings. Assuming houses and flats would not be replaced quicker than they were in 2003, each new dwelling would have to last 1,000 years. The average age at which entry to ownership could be afforded rose into the mid-thirties. In 1997 the average deposit a first-time buyer had to put down was just £4,600 but by 2004 that had risen to a hair-raising £26,000.

Barker also said something weird. There was effectively no housing 'market'. In a market, supply should increase as prices rose. Yet fewer dwellings, private or social, were constructed in the years since 1994 than at any time since the late 1940s – and this at a time when the number of households was growing sharply.

Various reasons were advanced. Planning bars and 'not in

my back yard' obstructionists (NIMBYs); too few brickies; 'developers' who made more from hoarding plots for later resale than from building houses on them. And tax. Successive governments, including Blair's, had been pusillanimous in not thinking about how to tax speculative gains from property. This wasn't money you earned or worked for. The driest of classical economists justified tapping into such ill-gotten wealth. It was true that house prices had risen enough to tip greater numbers towards the threshold at which their relatives would have to pay inheritance tax. Since 1997 the ratio of average house price to the inheritance tax level rose from 32 per cent to 65 per cent. But the tax system generally got nowhere near the additional wealth that scarcity was piling up.

## Leave it to the Bankers

Housing might forever be blowing bubbles for Blair, and Brown showed no taste for pricking the phenomenon. Matters were left to the Monetary Policy Committee (MPC), which meant controlling house prices took precedence even over the cost of borrowing money for business investment. No wonder UK investment levels disappointed. Interest rates were pushed up, sterling's value rose, borrowers were squeezed, in order to dampen down mortgage demand. Almost since the September 11 2001 scare was over, the MPC had been predicting that house price inflation would be cut. Only two-and-a-half years after back-to-back interest rate rises did the housing market cool. Brown talked of trying to move people to fixed-term mortgages to lessen the volatility.

From day one Brown had refused to wear the traditional white tie get-up at the City functions he was obliged as Chancellor to attend. But in the City or presiding over economic policy he turned out to be no more 'left wing' than Blair. The Chancellor had not just accepted the supremacy of market forces but embraced doctrines brought down from the mountains of classical theory by Mrs Thatcher's one-time guru, Friedrich Hayek. Brown emphasised 'rules', which usually meant inhibitions on the action of democratically elected politicians.

Were the monetarists to whom democracy had delegated its economic fate up to it? If Gordon was a lucky chancellor, so were the governors of the Bank of England. Global trends (more intense competition between companies) seemed to be keeping prices down. The Monetary Policy Committee was not tested by what economists call external shocks; September 11 2001 was nothing like the oil turmoil of the early 1970s. But at least, as *Observer* columnist William Keegan observed, monetary policy was not 'adding to the volatility of the economy in the way it did in earlier decades'.

Brown told the Bank he wanted annual inflation at 2 per cent or less. Which implied that the supply of money caused prices to rise, the classic monetarist doctrine. Yet there the Chancellor was, in spring 2004, saying pretty much what chancellors had been saying since the days of Reggie Maudling: we will tolerate no pay 'irresponsibility'. There would be 'no going back to the old days of inflationary pay deals'. But if inflation was something caused by greedy trade unionists (a difficult assertion to make now that unions were so weak) or weak employers, it wasn't the monetary phenomenon the Bank of England was going to be able to control.

## Productivity

Still, if Brown followed Hayek on the Bank of England, his mentor on productivity was more like Harold Wilson. Like the former Labour Prime Minister he too wrung his hands over the UK's lower performance relative to other countries on output per head, while not knowing quite what to do about it. The Bank of England could not make the economy grow. Indeed, by keeping interest rates higher it kept the value of sterling up and penalised exporters, especially in manufacturing, which shrank. Growth became unbalanced, far too reliant on house prices rising.

At best the Bank was part of an 'envelope' in which markets would flourish. But inside it, markets were quite happy to employ underskilled workers, incompetent and overpaid managers and tolerate investment levels that lessened capacity. Here was a 'market failure'. Labour's response was more and better education though no one had quite figured out any direct linkages between the GCSE pass rate and growth in output per head.

Output depended on investment and it fell – corporate investment dropped from 11 per cent of GDP in 1997 to 9.5 per cent in 2004. So celebratory bells rang when new data from the Office of National Statistics in February 2004 showed the UK reaching German levels of productivity and catching up with France. But then, far from unsympathetic to the government, Martin Weale of the National Institute for Economic and Social Research revised the revisions, saying the UK remained 18 per cent behind the French. If employment rates increased in France and Germany to UK levels, their growth rates would shoot up.

Among the causes of lower productivity were a lower propensity on the part of firms to innovate and invest and poorer workforce skills. Those who added 'concern over the regulatory environment' to their list of causes had a problem explaining why the well-regulated French and Germans did so well.

## Foreign Investment

Indeed, for all the apparently attractive flexibility in the UK labour market, foreign investment in the UK fell 48 per cent in 2003 compared with the previous year. Of the pool of international capital investment the UK attracted less than a third of the amount going to (inflexible) France. The number of jobs being created by new foreign investment fell to its lowest level since 1997. But these data were not so straightforward. Foreign investment was falling across the globe. British companies were not being bought so readily, but foreign-owned operations in the UK were expanding, funded by capital from UK banks. Was it a sign of the UK's emergence as a fabled 'knowledge economy' that the software industry was the largest single generator of inward investment? It would need to grow quickly, however, to compensate for, among others, the disappearance of 17,000 manufacturing jobs (2003–04) in the ostensibly high-tech sector of electrical and optical equipment.

## Science, Research and Development

The UK did well on measures of scientific output but less well on the appliance of science. The Patent Office compiled a list of organisations filing the most applications and put Japanese and American companies, NEC, Motorola, Hewlett Packard, top. Highest UK seeker after patents was . . . the government, in the shape of the Ministry of Defence. Under Blair, the UK weapons industry fared well.

In 2002 UK scientists had a remarkable 11 per cent share of citations of scientific papers across the world. Brown went to Cambridge to open new labs with commercial potential. But while over the year to 2002 patent applications rose by 8 per cent, the number of 'spin-off' science firms fell by 14 per cent. In the same year, university staff in commercialisation liaison offices rose 19 per cent.

The Department of Trade and Industry said it was an achievement that it had written a plan for the UK to become a world leader in turning knowledge into new products and services. Except it was not a 'plan' at all; the elements were not joined up.

The DTI's agreement with the Treasury included the aim of turning the UK into the 'leading European country in business research and development investment and patenting by 2013'. This was a classic example of the mindlessness of targetry as practised under New Labour. The DTI did not have the tools to reach into individual firms and change their behaviour; and why 2013 for realising this end, not 2012 or 2014; and who was going to measure 'leading'?

Perhaps the best that government could do was bang the drum. But research and development spending fell 1 per cent in the year to 2004. Biggest spenders were pharmaceuticals and biotechnology followed by aerospace and defence. Ford, Shell and BT were among the top ten spenders on research. The government did try to pick winning sectors itself, spending £90m over six years to promote micro- and nanotechnology in firms. On most measures, interactions between universities and business were improving.

## Trade

In 2004 the UK was the fourth largest economy in the world but China was coming up fast. A cliché of the speechmakers was that India produced a million graduates a year. Product cycles were shortening, Brown said, and the UK response had to be 'relying on our creativity and innovation'. UK exports as a share of the world total had been relatively stable, falling slightly in 2003. The need to export more was symbolised by figures for the oil trade in July 2004: imports exceeded exports for the first time in thirteen years. Overall in 2004 there would probably be a small surplus in oil but a slide into permanent deficit looked unavoidable – unless oil prices went so high rusty rigs out in the North Sea suddenly became viable again. But it wasn't just oil. The three-monthly deficit in trade in goods reached a record £15bn.

Labour was not even tempted by protection, unlike the Democrats in the United States. Brown and Blair were resolute liberalisers. World Trade Organization talks at Cancun in Mexico in 2003 had failed. The developed world – the EU and the United States especially – failed to meet demands to wind down trade-distorting agriculture supports. The DTI pointed to subsequent reforms to the Common Agricultural Policy and agreements on intellectual property rights as evidence that things were still broadly going in the direction of freeing movement across boundaries.

## Industrial Policy

As for what to produce at home, the plan, it seemed, was to throw a handful of multicoloured balls in the air and hope some of them landed in the right holes. Science was a sparkler and the DTI committed itself to achieving world-class labs and university departments (though they depended on what the Department for Education and Skills was doing to student fees and university funding). Another ball was 'ensuring fair markets', another transferring knowledge, while others were maximising potential in the workplace, extending competitive markets, strengthening regional economies and 'forging closer partnerships'.

Such a list won full marks for inclusiveness, but a low score for what it was, precisely, governments could and should do to make companies more successful. What if rigged markets (the opposite of fair) might spawn companies prepared to invest? The French had showed that could work. Labour had no 'industrial policy', a pretentious anachronism, said White-hall. But without a policy, confusion reigned. When Brown met Sir Nick Scheele, the chief executive of Ford Motors over the Coventry closure, he had no scheme for motor produc-tion in the UK to put before him, for research and develop-ment, the supply chain, ancillary industries. That was not the New Labour way.

Yet in some sectors a kind of strategy was followed. A plan for England's ports was devised by the Department of Trans-port, though it would not come into effect until 2005, and in the meantime important decisions on container ports were left to be decided on local planning criteria. Some evidence of joining up was found in the expansion of rail links to Felixstowe. Still at sea, the Department of Trade and Industry claimed to have 'mobilised' the UK leisure marine industry to take a larger share of global business.

## Cashing in on the Media and Communications

Labour ministers boosted film production, partly by divert-ing lottery money. Some £1.2bn was spent on film produc-tion in the UK in 2003, including the third *Harry Potter* and the second *Bridget Jones*. This was double the previous year but the renaissance of UK filmmaking had been glimpsed through a lens several times before.

There was, also, a sort of industrial policy for some of the media. Labour had made money from the sale of radio spectrum and in March 2003 the UK became one of the first countries in Europe to launch G3 mobile services. Labour's forward policy on phasing out analogue broad-casting gave the UK a theoretical lead in digitisation of television and radio. Sales of set-top boxes gave the UK, at 50 per cent, the highest digital television penetration rate in the world (though most of the equipment was likely to be imported).

The regulatory regime for telecommunications, the new Ofcom, was intended to further the interests of citizens and consumers in the new age. This left open the question of industrial policy – how many companies, how many jobs? Ofcom considered breaking up British Telecommunications but had no idea whether this would increase investment in broadband technology. The DTI's stated targets included giving the UK a 'more competitive and extensive broadband market'. A 2003 benchmarking survey showed the UK to rank seventh in the world in its take-up and use of information and communications. But what was the role of the state itself, a major investor in ICT, and how was government, severely short of IT practitioners and strategists, to ensure the greater integration and use of ICT within companies?

In thrall to Rupert Murdoch, Labour had soft-pedalled on the regulation of media ownership so it was gratifying, after amendments to communications legislation, to see News International, Murdoch's company, concerned that Ofcom would take a position on mergers – such as a proposed link between Channel Four and Channel Five, owned by RTL. Ministers said they had no intention of privatising Channel Four but equally denied it a trust status that would have permanently protected its non-profit status.

## Post Office

One of the few remaining nationalised industries, Royal Mail lost 30,000 jobs and restructured as its letters business returned to profit. There was an outcry – and many delays over negotiations – as 30 per cent of Royal Mail business was prised open to competition, but it retained 97 per cent of the postal business, mainly because it retained the advantage of VAT exemption. As Royal Mail missed target after target, privatisation was again in the air. The *Financial Times* reported that candidates approached for a director's position were told they would become millionaires in the next three or four years, when the company was sold. So much for any rational connection between performance and reward.

## Competition

The mantra was competition. A review placed the UK behind only Germany and the United States in the effectiveness of its competition regime. The Office of Fair Trading was reorganised in conjunction with a new Competition Commission, both with more teeth and more autonomy, though the division of labour between the quangos was not obvious. Together they approved the merger of Carlton Communications and Granada and the sale of Safeway to William Morrison. The OFT, stating the blindingly obvious, concluded the £2.5bn market for estate agency in England and Wales 'could be made to work better for consumers'. Better self-regulation was its recommendation.

## Financial Services

In his book *The Prudence of Mr Gordon Brown*, William Keegan acidly noted that Brown did hold close the welfare of a particular 'industry'. Not manufacturing, for all that his Fife constituents had depended on it. The industry singled out in his five tests for joining the Eurozone had been financial services, 'more commonly known as the City of London'.

Once, in the old days, Michael Heseltine had teased Brown's mentor John Smith for eating his way round City lunch rooms to try to win credibility: never had so many crustaceans died in vain. The taste of the *crevettes en sauce rose* must have lingered. Gordon Brown nurtured the City's welfare: however excessive the boardroom pay rise, however unjustified the golden goodbye payoff, not once could he bring himself to criticise the behaviour of one of the nation's great cash cows.

A big, all-encompassing regulator had been created in Labour's first term in the shape of the Financial Services Authority (FSA). This quango could justify paying its chief executive £365,000 a year (in 2004) because it was paid for by a levy on private companies, many of which paid their executives a lot more. The FSA fined Morgan Grenfell £190,000 for failing to manage conflicts of interest; ouch, was that a gnat that just bit? Was the FSA indeed a public body? When a responsible newspaper, the *Financial Times*, gave space to a whistle-blower's report to it, his company sued the paper for libel. The FSA kept suspiciously quiet.

It was moving, it said, to a 'lighter touch' regime. Critics said it failed to tackle the very reason it existed: asymmetrical knowledge between suppliers of services and customers. Look at endowment mortgages. Mis-selling (otherwise known as lying) had cost customers at least £1bn.

Surveys showed people to be ignorant of even basic financial facts and it was little wonder they fell prey to sharp practice. The FSA pushed companies to disclose commissions, to unpack 'with profits' policies. MPs opined that the FSA – together with the Financial Ombudsman Service, paid for by a levy on the banks – had 'made a positive impact on levels of confidence'.

The CBI called for a moratorium on financial services regulation amid fears it could jeopardise the industry's role. But this industry had shown it could not be trusted, which was why the FSA imposed new capital adequacy rules on life and general insurance companies. New rules were coming from the international bankers' organisation and from the European Union on the ratio of capital bankers should hold before lending on; similarly, from January 2005, companies would have to account under International Financial Reporting Standards. Was the UK record so stainless companies here should be excused rules their competitors seemed happy to accept?

The FSA proposed new tests for banks issuing shares and restrictions on the release of price sensitive information, regulations on money laundering and 'knowing your client'. Companies wanting to list shares on the main London market were offered a more liberal regime. The FSA was surprised by how little appetite UK investors showed. Behind their reluctance lay a preference for what was talked up as the British way of financial regulation based on 'principles' rather than explicit rules, such as the American Sarbanes–Oxley law. This allowed companies a margin for interpretation . . . it was a doctrine with some kinship to the idea that gents who wear the same school tie know how to behave without regulatory oiks writing everything down.

## Enterprise

Brown was more comfortable with 'enterprise', doing things in markets somewhat less virtual and ineffable than finance. He hectored graduates saying more should become entrepreneurs and start up their own businesses, typically making an unfavourable contrast between the UK and the US where 18 per cent of graduates started up their own businesses against 7 per cent in the UK. He backed a new council to support graduate entrepreneurship. A similar invocation was addressed to the unemployed and those on welfare benefits. Brown wanted a more enterprising culture and he aspired to cut the gap in Value Added Tax registrations between the better-off regions and poorer areas. In 2001 a survey found one in eight people considering starting a business or becoming self-employed, but there was not much evidence this increased.

What was the politics of this? There was some evidence that small- and medium-sized firms were increasing their productivity faster than larger firms. Smaller firms could be a source of jobs growth, but the small business mentality was still anti-training, anti-regulation, anti-union and, as voiced in employer organisations, anti-Labour.

## Business-Friendly Labour Rebuffed

This paradox marked Labour's dealings with business. On the back of Labour's increases in spending a new business sector boomed – companies doing exceedingly well out of providing lucrative outsourced services to councils, the NHS, defence and Whitehall. That meant that a number of FTSE 100 companies were, effectively, state dependents. Yet the fact that they were beneficiaries of the spending boom seemed to do little to change the predominantly carping anti-tax tone adopted by business organisations.

On one occasion six senior ministers turned out for a conference of the British Chambers of Commerce but one after another business leaders pronounced themselves 'disillusioned'. Martin Taylor, former chief executive of Barclays and erstwhile friend of Blair, berated the government for spending money ineffectively on public services: its response to the collapse of Railtrack exposed Old Labour tendencies. Instead of rebuttal, ministers tended to roll over. When local government minister Nick Raynsford was pressed by local authorities to put local business rates back under their control, his refusal was couched in terms of the damage local taxes (which might or might not rise) would do to companies' productivity and competitiveness.

This supine, almost pleading attitude left ministers with little to say when companies were badly run or underperformed. The CBI, Institute of Directors and chambers of commerce became more formidable foes in Labour's second term. Like competing teachers' unions, they were outbidding one another to attract members in their extremism in public, though the CBI was more conciliatory and worked with the government in private.

## Regulation

Business bleated about red tape and regulation but its arguments were tainted by self-interest; it failed to make a compelling case that the UK was in some measurable way over-regulated. In 2004 the Better Regulation Task Force plucked a figure from the air. 'Regulation' cost 10 per cent of GDP or £100bn a year, of which £25bn was spent enforcing rules.

On the back foot, Labour established regulatory reviews galore. But the manifesto for Labour's policy on business and competitiveness – a study by Harvard business school professor Michael Porter for the DTI – had denied the UK was tied up in red tape, judging that in 2003 the UK had 'the lowest rate of product and market regulations in the OECD'. Porter had recommended a 'productivity driven regulatory context'. But it was far from clear what this would look like; stripped of its academic varnish it could sound remarkably like the arguments mill owners had once used to justify employing children. Without regulation there would be no minimum wage; without it how much would employers do to consult, train or treat workforces fairly? How was the food industry to be persuaded to cut sugar and salt?

It was true that UK law and European Union directives could be over-specific and were not always tidied away when regulations were updated. There was a case for example for a general injunction on businesses to trade fairly, replacing a mass of sector-specific norms and rules. Blair responded that for every new regulation brought in, one had to be rescinded.

But the anti-regulators had to accept that beliefs could be as important as rules themselves. Newspapers, rarely bothering with reliable numbers, pontificated about the 'compensation culture' and the avalanche of petty claims clogging the courts, preventing teachers taking children on school trips, forcing up the insurance bills of firms. It was a myth. Insurance claims were dropping in several categories. The cost of litigation in the UK was a fraction that of the US. There had been a burst of ambulance-chasing when Labour, following a Tory lead, made no-win, no-fee litigation easier. But the courts were not turning overnight into champions of the little people.

## Company Tax

Labour wondered about reforming the principal levy on businesses, the corporation tax, reduced in the first term to 30 per cent. That had put the UK at the lower end of the international tables and it suited Blair and Brown to boast about it, though they were pleased enough with receipts equivalent to 3.5 per cent of GDP. But other countries, including other EU countries, followed suit and UK corporate tax ended by 2005 in the middle reaches of the table. It was lower in Germany where corporation tax was only 1 per cent of GDP. The tax needed reform. Its allowances for investment were wildly out of kilter with what companies depreciated on their balance sheets and sooner or later the EU or international accounting standards bodies would get to grips.

## Corporate Governance

Neither the Chancellor nor Prime Minister found a satisfactory language that dared suggest to business that they had responsibilities as well as rights, as surely as individual citizens. But maybe their pragmatism about how companies should conduct themselves secured some improvements.

In the second term there was a fair amount both of explicit companies legislation and code making, which companies said they much preferred as long as the codes were voluntary. The CBI and Institute of Directors were quick to denounce unwarranted interference by the state but seemed unable or unwilling to explain why corporate boardrooms had become so fat and self-absorbed. Patricia Hewitt, secretary of trade, aligned herself with shareholders, hoping that if they became more active, directors would get away with less. Shareholder activism, however, was sporadic, depending often on whether the National Association of Pension Funds – with lots of shareholder votes in its pocket – would pick up the cudgels.

Some noisy annual general meetings ensued but not one board was overturned, even where pay structures had become notorious. With a fair wind of indignation behind them, Labour could have taken action, at least as a symbolic gesture of disapproval for corporate greed, but instead they stuck doggedly to a 'self-regulation' model. A banker, Derek Higgs, had reported to the government in the wake of the Enron scandal. Much song and dance accompanied the adoption of his mainly sensible recommendations into a 'combined code' applied by the stock exchange to companies from January 2003. They would, in principle, make non-executive directors much more responsible for the good governance of public companies. But Higgs turned out to be very voluntary as only a fraction of companies adopted the new principles. Labour's second term saw marginal increases in, for example, the number of women and minorities in top boardrooms, let alone talent from outside the charmed circle. Business ranted and raved about obstacles to competitiveness but chose not to tear the veil on the holy of holies, the boardroom, and modernise corporate governance. Blair did not insist.

UK business did raise its corporate voice to denounce plans developed by the European Commission to legislate for corporate governance in the wake of scandals at Dutch company Ahold and Italian Parmalat. Were UK companies so well run? After the allegedly titanic struggle for control of Marks and Spencer (surely an example of consistent corporate failure) barely 40 per cent of its share capital owners bothered to vote at the annual general meeting, 10 per cent down on the previous year. The DTI explored changes in company law, updated the treatment of insolvency and sought to enhance the powers of its own inspectors to investigate. But the government delayed putting into effect its demand that alongside the annual reports companies should state clearly – in an 'operating and financial review' – the factors affecting past and future performance, which might give shareholders a better guide to whether those fat bonuses were justified. As for environmental audits, warmly praised by Tony Blair in 2000, when he had challenged top companies to issue them regularly, they were largely ignored.

## Consumers

The DTI said the UK compared well in the rights consumers enjoyed, in being able to return goods and secure redress through small claims courts. Consumers, rather than shop workers, carried the day as Sunday trading was further liberalised. Impressed with the success of NHS Direct, the government wanted to offer consumers a national hotline for complaints and queries. There was certainly an appetite. Enquiries to Citizens' Advice Bureaux about debt mushroomed, up 74 per cent since 1997. The DTI proposed restricting cold calling and allowing consumers more time to cool off if they did sign on the doorstep.

The Enterprise Act 2002 was intended both to strengthen enforcement of consumers' rights and better to join up the work of the principal quango, the Office of Fair Trading, and council trading standards departments – for example in dealing with email and text messaging mass marketing scams. The OFT received more complaints about misleading adverts in 2003–04 than ever before. It was not the only quango in town. The NAO wondered if specialist consumer bodies for the Post Office and energy were cost effective. A proliferation of obscure consumer bodies in other areas, such as Water-Voice and the Rail Passengers' Council might have been asked the same question.

## Regions

The UK would be markedly more prosperous if the tempo of economic activity in the North, West Midlands, Wales, Northern Ireland and Scotland were to rise. Indeed, the Treasury set itself the task of reducing 'the persistent gap in growth rates between the regions'. But how? Brown was not prepared even to think about 'directing' jobs. That was Old Labour talk. In this globalised world, you took what the markets gave you; the state was a sort of street sweeper.

The formula was business-led development agencies working with a business-oriented quango, the Learning and Skills Council, to improve the capacity of staff and increase the number of small firms starting up. Disparities in growth rates seemed, if anything, to grow. In fact the public sector

remained a prime mover in such regions as the North and
Northern Ireland. Whitehall was torn. The logic of Brown's
policy was to have pay rates in the regions rising but in the
meantime he extolled local pay bargaining, in an effort to
lower costs.

## Fiscal Policy

In the eyes of the owners and manipulators of money,
Gordon Brown was constantly under suspicion of wanting
to spend. Their word was 'loosening', as if he were an old
maid ever looking for a chance to undo her stays. The years
of budget surplus did end. Revenues exceeded spending by
1.6 per cent of GDP in 2000–01 but by the end of 2003,
spending exceeded income by 3 per cent.

Doom-mongers over-predicted the deficit. Brown insisted
that the deficit conformed with his self-imposed rule specifying the budget balanced over 'the cycle'. It was in average
surplus to 2003–04, he said; deficits were justified by the
growing rate of public sector investment. (The Treasury got
to identify the cycle's start and so the rule was upheld. Rule
radicals, who now included the Tories and Liberal Democrats, wanted the National Audit Office or some independent
body to set the parameters.) Public sector debt, what the state
owed, would rise to 2006, then stabilise at 36 per cent of
GDP, lower than the United States and the Eurozone. Still
lower than Labour had inherited in 1997.

Brown spent, keeping strictly to Labour's repeated pledge
not to raise income tax rates, but he also did not borrow
much (at least by historical standards). So where did the
money come from? Brown's overt tax increases since the
2002 budget were few and contradictory. In 2002 he sur-
charged profits from North Sea oil, an old standby; in 2003
he abolished petroleum revenue tax to encourage new ex-

ploration. Otherwise, he was a great freezer – holding petrol and alcohol duties in 2002 and freezing duties on spirits and champagne in 2003. Environmental taxes fell as a proportion of the total, further dulling the Blair government's green credentials. It wasn't some great improvement in tax collection either. In 2002 tax inspectors raised six times as much in tax as it cost to mount an inquiry; that fell to 5.6 to one in 2004. For small businesses the ratio was much lower: £1.30 in tax back for every pound the tax operation cost.

## Income Tax and National Insurance

Brown's conjuring trick was 'fiscal drag'. No, not the chairman of the Board of Inland Revenue dressed in frillies – as incomes rose, so more people moved into the higher-rate bands for income tax. Standing still, as it were, income tax would rise from 10.9 per cent of GDP in 2004 to 11.6 per cent in 2008. Each year during the second term those taxed at 40 per cent on income above £31,400 a year were joined by 150,000 new people. Correspondingly, the number paying no more than the 10 per cent rate was cut in half, on Brown's watch, from 7.7m to 3.4m.

That sounds uncharacteristically hard on the lowest paid. But in fact it wasn't quite that simple. Among earners with children there were millions more gainers as they received ever more generous child tax credits from the Inland Revenue. The astonishing fact was that by 2005 an earner with a child paid virtually no tax until their earnings reached over £25,000.

## How Heavy was Britain's Tax Burden?

Polls of ABC1s, the top people, showed 60 per cent of them believed they had not prospered under Labour and nearly 70 per cent thought their tax bills had risen. A calculation in mid-2004 took all direct and indirect taxes and concluded the 'burden' on a £50,000 a year earner had risen from 35 per cent to 50 per cent since 1997. But these oft-quoted figures need careful examination: it turns out this assumed he/she had bought a house in 1997 and again in 2004, and so paid stamp duty twice – Brown had done a little to quieten house price inflation by increasing the rate of stamp duty. Leave out stamp duty and this high earner was only paying 2 per cent more of his/her income in tax.

Stamp duty was one of Brown's trumps, raising three times as much in 2004 as in 1997. Council tax, too, carried some of the weight of Labour's extra spending. Like all previous governments, it put extra burdens on councils but did not always give them enough extra grants to pay for them. With tremendous regional variations washing through a system Labour tried to make fairer (at least as far as poorer areas went) council tax take rose, doubling in value between 1997 and 2005.

During the first term net tax and social security contributions had risen from 34.9 per cent to 37.4 per cent of GDP, then fell between 2001 and 2003 before rising slightly to 36 per cent of GDP by 2004. It is projected to rise to 38 per cent in 2006. This tremendous level – 38 per cent – had last been reached under Mrs Thatcher in the mid-1980s. It had then dropped back to 33 per cent before Kenneth Clarke started pushing it up again under John Major. Was this progress or backsliding? Martin Weale of the National Institute for Economic and Social Research noted the tax-and-spend epithets being thrown at Brown, and asked wryly, 'Do people characterise Mrs Thatcher's heyday as tax and spend?'

It was easy for pollsters to elicit anti-tax replies. The public wanted lower taxes by a margin of five to one, said the Taxpayers' Alliance. Yet – bear in mind the majority of taxpayers got nowhere near the threshold for paying higher-rate income tax at 40 per cent – the burden had not risen much. The tax take on a £30,000 a year earner had increased by only 1 per cent to 32.2 per cent. For some people the fact a reasonably well-paid person was still paying less than a third of their income in all taxes after seven years of a Labour government was itself the scandal.

## Value for Money?

Brown's annus mirabilis was 2002. His budget in March and his spending review in July did two things. They pushed up public spending to what may come to be regarded as the nearest the UK will ever approach social democracy, with public spending set to rise towards 42 per cent of GDP. This was the target for 2005, which would mean spending had risen by five percentage points of GDP since Labour took office, and of course GDP grew strongly. These were therefore plump years for most people in the public sector, though as ministers often complained, few ever publicly thanked Labour for the largesse.

After a well-planned softening up of the public with the Wanless report revealing the parlous state of the NHS, Brown raised National Insurance in the budget, explicitly linking it to increased health spending. Business complained, but that extra 1p on NI made it a popular budget, even if NI was indistinguishable from income tax, which Labour had promised not to raise.

However, Brown was often – to coin the phrase used by former Tory minister Iain Macleod – too clever by half. His aides talked of 'progressive universalism' which meant improving public services for all but bending them here and there in favour of the poorest. 'We want universal provision but we want to do more for those who need it most,' Brown said. But at the moment of triumph, Labour offered large hostages to fortune. The first was delivery. Labour could have justified all this extra spending as a necessity to bring services up to civilised levels. Instead, they promised galloping improvements. Expectations were ratcheted up so that any instance of shortfall became proof, certainly in the eyes of the newspapers, that money was being wasted.

What became clearer than ever during Blair's second term was how little ministers really understood of the complex system over which they presided; this was especially true at the top of the Treasury. There were no reliable figures linking money spent and outputs. For all the 'public service agreements' between Whitehall departments and the Treasury, renewed with each spending review, no one could quite pin down the value of education or policing, which evidently went far beyond the immediate work of a teacher or the presence on the street of an officer. Late in the day – in 2004 – the warden of Nuffield College Oxford, economist Sir Tony Atkinson, was commissioned to study public service productivity. But by then Brown had embarked on a hazardous course. Barely a year into the spending period that began in 2003, before the fruits of Labour's additional spending could possibly be assessed, Brown determined to excise 'waste'.

Employment growth owed a lot to public spending, half a million positions created between 1998 and 2003 and some 360,000 since the second term began. It was likely to see public sector jobs grow by between 400,000 and 500,000 in total. Suddenly, these were seen as too many. A study was commissioned from a businessman, the Marconi executive Sir Peter Gershon, who had been recruited to head an office newly created to oversee more efficient public sector procurement.

## Public Sector Pay

Gershon's review was partly political cover. It protected Labour against Tory charges that only they were concerned with administrative costs and cutting that 'red tape' that in fact had not been used in government offices since the days gents in frock coats snuffed out the candles at night. But it also lured Labour into a simplistic and utterly misleading distinction between the front line and 'back offices'. Within months of this efficiency review, ministers were calling staff working on tax credits 'front line'. So they were, but it made a nonsense of the plot.

Between 1998 and 2002, public sector pay had grown relatively fast, faster than the private sector average. Public had not caught up private, though. Growth in rewards was inevitable. Teachers, police, NHS lab technicians and nurses had to be recruited. Then from 2002, private earnings rose faster again. Brown could not quite bring himself to face the dilemma over pay. The way to reduce unit costs in the public sector was simple: cut salaries in relative terms. But then holding down public pay was a sure-fire way of signalling that public services were less important than private consumption, less worthwhile, and would again attract lower quality staff.

## The Unions

You could not call Labour's approach to business and unions evenhanded. Business was given seats, often the direction of regional development agencies, industrial development boards and the like; the Trades Union Congress and its members had sometimes to struggle to be heard. Blair's anti-regulatory instincts and Brown's yen for flexibility did not make the unions easy bedfellows. The government insisted on retaining its opt-out from the European working time directive.

Applications to employment tribunals were down from a peak in 2001 but the government seemed to listen more to employers when it introduced new regulations intended to reduce the number of cases.

At Labour's national policy forum at the University of Warwick in the summer of 2004, Blair struck a deal with the unions. The concordat covered redundancy, Bank Holidays, pensions and skills. Much was a restatement of what Labour was already doing. But the nub was meant to change the fate of staff if a public body outsourced its work or contractors took over. They had secured an agreement over councils; Warwick extended it across the public services. But the 'it' would, however, have to be negotiated time and again in specific contracts. Employers were not rolling over. Alan Leighton, chairman of the Royal Mail, said pugnaciously, 'Warwick can't be binding on the company.'

## Rich Profits

If you wanted to see fat cats, you did not go to the public sector zoo. Company directors were having a whale of a time under Labour. In 2004, directors of 350 FTSE companies received £263 for every £100 they earned in 1998. The stock market crashed in 2000, yet in that year FTSE directors' total cash remuneration rose by 14 per cent (national average 4.75 per cent). In 2004 their cash rewards went up 16 per cent (national average 4 per cent). Incomes Data Services showed in successive reports that directors' pay rarely had an obvious relationship with company performance or performance targets.

Given the failure of the top companies to put their own house in order, it seemed remarkable they should somehow manage to blame Labour when the stock market went into reverse. In the six years to 1997, stocks rose by 78 per cent on average, better than the 63 per cent rise in equities in the world at large. Between 1997 and 2004, world stock prices fell by 5 per cent, but the UK market fell 12 per cent (though it was recovering in later 2004). These differences in timing could be due to cyclical differences; UK equities fell no further than those elsewhere, but fall they did. The FTSE had reached an all-time high of 6930 in 1999. But then some £200bn was wiped off stock values and Labour was blamed. The equation was obvious: higher taxed companies produced lower after-tax profits leading to lower share prices. But Brown had cut corporation tax in the 1999 budget.

## Pensions

What really angered companies was something he did subsequently, in trimming the pension pots of the very highest earners. He refused to lift the cap on the amount of money top earners could accumulate in tax-free pension funds – at £1.4m still a vast sum tax free. The Treasury claimed this would affect only 5,000 people. It turned out to trap many more, which was only a further signal of how top incomes had soared away into the stratosphere under Labour. Ministers complained that whenever they had meetings with captains of industry, it was hard to engage them with matters of pressing economic importance: too often their own pension cap was all that they wanted to discuss.

Fitting the cap was a small matter compared with the political explosion over pensions under Blair and Brown. Vehicles converged from different directions, demography, actuarial failure, means testing and created a policy jam that whoever is in power from 2005 onwards will have to unblock.

When Labour took power some 63 per cent of the workforce had pension rights (occupational or personal) outside what the state offered. With the benefit of hindsight, we can see that many of the funds on which these rights were based were unsound, but the actuaries never saw it coming. Pension payments needed a guaranteed fund, bonds or government debt, but too much was invested in volatile stocks. During the fat years, when company profits were rising, some employers had taken a pensions holiday. They had been allowed to stop sharing their revenues with their workforce, to the tune of some £18bn before 1997.

## Pension Funds Fall

Meanwhile, in the background, there was a worldwide movement to make company accounts more honest. This would have had an impact whoever was in Downing Street. Whereas in stock market downturns before, a blind eye had been turned to the true effect on company pension funds, balance sheets were now required to show tomorrow's liabilities, including pensions: traditionally they had been shuffled off into appendices and separate reports. A new accounting standard FRS17 came into effect at the same time as pension funds were losing value from the stock market fall – wiping hundreds of billions off their value. Company balance sheets now looked bad, risking throwing the entire company into insolvency.

Now the deficits had become transparent, companies needed to put enough into their pension funds to match their liabilities. By the end of 2003, the 350 biggest quoted companies had a hole in their accounts worth £64bn. There was much panicky wild talk. One estimate of the extra savings needed to preserve today's ratio of pensioner living standards to average income said they should rise from 3.8 per cent of GDP to 7.6 per cent, that is by about £40bn.

## The Pensions 'Plunder'

By unlucky timing, just before the stock exchange fell, Brown had removed tax credits from share dividends. In the circumstances it seemed a reasonable clawing back of some of the tax privileges surrounding this form of saving. Pension tax relief has always been a huge unseen handout to the well-off, a hefty part of the unacknowledged middle-class welfare state.

This 'plunder' of pensions was later held against him, because it reduced by £40bn over seven years the value of assets held in pension funds; his parallel move to cut corporation tax was held not to have compensated. It was less often noted that pension fund tax rebates continued to be worth almost half the annual cost of the basic state pension – regressive in effect, since the rebates were slanted towards the better off.

Under balance sheet pressure some employers tried to bail out and abandon promises made to their workforce; the government tried to stop them. It tinkered with trusteeship arrangements when the real problem, critics said, was money. The government said it was putting aside £400m for pension funds that previously had gone bust and it brought in new protection arrangements for any future employees of bankrupt companies. Brown promised to do what it took to help staff who found their pensions destroyed.

Finance directors in small and medium-sized firms were shown to have deliberately blocked staff from joining even existing schemes. Companies, frightened by the red ink on their balance sheets, started closing to new entrants their 'defined benefit' or final salary schemes – where pensions were linked to earnings. Much safer, for them, were 'defined contribution' schemes where pensioners only got what the fund could afford at the point they retired.

## Stakeholders at the Stake

Medium and larger employers continued to make pension contributions; the proportion of the workforce in company schemes rose slightly. The 4 per cent fall since 1997 in the proportion of the workforce with an occupational or personal pension (one million people) was mainly about a big drop in those with personal pensions, the great hope of the Thatcher years. Actuaries, guilty of professional negligence in the go-go years, started to panic. A new 'longevity risk' was pronounced: company pension schemes had not reckoned with people surviving longer.

It wasn't that Brown was inactive, rather that his schemes did not catch fire. Labour asked financial institutions to provide a 'stakeholder' pension, with lower charges that was designed to appeal to lower-paid workers. Launched in April 2001, some 1.9m had been sold by March 2004, but it seemed people were transferring money into them from other savings; average contributions per month fell from £353 at the launch to £161.

Some three million people were said not to be saving enough to allow them to retire without recourse to means-tested benefits. By 2005 the Department of Work and Pensions was issuing some eight million pension forecasts and was pressing employers to do the same; the 2008 target was fifteen million forecasts. It was developing a web-based planner, so people could calculate their likely pensions, from both state and private sources, and issued 1.6m pension forecasts to the self-employed by May 2004.

Brown's Minimum Income Guarantee for pensioners was a disincentive to save, it was alleged. However, this was doubtful since the evidence suggested most people were clueless about current, let alone future, levels of pension provision. More to the point, the commission the stakeholder providers could charge was so low that they made too little effort to sell them, and the people they were targeted at were hard put to get their foot on the property ladder, let alone have anything left over for a pension. What was obvious was that the roaring consumption powering growth (along with government spending) during the second term was incompatible with the savings rates needed if the working-age population were to enjoy comfortable retirements – whenever they began.

## The Turner Report

Malcolm Wicks, pensions minister, said mandatory retirement ages should be thrown into the 'dustbin of history'. And so Labour almost nonchalantly fomented a great pensions debate. The idea had been to commission a general report but leave specific policy recommendations until after the general election. Former CBI man Adair Turner obliged by stating the problem but leaving the prescription open for another report, later.

A government which had extolled 'partnership' between public and private sector and had, once, made the 'third way' its mantra, proved curiously reluctant to embrace pensions as a defining issue, even though they necessarily would have to marry state and individual provision and varying proportions of compulsion and choice.

Turner spelled out a relentless and unpalatable logic. First there was growing life expectancy. In 1981 actuaries said an average man would live for nearly fifteen more years when he reached sixty-five; now the prediction is nineteen years. In retirement, people either receive income from savings or from taxpayers, so the basic arithmetic was stark. In 2002, total transfers to pensioners amounted to just under 10 per cent of GDP, the bulk of which (6.1 per cent) came through the state. All things being equal, by mid-century over 15 per cent of

GDP would have to be transferred to maintain today's living standards (that figure assuming women start retiring at the same age as men).

Arithmetically, the simplest of Turner's options was to push up everyone's retirement age. The status quo (pensions at 10 per cent of GDP) would be preserved if retirement age rose to seventy. The 'fundamental point', said the Pensions Policy Institute, 'is to encourage people to work longer and to accept that pension must start to be paid later in life'. But working longer would take heroic changes in organisational structure and culture, let alone people's attitudes and expectations. Turner said the other options were to increase tomorrow's tax or to start saving more. Or for tomorrow's pensioners to be relatively poorer than today's. The pensions problem would not manifest itself today or even tomorrow but in the years after 2020.

For Gordon Brown, the centrepiece of pension policy had been his 'Pension Credit', a top-up for the basic state pension paying about £40 a week to some 3.2m households. The credit looked like a medium-term stopgap solution to the problem of inadequate saving in the past. The credit should remain until the problem of 'abject pensioner poverty had been solved', said Alan Johnson, who had replaced the Brownite Andrew Smith as secretary for work and pensions in September 2004. When would that be?

## Conclusion

Brown's object was simple: to create conditions of stability within which private business could flourish. Planning spending in advance, sticking to fiscal rules, letting the Bank of England make technical adjustments in pursuit of a certain level of price inflation – the clock wound up, the Treasury could then take tea.

Except British business could not be trusted to invest, innovate, re-train or play fair. Under Labour, government was not going to retreat from inspecting or worrying about markets, but then neither had it really retreated under Thatcher. Brown's problem was that he had no model for intervention. At best he was more the assistant referee than a striker. The state ensured people were educated and not hungry. After that the markets were supposed to provide work and incomes. Labour ministers more often than not were tempted to regulate – to give staff rights, to make directors more responsible, to protect the climate, to encourage training, and so on. But Blair took business complaints to heart. An anti-regulatory apparatus grew up to police the regulations imposed on business. Blair promised to make the drive on regulation the centrepiece of the UK presidency of the European Union due to start in July 2005.

Business whinged increasingly as the second term went on. The public, better employed, with higher incomes, sometimes joined in, bemoaning higher taxes which were in fact minimally extra on most middling earners. Stability and prosperity, Brown's calling cards, were not enough to secure gratitude.

**Gross Domestic Product (GDP)**

Percentage changes on previous year

forecast

1986  1988  1990  1992  1994  1996  1998  2000  2002  2004  2006

**Source: HM Treasury**

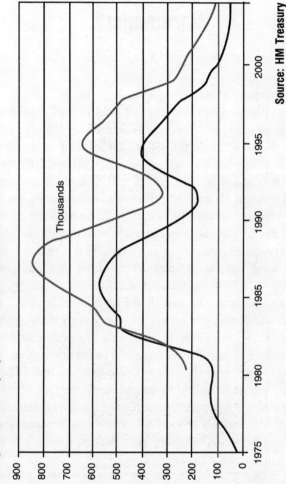

**Long-term Unemployment, Youth and Adults Over 25**

Thousands

900
800
700
600
500
400
300
200
100
0

1975    1980    1985    1990    1995    2000

**Source: HM Treasury**

— Youth: aged 18–24 unemployed for more than 6 months
— Long-term: aged 25+ unemployed for more than 18 months

# CHAPTER FIVE

# Warmonger?

Critics of Blair's conduct of foreign policy in his second term far outnumbered his defenders. Their fire concentrated on his biggest decision, to tie the UK to the chariot of war being whipped along by US Defense Secretary Donald Rumsfeld and Vice-President Dick Cheney and their neoconservative circle. President George W Bush relied on them for his Iraq policy. The reverse applied to the UK Prime Minister. He had worked out a view of the world, and the refusal of his cabinet and party colleagues to put up intellectual resistance helps explain why, despite the extremism of his view, he predominated.

Labour's decision to bed down with Washington had a context, which was the American response to the assault on September 11 2001. Whoever occupied Downing Street on that date would have been consumed in the consequences of 9/11, whichever way they turned. Whoever occupied Downing Street would have had to weigh heavily the past tilt of UK defence and foreign policy towards the US. Tony Blair chose a kind of national self-abasement, which was the usual stance of postwar prime ministers of both parties, Britain's instinctive default position.

His misfortune and his misjudgement was that the occupants of the White House were incompetent as well as politically extreme. Previous prime ministers had had to deal with a more or less consensual American policy line. But the partisan and blinkered stance taken by the Bush–Cheney–Rumsfeld axis contradicted large blocks of opinion in the American military and foreign policy establishment. Blair embraced what, in American terms, was a dangerous and (in the long run) untenable position.

However, few of the paths open to Blair in the wake of 9/11 were not strewn with landmines. Some Western leaders pulled the bedclothes around their ears. Let others do the heavy lifting while we keep our hands clean. If Blair became the villain in Europe, neither Chirac nor Schröder, in their different ways, could claim much nobility or coherence either.

But the path Blair chose, as lapdog, stained Labour's record. The shame of it, among other reasons, was that Blair had been moving towards a new and creditable doctrine for the use of British power abroad, one that complemented Labour's fulfilment of its pledges on overseas aid.

## Blair's Theory

A theory of pre-emption had been formulated during Labour's first term; it would use military force not just to keep the peace in civil conflicts. The doctrine did not, however, offer much on what happened after the pre-emptive strikes, as detachments of British troops remained littered in far-flung spots around the globe. UK armed forces were being reconfigured, slowly, to take on the task of intervention, preferably in a country with a coastline. But how long ought troops to stay to rebuild not one but a growing list of nations?

The irresponsibility, even the vacuity, of American neo-conservative thinking was to be demonstrated in Iraq. Did Donald Rumsfeld honestly believe that civil society would spring back into life, safe and sound, once Saddam had been toppled, allowing American troops (insufficient in number in the first place) to withdraw fast?

Some commentators, sympathetic to Blair, saw him hark-
ing back to an earlier tradition in British foreign policy. Blair
led intervention in Kosovo on a more muscular notion of
using military power to constrain oppression, and create
space for a people or ethnic group to live. His moving speech
in Chicago in his first term about the duty to do good where
you can helped sway Clinton and America behind intervention to save the fleeing Kosovans.

The failure of American policy in Iraq pushed Blair back to
handwringing. The news cameras captured him in Khartoum
in October 2004 bleating, almost literally, about the fate of
people in Darfur. Once he would have threatened intervention. Now, with daily death in the streets of Baghdad thanks
to the incompetence of the interveners, that option had
evaporated. Blair said Africa would be a top priority for a
proposed European Union (EU) rapid reaction military force,
1,500 strong. But now the political conditions for European
agreement on anything military post-Iraq did not look propitious, let alone how intervention of any kind would play at
home.


## Channel and Atlantic

Defenders of the Prime Minister over Iraq, few in number it
must be said, argued the UK had no alternative but to take
the White House position, despite deception over weapons of
mass destruction. There was no 'European' nor United
Nations (UN) option. In the diplomatic circumstances of
2002–03, they had a point. Jacques Chirac played to the
French domestic gallery. There was no competing French
analysis of terrorism, Saddam or the threat of weapons of
mass destruction (WMD), just a bid to win a deuce game
against the Anglo-Saxons. (It later turned out the French had
not been entirely sincere in applying UN sanctions either.) As

for Gerhard Schröder, his focus was also intensely domestic. Anti-Americanism, some of it an astonishing throwback to the 1960s, had won him the 2002 election, yet his political strength had waned by 2003. Could Blair really have concocted some coherent, effective, world-leading alternative European policy on Iraq from such feeble elements?

But Blair never tried, nor was he remotely inclined to turn across the Channel when the Atlantic beckoned. One result was the incoherence of his engagement with Europe during his second term. He allowed opinion in the UK to shift even further in a Eurosceptic direction. The government's policy on accession to the Eurozone was set up to produce at best a temporising and at worst a negative decision – that was the point of Gordon Brown's five tests. Blair's old notion that he, the British Prime Minister, would at last become a leader at the heart of Europe had never seemed further away, even under Margaret Thatcher.

At the end of Labour's second term its foreign policy dreams had become a nightmare on the streets of Baghdad. Will Blair's closeness to such a reckless and irresponsible White House prove to be the tipping point that breaks a fifty-year reflex in UK foreign policy? What if Gordon Brown were to succeed Blair? His pro-Americanism and anti-Europeanism are more deep-seated still. He never questioned the Iraq war, when his intervention at various points would have been decisive. Only two members of the cabinet resigned. The rest – implicitly – agreed with Blair that in trying, unchosen circumstances the UK had kept as close as it could to the 'ethical' foreign policy enunciated in what now seemed distant and innocent days when Labour first came to power. But how many really believed, as Blair seemed to, that Rumsfeld, Cheney and Bush could be its agents?

## The World in 2001

In June 2001, the Taliban terrorised the women of Kabul, the Pentagon war-gamed conflict with China. There was anxiety about proliferation of nuclear weapons and hawks muttered darkly about strikes on Teheran, though few wanted to work through a similar assault on Pyongyang. Saddam was a blip on the radar of mainstream Washington.

The pre-9/11 world was America-dependent. Who else could begin to broker a stand down between the nuclear powers of India and Pakistan? Who else, with the assistance of a handful of British war planes, would have forced Saddam back into compliance with UN resolutions in 1998? Surveyors of Saddam's labs and weapons dumps, checked and deceived at every turn, kept reporting that sooner or later he would have to be disarmed; if not, sooner or later, he would acquire destructive offensive potential. (This was the conclusion of the survey group commissioned after the Iraq invasion by the Americans themselves: there were no WMD for use in March 2003 but given time and space Saddam would have tried to acquire them.)

Counsellors to George H Bush, now advising the son, dreamt of toppling Saddam and fed Oedipal fantasies in George W Bush, but no planning was done. Blair, however, had worked out his own case for regime change. In London, apparently, Saddam was taken more seriously than in Washington. Paddy Ashdown's diaries recorded him saying in November 1997 that the intelligence reports on Iraq were scary; since then he had become an even more assiduous reader of the products of the Secret Intelligence Service.

What Blair had and what Washington lacked were the beginnings of a theory of intervention, based on an appeal to universal moral principles – 'hard Wilsonianism' someone called it. Close as they had been, Blair had brushed with Bill

Clinton over the use of force, not just in the Balkans. Blair had seized the case for toppling Saddam in the winter of 1998 when the Americans bombed his airfields. His critics said he was a sort of cut-down Gladstone, impatient to intervene to satisfy emotional urgings. Blair himself, in his Chicago speech in 1999 and then at the Labour conference in 2001 (after the New York and Washington attacks but actually long in gestation), exulted in reconnecting with a tradition in British foreign policy that went back to Palmerston and his master, Canning, mixing strong forward positions on international problems (such as climate change and Third World poverty) with a readiness to deploy British forces in pursuit of human rights and democracy, and use them proactively if necessary. For him, liberal imperialism was not an oxymoron.

## 9/11

It was this theory that made him and his advisers much more intellectually prepared to deal with 9/11. Blair knew the American response would be retaliation – a bigger version of Clinton's cruise missile attacks on Sudan after the bombing of US embassies in East Africa. (Why the demonstrated link between those blasts and al-Qaeda did not prompt an earlier – and better considered – war on terrorism is a question only answered by pointing to Clinton's political weakness and the arrogance and myopia of the incoming Bush administration.)

Blair's priority was to head off American unilateralism, because the world could not afford an isolated, introverted America. Was he right in taking on an almost personal burden in trying to secure Leviathan or was this an early sign of the Messianism which showed more than once in later months?

Or were such personal charges – liberally levelled at him –

unfair? After 9/11, wrote a sympathiser, Peter Riddell, he sought to 'emulate the presidentialism of Clinton' in the arena of foreign affairs where he would be unconstrained by Gordon Brown's dominance in domestic affairs. Yet between 9/11 and the first missile strikes on Afghanistan only two cabinet meetings went by without discussion of terrorism and the American response. After that Blair's cabinet talked and talked about Iraq. In *Did Things Get Better?* we pictured Don Quixote and his red-headed Sancho Panza girding up to tilt at the windmills of global injustice. Sancho could not understand why he was ejected from the Foreign Office; but Robin Cook, as Leader of the Commons, had ample chance to deploy his knowledge and experience on foreign affairs.

Blair's cabinet accepted the arguments made to them, or, to put it more negatively, they could not come up with better ones. Cook rejected the criticism that Blair sidelined the cabinet: 'on the contrary over the six months [from March 2002] we were to discuss Iraq more than any other topic'. So why so few dissidents?

The American assault on Afghanistan was as near as possible a (Western) consensual operation. But it was no UN war. Lawrence Freedman was not alone in doubting whether that phrase had any meaning. Even if it had – in Korea, in Iraq in 1991 – there were anti-Blairites to condemn all war absolutely and unthinkingly. UN approval, to be mythologised as the invasion of Iraq loomed, depended on games and tactics in the Security Council and (Freedman again) a good many of them were not devoted to logic or the rule of international law. Kosovo had shown that the right course of action could and should be taken without the UN's assent.

## The Build-up to the Iraq War

After Afghanistan was invaded the game changed. A dispassionate analyst would have said: pacify the entire country (which would take a long time); begin to establish a functioning and fair state (ditto); then build outwards, along myriad channels to seek simultaneously to destroy nests of terrorism while diminishing the disposition of individuals, groups and nations to join or succour them.

Conventional wisdom had long said that the volume of terrorism both within the Middle East and elsewhere would diminish in proportion to 'resolution' of the problem of Israel and Palestine. The best shot at this looked like the creation of a Palestinian state which would have an incentive to augment its autonomy by reducing terrorism launched from within its borders. Defining its borders was only one of the complexities. Intellectually, Blair signed up to this model: action on Israel/Palestine was a precondition of stabilising the rest of the Middle East. One of his domestic political problems was that the Bush White House simply did not agree, whatever the State Department might signal.

Blair was aware fairly early that Washington had no intention of consolidating in Afghanistan: Hamid Karzai was left to struggle with a tiny international force and a budget an infinitesimal size of the worth of the flourishing opium crop re-grown by the war lords.

## The Justification

The White House now openly linked its anti-terror campaign with the destruction of Saddam, despite the lack of evidence then or since of any association between the Iraqis and al-Qaeda.

Nuclear weapons were another issue, which embraced Iran

and North Korea, Pakistani secret-sellers, the debris of the
Soviet Union's arsenal and so on. Saddam's intentions were
known but what was not known was his capacity. However,
there was an effective inspection regime squeezing him and
(limited) military capacity in the Gulf region.

In his speech to a joint session of the US Congress Blair
asked the key question: Can we be sure terrorism and WMD
will join together? No, he said, but history would forgive
Blair and Bush for destroying Saddam even if there was no
immediate link. History would not forgive them for inaction.

What he forgot was the third danger – action that would
make the lethal linking of terrorism and WMD *more* likely.
By botching the invasion and its aftermath, the Americans
might have widened the scope for terrorism and, simultaneously, reduced their and other countries' capacity to do
much about WMD. In the aftermath of the invasion of Iraq
the risk of nuclear proliferation increased, and strengthened
the hand of rogue nuclear powers in Iran and North Korea.
Iran may now be the great regional winner, with dominance
over both Afghanistan and Iraq long after the Americans
have gone. The Foreign Office said after the event, 'the action
in Iraq sent a powerful signal to regimes who persistently
flout international law'. But wasn't the message about the
limits of Western will, and the likelihood, after Iraq, of too
many people saying 'never again'?

In answer to Blair's complaint about what friends of the
United States might have said in the summer of 2002, the
response could have been: to meet your strategic anxiety,
disaggregate the problems. Factor in American–Saudi relations, the peculiar way in which the United States had winked
at Saudi support of Islamic extremism for the sake – you did
not have to be a conspiracy theorist to see it – of security in oil
supplies. But such security was only medium run because the
Saudi regime was endangered; and besides Saudi supplies

were diminishing as a proportion of total US consumption. A reviewer of Seymour Hersh's book *Chain of Command*, detailing the complicity of senior figures in the Abu Ghraib abuses, said Blair's decisions on Iraq hinged on a colossal fraud in Washington. Here was Blair talking principle while there were Bush and Rumsfeld pursuing sectarian interests.

## Regime Change

What Blair had bought from a small cabal around the President was the imperative for 'regime change' in Baghdad. That meant deposing Saddam. We now know how perilously little thought had been given on either side of the Atlantic as to what ought to come next. Blair's problem, and the crux of the charge against him, was that instead of directly facing and selling this policy, he hid behind the threat of WMD. In another age, his defence might be *raison d'état*: putting wider national interests before immediate truth. The wider concerns, Blair implied, were keeping in with the Americans for fear a) of what they might do if left alone and b) to keep the UK's place at the top table.

In global affairs the UK might be below the salt but its place setting was still above, as a nuclear power (just) with a permanent seat on the UN Security Council. This chair, said the Foreign Office, was a 'crucial asset'. Polls might show people deeply confused about the UK's place in the world but they mostly agreed in wanting it to be somewhere near the top. Blair, it is said, will never be forgiven for Iraq. Would he have been forgiven if he had lost the UK's strategic position, which was in the gift of the Americans? The problem with this, once again, is that it confuses the Bush White House with longer-run American interests.

The Bush White House appreciated having Blair on side. It was even willing to give Colin Powell a few more days in spring 2003 to persuade the Security Council to come round. But Paul Wolfowitz blurted out the truth. WMD were a pretext. The real reason for the war was peculiar. Regime change in Baghdad would allow the Americans to transplant their troops out of Saudi Arabia, removing a cause of resentment. (The neoconservatives ruled out Israel/Palestine as another cause of resentment.)

Blair sympathised with the goal of regime change. You played the hand you were dealt, he said, when asked over and over: why Saddam and why now? But his great failure was that the cover for this policy – the threat of attack with lethal weapons – was blown. In striving to make this case, Blair stumbled.

## Blair's Failure

First, he allowed his political fate (and the future of the Labour Party) to depend on the whim of the White House. Second, he consumed his party's energies and loyalties in defending a position that was indefensible: Saddam was being toppled for reasons other than his possession of WMD. Third, by being forced on the defensive he had to concede portentous, time-intensive inquiries into the operations of government.

Lord Hutton, deputed to investigate the circumstances of government scientist David Kelly's death and Lord Butler, to investigate intelligence, both comforted Labour's enemies, whatever their actual conclusions. They exposed the innards of government. In evidence ministers and officials allowed the inherent ambiguities of governing to be reduced to a simple courtroom yes and no while the multi-levelled uncertainties of decisions became tabloid newspapers' 'lies'. No effort was made – perhaps in the circumstances it could not be made – to explain how government was not simple; how 'intelligence' was often anything but. Blair may, inadvertently, have made governing Britain – especially projecting British power abroad – very much harder for any successor.

## Kelly

The Kelly affair and its aftermath followed directly from Blair's over-inflating WMD as the reason for war. Kelly, a Ministry of Defence scientist, did not believe the survey evidence was conclusive. He was right. But all he had to offer about what happened to intelligence reaching Number Ten was an opinion. The BBC wrongly presented that opinion as a fact. Downing Street responded with disproportionate outrage, Kelly committed suicide and the Hutton report was commissioned. Published in January 2004, it blamed the BBC for refusing to apologise for a false report and amid a welter of recriminations the BBC director-general Greg Dyke and chairman Gavyn Davies resigned.

Showered with criticism about his spurious claim that there had been an immediate threat, Blair commissioned the former cabinet secretary Lord Butler of Brockwell to examine the paper trails. Neither Butler nor Hutton, to the dismay of the conspiracy theorists, found evidence of deliberate tinkering with material. They showed, however, that thin evidence had been overused and over-interpreted. Naive people suggested the intelligence services, pristine and pure, had been sullied by the way politicians had used their material, conveniently forgetting the origins of the Security Service in dishing dirt on political dissenters and the role of the Secret Intelligence Service in campaigns against liberals, socialists and Nobel prize-winning anti-colonialists as well as Communists.

One lethal memory branded into the minds of British voters was Blair's breathtaking claim that Iraq had WMD capable of being launched within forty-five minutes. What was even more breathtaking was his subsequent admission that he had never bothered to enquire what sort of weapons – battlefield or mega-death? The reason can only have been his desperate search for justification for action to which he was committed because he knew the Americans were committed.

## The Aftermath

The great statue toppled as coalition forces removed Saddam's regime, but they were not able to establish themselves on the ground with sufficient speed and precision to avoid a damaging period of lawlessness during which much of the potential goodwill of the Iraqi people was squandered.

The CIA presented a national intelligence estimate in July 2004 which effectively said the Americans were losing the continuing war. Joe Klein, in *Time* magazine, asked why Bush did not embrace this report with the enthusiasm he had given a CIA national intelligence estimate in October 2002 saying Saddam probably possessed WMD. 'If the [2004] estimate is correct we are facing a far more dangerous world than existed before the war,' Klein concluded, looking nervously at Iran, military overstretch and indeed American will and credibility in dealing with any future threat.

It was the failure of the Americans to pacify Iraq that was more instrumental in returning even the Bush administration towards a kind of multilateralism than anything Blair effected. The UK's leverage on the United States over Israel/ Palestine amounted to zero. But equally none of the apocalyptic predictions about the end of Nato and a permanent transatlantic freeze as a result of the war came to pass either. In Australia, a right-of-centre government acting in parallel with Blair had also been forced to mount inquiries, suffering slings and arrows from domestic critics and yet John Howard won re-election in October 2004.

Nato's troubles antedated the Iraq war. Its problems in persuading European members to meet their promises of even small troop commitments in Afghanistan, which was an intervention with the UN's approval, showed how little appetite there was to shoulder responsibility for global security. As for the UN, in the same week that Kofi Annan, the Secretary-General, told an interviewer that the intervention in Iraq had been illegal, its impotence was demonstrated by news of continuing death and mayhem in Darfur. Despite UN promises, there was no sign of effective UN action, and all this at the same time as the tenth anniversary of the UN's shameful inaction over Rwandan genocide was being commemorated.

## Human Rights

The UK sought to 'depoliticise' the UN Convention on Human Rights, behind which serial abusers such as Zimbabwe's Robert Mugabe had managed to hide. Labour could usually be found on the right side of condemnations, of insurgents in Nepal and the Burmese junta, for example. But painful action (against the Chinese, say, or the Russians because of Chechnya) was not forthcoming. UK leverage with the United States secured no movement on its refusal to reconsider its renunciation of the Rome Treaty establishing the International Criminal Court. The painfully slow prosecution of Slobodan Milošević at the Hague demonstrated the limitations of such tribunals.

## The Foreign Office

. . . was in decline. Foreign offices across Europe had been losing influence. In France the Quai d' Orsay had become one of the president's outer offices; in Spain, José María Aznar was principal foreign policy spokesman; there was nothing exceptional in Blair's drawing on the best people from the Foreign Office and taking a leading role.

The Foreign Office said it was shedding assets, selling 230 ambassadorial homes since 1997, but why couldn't it share officials with other EU countries? If UK strategic priorities were terrorism and immigration, what were France's or Germany's? The EU had an External Action Service to run joint missions, but the precondition for such rationalisation was a closer engagement with the EU which Blair had promised but did not deliver. By the end of his second term, he appeared to have lost his appetite for it.

## Europe

When he was interviewed by the European Parliament to confirm his nomination as a member of the European Commission in October 2004, Peter Mandelson chose to distance himself from his past. He was, he said, no longer a member of Blair's cabinet; he was a European.

It was a worthwhile distinction. Despite pledges, nothing much had happened on Labour's European front, except the emergence of the Treasury as the site of genteel but convinced Euroscepticism. For Brown, the test to be applied to 'Europe' was that it should be more British – a depressingly familiar UK stance. It must embrace flexibility and reform, resist federal fiscal policies, reject tax harmonisation and tackle, root and branch, the 'waste and excesses of the Common Agricultural Policy'. No wonder anti-European sentiment sharpened.

Two years after coming to power Blair famously declared 'once in every generation, the case for Europe has to be remade from first principles. The time for this generation is now.' But Blair's second term was not to be that 'now', it turned out. 'Nobody has been making the damned case for Europe since 1985' said the pro-European Labour business-man Lord Haskins. They didn't start. Robin Cook was either being uncharacteristically naive or all too knowing when he wrote in his memoirs, 'Tony Blair is arguably the most pro-European prime minister in modern times, certainly since Edward Heath.' First consider that 'arguably' and then list the premiers since Heath – Wilson, who called the referen-dum, Callaghan who probably voted against, Thatcher then Major. Blair did not have to do much to distinguish himself in that list.

The problem was partly Europe. Had the French and German economies been booming, the Treasury could never have adopted its snooty tone (which conveniently ignored such indices as productivity, where the French were streets ahead). The fact was, however, that the Ger-man economy had stalled – though smugness from Britain was hardly in order. German fundamentals: productivity, trade, investment, were still far stronger than the UK's. The French growth rate had slowed to half the UK's, its unemployment was far higher; but its GDP per capita was still higher. Eurozone interest rates were lower, but the growth and stability pact which underpinned the Eurozone was not working. First the German then the French gov-ernments burst the bounds imposed by the pact. Then they used their muscle to manipulate the agreement to avoid censure.

What of the goals agreed at the Lisbon summit in March 2000 to 'make the EU the most competitive and dynamic knowledge-based economy in the world'? The Treasury said the competition regime was being harmonised along with rules on government assistance to business. But the UK continued to adopt a holier than thou attitude on employ-ment and market flexibilities, even though GDP per person employed in the UK (productivity) was exceeded by the average for the fifteen-strong EU and even by Italy.

This was not an era when European leaders stood tall in the gaze of the world. The EU proved incapable of dealing with the crisis over those anomalous tracts of Moroccan Africa still held by Spain – Colin Powell had to intervene. The EU lacked leverage in Cyprus, despite holding the fat carrots of entry over both the Greek Cypriots and Turkey. As for a more general willingness to remake the EU as a 'force', all the EU could threaten were trade sanctions. A country intending to acquire nuclear weapons, Iran, was unimpressed.

The EU operated on a basis of laws and open, cooperative security, but dealing with the wild world required force, preventive attack, deception. This Manichean view had some merit. The member states of the EU were reluctant to commit resources to a common defence and security policy, reluctant to take on the burden of peacekeeping, let alone peacemaking. Had the Madrid bombings come before 9/11, would the EU have concerted action of any kind? The member states cooperated on security, up to a point, but not on preventive action. That burden was left to the Americans but, as Blair complained, when they acted, it was condemned as cowboy unilateralism. All this made selling the EU in Britain even more difficult.

The five tests instigated by Gordon Brown were judged in June 2003. Stage-managed by the Treasury, the conclusion was foregone. Theatrical boxes of documentation were dumped on each member of the cabinet, defying them to read the papers let alone criticise them. With that infuriating arrogance economists have – despite the non-scientific nature of so much of what they do – the Blair cabinet was dared to challenge the Chancellor's position of 'certainly not now, and I'm not really sure ever'. Brown said the key was maintaining the macroeconomic stability that was his principal calling card. Would joining the Eurozone jeopardise it?

Road shows had been due to trundle out round the country in the same month advertising the benefits of joining. The wheels must have fallen off the buses because they never left the garage. Charles Grant of the Centre for European Reform quite rightly said you couldn't blame Blair alone: where were the cabinet's pro-Europeans, why so silent and shy?

## The New European Constitution

Blair could be blamed for mishandling the politics of the European constitution. Everyone knew that enlargement, taking in another ten countries to the EU, required re-engineering. So the government tried to present the convention which began work in spring 2002 as a technical exercise. No chance, however, when it was chaired by the subtle former French President Valéry Giscard d'Estaing. Labour could have presented the writing of a new constitution for Europe as a wonderful recognition of the new entity that would be formed once the Eastern European countries with Malta and Cyprus had joined, but instead the government tacked defensively, as if embarrassed.

There were differences of view, pounced on by the Eurosceptic press, but how far did Blair personally object to those references to 'ever closer union' that had to be excised at all costs? The UK gave the impression abroad that it was clinging to the last scraps of a threadbare garment. Every other country was in the same boat and the 'red lines' drawn to prohibit European ruling on tax had opponents elsewhere. Indeed, other countries might have shared the view – if this was indeed the Blair government view – that integration had ground to a halt and the constitution was about providing a machine for a new, looser give and take. It might also necessarily have to accommodate an ever closer union between France, Benelux and Germany.

Here was a Prime Minister prepared to go to war thousands of miles away for the sake of fundamental rights, in Sierra Leone, in Iraq, yet who blushed when the CBI attacked the constitution for attempting to lodge social and employment rights understood across the rest of Europe to be fundamental to civilised economic relations.

Then suddenly, in April 2004, the government spun on its heels and agreed the constitution was not a cleaning-up exercise after all. In autumn 2003 Jack Straw had said firmly that it did not affect parliamentary sovereignty, yet six months later it did. Blair promised to hold a referendum once the final version had been agreed. No matter that the Single European Act in 1986 and the Maastricht Treaty in 1992 had a far greater impact on pooling sovereignty, yet needed no referenda. A plebiscite had become a political imperative for Labour, as it was clear that Europe and fears of lost sovereignty would, to Tory glee, dominate the 2005 election unless they could be parked by promising a vote afterwards.

Timing was left vague. Perhaps (ministers whispered) some other country's voters would vote it down before the UK's turn came. Chirac was soon forced to concede a referendum too. Labour might then be spared the embarrassment of campaigning for a document they had spent months saying was relatively unimportant. When it was finally signed, in June 2004, Blair returned from Brussels with a glowing endorsement, but a referendum was safely at least a year away. In October he travelled to Rome to sign the treaty embodying the new constitution amid more confusion. The European Parliament had just forced the membership of the European Commission to be refigured. Was this an example, at last, of effective European governance? There were no answers.

Yet you could say Blair, accidentally and on purpose, had effected a great shift within Europe and in the direction favoured by the UK. We shall never know if Blair might have forged a better European response to America over Iraq, but it would not have been easy. Afterwards, if the UK was battered by its closeness to Bush, the French game was up too. The Gallic – Gaullist – version of Europe had gone, never to be resuscitated. The Franco-German engine sputtered. The Iberians altered the balance and the Eastern Europeans shifted it further away from the entity conceived by Robert Schuman and Konrad Adenauer.

Here was a sign of things to come. Only eleven of the thirty-two commissioners who were to take office in November 2004 spoke French; they all spoke or claimed to speak English. Leadership of the new Europe was up for grabs.

## Defence

Europe was hardly mentioned when Labour reviewed UK defence, first in 2002, when the 1998 Strategic Defence Review was updated, then again in a December 2003 white paper. It was still nowhere to be heard in July 2004 when the Ministry of Defence reassessed its stance according to the government's revised spending priorities and the interim lessons of the Iraq war. Troop deployments to Afghanistan and (46,000 strong) to Iraq had been relatively inexpensive; the Treasury put the extra cost for 2001–05 on top of defence spending (which was trending downwards) at £4.4bn.

British military planning was oriented west. Implicitly, it was acknowledged, British operations would take place with American support or, at worst, indifference; practically they would depend on the supply of American munitions. There was virtually no independent capability. That did not, how-ever, make the Americans any more likely to give the UK a waiver from its regulations on international traffic in arms for example. Post-Iraq who expected gratitude from the Pentagon?

An audit of the war by MPs found equipment supplied well enough, despite a fuss in the press over body armour. The British effort was augmented by the 'unique capability' of special forces. Tours of duty in Northern Ireland seemed to have given the British army a set of skills which were unique and invaluable for operations in the twenty-first century. It meant that in Iraq, in the area around Basra allotted the British, forces managed the transition from fighting to peace-keeping swiftly.

Given the chance to think about future conflicts, Blair's government imagined more of the same as Iraq. Blair's wars had helped push the armed forces to adapt to their more mobile post-Cold War shape. 'Lift' – the capacity to move forces and equipment over a distance – proved sufficient in Iraq. But the UK's was a 'one operation' force, after which lengthy recuperation would be needed. The Iraq commitment ruled out any others at the same time.

Labour had proved much more adept than the Tories at restructuring, partly because they were spending more. The army would need fewer heavy tanks and artillery pieces but it would need more lightweight armoured vehicles and more aircraft carriers. And personnel. Iraq operations had relied too heavily on reservists.

Mobility and far-flung operations demanded ships and Labour inaugurated the biggest naval construction pro-gramme since the Second World War ended, with two new carriers to enter service in 2012 and 2015. Some £2.9bn was allocated: the likely cost would be more like £4bn, with a lot of politicking on the way. That kind of money would keep jobs going in some of Labour's heartland seats, Govan, Wallsend and Rosyth among them, at least if the American master-contractors had any sense. It would need air support which (everyone hoped) the Eurofighter Typhoon would supply, replacing the ageing Jaguars. Fewer aircraft in total, fewer ships and smaller forces.

Defence Secretary Geoff Hoon proposed the armed forces reduce in size from 203,000 to 179,000 over four years. Personnel would be used to greater effect by the use of Net Enabled Capability, or e-war, a system linking electronic sensors with command. Needless to say, the technology was American. But critics wondered how it would work on the streets of Samarra where spies in the sky were blind and every car could contain a bomb. Was this a high-tech gamble? Generals used to expend men; now the imperative was to substitute machines for bodies.

## Overseas Aid and Debt Relief

Labour's record on development aid from 1997 had been worn as a badge of honour and Gordon Brown won plaudits for the Treasury's (relative) generosity.

But if by 2005 Labour had almost doubled the UK aid budget it remained a long way short of the UN target of spending 0.7 per cent of GDP in overseas aid. The UK figure would rise to 0.47 per cent by 2007 and at its current growth rate Gordon Brown announced it would finally reach the threshold for the first time in 2013 – joining ten other EU countries that had already, or would by then, have reached the target.

Despite that, the Department for International Development (DfID) was the department of Labour's conscience and the replacement of Clare Short by Hilary Benn after the invasion of Iraq was a masterpiece of party symbolism: could New Labour be all bad when the son of Anthony Wedgwood-Benn was one of its cabinet ministers? Its aim was 'to eliminate poverty in poorer countries' and by 2005 it was pushing £9 out of every £10 in UK aid to low-income countries. Half of DfID's bilateral aid went to Africa, which also received the attention of a prime ministerial commission, launched in February 2004.

Labour counted among its best acts the decision to write off 100 per cent of the sovereign debt owed to the UK by the designated 'heavily indebted poor countries'. But irrevocable debt relief had to be multilateral and progress was slow; the Treasury said it would be 2006 before its own target of three-quarters of eligible poor countries were helped. This and myriad grants and schemes – nearly £3m to Iran after the Bam earthquake in December 2003, a large share of a $21m HIV/Aids programme in Burma – were commendable. The government, keen as ever to quantify and monitor all its outcomes, said the aggregate result of its efforts lifted two million more people permanently out of poverty each year – cheaper and easier to do abroad than at home.

Gordon Brown was critical of the EU's aid programme which dispensed £6bn a year. Instead of hitting the most extreme poverty, money flowed to favoured areas, notably the Balkans where it would have flow-back economic benefits. The EU said it had moral and practical obligations to the region after the Kosovo war. UK policy was not without certain confusions. DfID helped India increase primary school enrolment at the same time as Gordon Brown was warning of the threat to UK competitiveness of India's annual output of one million graduates and public sector unions worried about the threat to their employment being caused by outsourcing of data processing to Bangalore. There was DfID doubling its support to Yemen, 'with an increased focus on education for girls', while Yemen's northern neighbour, Saudi Arabia, oil rich and de facto peninsular power, allowed schoolgirls to burn to death in a blazing school from which religious 'policemen' refused to allow them to escape, unless they returned into the inferno to recover their face scarves. DfID was embarrassed by the disclosure that over six years Clare Short had paid out £34m from the aid budget for consultancy from the Adam Smith Institute, the prophets of privatisation. War on Want argued that DfID's 'commitment to privatisation' – demonstrated by the large sums it had paid out to ideologically committed consultants – was incompatible with its commitment to poverty reduction. Here, however, was the philosophy of Gordon Brown in action: government simultaneously able to provide the wherewithal for policies but disqualified from itself putting them into effect.

The UK could claim some share of significant reductions in HIV/Aids infection rates in such countries as Uganda. Gordon Brown applied a rod to his own back, accepting that on present rates of progress primary education for all would not arrive in Africa until 2030, at least fifteen years later than the target date set at the 2000 world summit. Indeed, only two out of eighteen millennium targets were going to be reached by 2015, halving the proportion of people whose income was less than $1 a day and halving those who had no regular access to safe drinking water. All the government could promise was that it would remain 'an influential voice' in the G7, the International Monetary Fund and the World Bank.

## Cultural Property

Some forms of international cooperation deepened. The UK signed the UNESCO convention on illicit import and export of archaeological and similar artefacts – the looting of Iraq during the war against Saddam prompted action. New UK legislation stiffened offences but a database of stolen items was slow to arrive. Organised crime recognised no national boundaries.

## The UK Abroad

Because influence is hard to measure did not mean to say it could not be exerted. Labour, however, did not seem particularly interested in projecting a UK view. MPs concluded that the failure to launch a BBC World Service television channel in Arabic was 'a missed opportunity to further the UK's wider diplomatic ambitions and interests in the Middle East and wider Islamic world'. Though the World Service was maintaining its audiences – in the face of stiff competition – neither the government nor the BBC itself enthused. The former tightened finance in the 2004 settlement; the latter saw the World Service as a dumping ground for domestic managerial retreads.

## Drugs

Foreign affairs, said the Foreign Office in its statement on UK International Priorities, are no longer really foreign. Despite the expulsion of the Taliban regime, some 90 per cent of heroin consumed in the UK still came from Afghanistan. Yet Labour's 2002 strategy blithely announced the government would 'reduce opium production and eliminate it by 70 per cent by 2008 and in full by 2013'. Since Hamid Karzai, Afghanistan's leader, was at the time pleading for an increase of the tiny international force of 5,000 which never went beyond Kabul, he had no chance of controlling the opium fields of the war lords. His entire government budget was less than the sum Britain spends on drug treatment.

But such blue-skies optimism permeated all international drug policy. The UN had an unrealisable target of its own: to eradicate all cultivation of coca, cannabis and opium by the year 2008 with the slogan 'A drug free world! We can do it!' The inability of the West to consider whether prohibition is what drives the growing drug crisis derived from the UN Convention on Drugs – itself driven by the United States – which obliged member states to criminalise production, distribution and use, with heavy threats and penalties to any country that refused to sign up. Still, enhanced cooperation between the UK and the Jamaican government resulted in more arrests of cocaine couriers.

## Conclusion

States had the right to non-interference in their internal affairs, said Foreign Secretary Jack Straw, but it was unacceptable to classify some situations as the concern of one national government alone. What were the criteria for defining which was which? Straw cited Darfur, Rwanda and Kosovo. So, a case for intervention having been established, what if the UN proved to be a broken reed? Blair had argued action could be right, regardless of the state of play on the Security Council. But after Iraq the UK's appetite was sated, as its capacity for action had been exhausted, physically, by the troop commitment in Iraq, where the UK could not withdraw without admitting the most profound errors of judgement.

Yet Blair had offered an engagement with the messy post-Cold War world. The British public was fickle and contradictory, wanting a seat at the top table, but unwilling to stomach the compromises it might require. Many of those who had voted for the UK Independence Party also harboured fantasies of independent UK military action. Blair's critics on the left had rarely thought through where they wanted the UK to be; many were anti-Blair and anti the EU, leaving no geopolitical space for their preferred model of a neutralist, passive Britain. Blair, too, was inconsistent. As the nuclear powers of China and India increased in economic strength, was anyone suggesting his doctrine of intervention should apply to their WMD? The UK maintained a rusting nuclear capability on board Polaris submarines, now approaching an age when they should be slung up on a rack in the Imperial War Museum. What was it for?

Some analysts pointed out that compared with the period of the Cold War, of the rise of the Fascists or even the later nineteenth-century rivalries between great powers, the early twenty-first century was looking benign. Vladimir Putin was an authoritarian but Russia posed no great external threat. In that bigger picture the world was in no bad shape. Terrorism might terrify many, but bands of religious maniacs from the caves of Tora Bora were neither about to dominate the world nor – the Cold War threat – annihilate it in a single nuclear strike.

In the end the Iraq intervention, led by an American President with uncertain credentials and maniacal inclinations, turned to ashes the vision Blair had laid before Labour's conference in 2001, about spreading good around the world. The triumph of democracy and human rights rolling out across the globe lost its attractions if it arrived on a gun-mounted humvee driven by cynics (Rumsfeld), neoconservatives (Cheney) or Christian fundamentalists. Why here, why now, they had asked Blair about Iraq. His answer was that it happened to be the opportunity available to bring freedom to these particular oppressed people. What he didn't see was the connection between means and ends: if Bush was the means, the end was tainted.

# CHAPTER SIX

# Safer?

Britain became a much more dangerous place during Labour's second term. The Prime Minister said so, the Home Secretary said so, and so did every pundit on terrorism. External attack was imminent. Yet on home ground, on the estates, even on roads that were getting busier, Blair's Britain was becoming a *safer* place. Safer than in the past, and safer than elsewhere: it's curious how little pride was taken in the attractiveness of the UK to migrants and refugees. Labour's leitmotif was control. No one doubted procedures needed tightening and administration improved, but was the new, harsh note necessary?

During Labour's second term aggregate crime rates went on falling. The risk of being a victim of crime fell 40 per cent from a peak in 1995 to 2004. Crime had not seen such a long sustained fall since Lord Salisbury was Prime Minister.

But the shape of criminal behaviour was changing, worryingly so. Amidst those tumbling figures for offences notified to the police, violent crime showed a 12 per cent increase over the year to 2003–04 – terrifying enough to give the tabloids the headlines they wanted. But how far was behaviour actually changing, as against the proportion of violent offences reported to the police? Improvement in the method of recording crime paradoxically sucked in more offences.

Labour's approach was to target the 100,000 offenders who committed half of all crimes – and the hard core 5,000 who committed a tenth of all crime. But, second term, Labour had not only to catch and cure the criminals, but to be believed. Sentiment departed from statistics. Attempts to put across plain numbers were greeted with accusations of fiddling. Criminologists might confirm a trend to safety but danger inflamed imagination. Perhaps car theft and burglary were rarer, people might acknowledge. But other anxieties crowded in: new migrants, vandalism, rowdiness, graffiti, abandoned vehicles, litter and all those forms of disorder bundled together by the government itself as 'anti-social behaviour'.

In mid-2004, the Home Office sent a peculiar leaflet to every household telling them what to do in the event of bombs, chemical, biological or radiological incidents. It contained first-aid tips for dealing with burns, bleeding and broken bones. Go in, stay in, tune in, said the hitherto unknown National Steering Committee on Warning and Informing the Public. It felt like the 'secret state' exhibition then on at the National Archives, with its yellowing civil defence instructions from the early 1950s about putting gumboots on when you went outside after the A-bomb dropped. Public reaction was stolid and mildly indifferent. Any home secretary trying to make the country feel safer had a perplexing task.

### Feeling Safe

After 9/11, right through Labour's second term, defence/foreign affairs/international terrorism topped people's list of concerns when they answered polls. Second came race relations/immigration/immigrants. Crime combined with law and order plus vandalism was third, with the state of the NHS fourth.

Of course something had to top the list and war and migration dominated the news. But perhaps here was some indication that domestic crime was being put in its place.

More coppers helped the perception: Blair's Britain became a policed state as, in the second term, 12,500 extra officers swelled the ranks, to the highest number ever. The effort to get more police officers out patrolling the streets, together with a new breed of street wardens – 4,000 community support officers in place by 2004 – made the forces of law and order more *present*. That visibility was to grow: the 2004 spending review provided for 20,000 additional community support officers by 2008.

Did it matter that officers pounding a beat would catch no criminals? The Audit Commission long ago estimated that, walking the streets, an officer would come within 100 yards of a crime being perpetrated only once every eight years, and even then probably wouldn't know it was going on. Effectiveness was what people believed when they saw a uniform.

In 2004 MORI found 24 per cent saying they expected policing in their area to improve, compared with 20 per cent who thought it would get worse. That was marginally better than expectations of health. People tended towards optimism about their own area. But they still thought the nation at large was going to the dogs. The Prime Minister's Strategy Unit racked its big brains over how to get people to draw impressions from their own experiences and local observation, and not the scares they read about or saw on television.

If there was such a thing, the national frame of mind was fearful and pessimistic. The 2004 British Crime Survey – results a bit less bad than in 2003 – found two-thirds of the public thought crime had increased in the previous two years and half of them said 'a lot'. But again, when asked about their local patch, people were a little brighter – only one in four people thought local crime had been rising a lot.

People were not joining up the dots in their own thinking. When they considered specific crimes, it turned out things *were* getting better. In 1994 26 per cent expressed a high level of worry about burglary and that fell to 13 per cent over the decade. In 1998 25 per cent said they were highly anxious about violence. Six years later 16 per cent were seriously afraid.

And it was right the index should have fallen. There was less to fear. In England and Wales, the proportion of homes burgled each year was 3.2 per cent – with wide variation between social classes and geographic areas. That is to say, of the fifty houses in a typical suburban street one or maybe two might be broken into; in fact it might have no burglaries while flats on an inner city estate suffered a number. People without alarms and decent locks were at a six times greater risk. Single parents were two-and-a-half times more likely to be burgled – not because they were single parents but because they lacked money. The paradox of burglary was that the poor who have less were more likely to be robbed than the rich, urbanites more than country dwellers. It was typical that crime reporting during the Blair years should be dominated by an entirely unusual crime, when a Norfolk farmer, Tony Martin, shot and killed a burglar, an incident utterly unrepresentative of the picture at large. But it lead to Tony Blair promising to support a change in the law to send 'a very very clear signal to people that we are on the side of the victim, not the offender' to give home-owners stronger rights against intruders.

## National Security

When Britain joined the United States in invading Afghanistan, and particularly after the Iraq war, the UK was assumed to be a target. 'When not if' said a grimfaced Prime Minister. In Spain multiple simultaneous blasts killed hundreds on morning rush-hour commuter trains in Madrid, helping unseat a government that had sent troops to Iraq. How long could London escape? The Metropolitan Police hinted at plots foiled. What proportion of the UK's comparative immunity was due to police work and intelligence, what to sheer luck?

Risk assessments remained high. Embassies abroad were strengthened; intelligence budgets boosted. Public opinion said Labour's foreign policy had made a terror attack more likely and few could doubt it, however little anyone knew about terrorist intent and capacity within or exportable into the UK.

There was one peculiarity, though. According to figures collected for the American government, the period since 9/11 saw less terrorism – defined as targeting civilians or property by non-state groups such as the IRA, UDF or ETA. The worst recent years had been 1985 and 1988. There were more deaths in 1998, with bombings of US embassies abroad and other incidents, than in 2001 despite the World Trade Center horror. Perceptions could deceive. Except in Iraq itself, swimming in blood.

Security forces were busy. The UK responded to the threat by suspending the clauses of the European Convention on Human Rights stipulating no detention without trial. Over 600 people were arrested, often with a fanfare of prearranged publicity in the press. By the end of 2004 only sixty-nine had been charged and only fifteen convicted. Meanwhile thirteen foreign nationals were locked away in a legal no-man's-land inside Belmarsh prison – though they were free to leave the country if they could find somewhere that would accept them (two did).

Citizens of the UK had been picked up in Afghanistan and taken to the prison colony at Guantanamo Bay – a place of multiple anomalies, American sovereign territory on the island of Cuba where American civil laws did not apply. Three young men were eventually released. They went back to their homes in Tipton, an unremarkable West Midlands town, where these boys from families with reasonable jobs had received an education. They were not poor or unemployed. What drove young Muslims, what teaching in which mosques recruited them to Jihad? Resentment among Muslims at arrests might propel more into terror than fiery imams imported from the madrasahs of Pakistan.

## Secret Service

In a secret world where the targets and performance measures applicable to other civil servants did not seem to apply, how was the public to assess security and intelligence? After an odd lag, by 2004 recruitment and spending was growing fast – the security and intelligence agencies were to expand by 1,000 by 2008, up by 50 per cent over 2004.

Iraq exposed technical deficiencies, the most obvious being the limitation of signals intelligence and the lack of reliable human intelligence sources. After 9/11 it emerged the CIA had not one Arab-speaker on its staff. Larger questions were put aside, the biggest of which was why the UK needed an autonomous intelligence-gathering operation in a world when the threats were increasingly directed against a way of life shared by all Western nations. But the service grew.

At home, the reputation of the security service, MI5, had recovered since it was revealed to be spending its time monitoring Labour prime ministers and bugging the phones of trade union leaders. But who was to know whether arrests were based on good information? While Labour warned sombrely of danger, the Conservatives pledged to follow the Americans in creating a department and a minister of homeland security, with all its implications of pulling up the drawbridge, circling the wagons and living in a siege mentality of permanent threat from the never-ending war on terror.

Labour tinkered with the way police intelligence was co-ordinated nationally. What had transmuted from the national drugs intelligence unit into the National Criminal Intelligence

Service became a separate department under the Home Office in 2001. It took on more functions and was due, by 2006, to form the core of a super Serious Organised Crime Agency. With 5,000 staff this was a national police force in embryo. To some, looking ahead to identity cards, more effective data sharing between police, customs, and other government departments, it brought fears for civil liberties. To others, it was belated recognition that crime had gone global and old distinctions (between, say, civil crime and terrorism) had dissolved.

## Emergency Services

After widespread flooding in 2000, the government reviewed emergency planning and moved to establish what it called a single framework for emergencies, though it still involved councils on the one side, separate police and fire authorities, and on the other Whitehall departments dispensing grants. In 2004 the Treasury doubled the annual £20m contribution to 'resilience' work by local authorities. New civil contingencies legislation was introduced in 2004 to move things along from the days of civil defence wardens with whistles. But if the modern face of emergency planning was a fireman in decontamination gear, he had his problems – one of which was gender. Despite a strike, white paper and two pieces of fire legislation, the fire services remained 98 per cent white and 99 per cent male.

The strike in 2002 had been provoked by fire staff rejecting the government's (generous) offer to buy out outdated practices in the fire stations and try to move the service into the twenty-first century: the future lay with prevention work rather than beefy men scrambling to race engines to a diminishing number of fires. Arson was reckoned to cost £2.2bn a year, and the total cost of fire some £6.6bn. 'The speed and efficiency with which the fire and rescue service responds to fires remains vital, but the best way to save lives and reduce injuries and other losses, is to reduce the number of fires that start.' Half of all deaths from fire took place even before the fire engines were called out. That implied much more community involvement by fire staff and more home visits – for which female fire officers might be a lot more suitable. A few more graduates might help: only one in fifty firefighters had degrees compared with one in four police officers. It would also imply recognising the stark social class profile of domestic conflagrations: fire at home was a poor person's danger.

Labour, sensitive about unions, chose not to push hard on obvious rationalisations, such as brigading fire and ambulances together, or insisting fire crew carry and use resuscitation equipment as part of their regular work. Ministers had, however, stuck to their guns during the fire strikes and welcomed an independent review by Sir George Bain, which advocated reform.

The Fire and Rescue Services Act 2004 gave the (increasingly anomalous) fire authorities a duty to try to promote fire safety, to coordinate and plan, but the future increasingly lay with regional rather than local bodies – better able to mobilise the equipment that would be needed in the event of a terrorist attack.

## Migration and Identity

Anxiety about aliens was easily stirred. Soaring numbers of people seeking asylum were front-page fodder in the early part of Labour's second term. Day after day the alarming impression was given of borders punctured and absorbent. A tidal wave of flooding metaphors inundated rational argument. But Labour did not help, refusing for a long time to accept that there were overlaps between those seeking asylum in the sense defined by international convention, and those seeking a better life in a country with low-paid work aplenty and, for all the anxiety about housing shortage, places to stay.

Newcomers would overwhelm Britishness, it was feared. Similar questions were being raised elsewhere in Europe, identities threatened and changing in the wake of growing migration. But what was Britishness? And within Britain, what weight should be given to the majority's complacent sense of Englishness? Some asylum seekers were dispersed to Glasgow, but, later, the Scottish first minister announced his country's borders were open to fresh migration and by his country he definitely did not mean England. Gordon Brown, a Scot in a cabinet disproportionately Scottish, made an attempt at definition of Britishness in a notable speech: to feel safe is to feel secure in a collective identity.

Citizenship classes were made compulsory in (English) schools. The Home Office invented a civic ceremony for newly naturalised citizens to mark their transition from otherness to one of us. Welcome was accompanied by questions about what should be demanded of them in return – to speak some English and understand the law and customs of the country.

On 1 January 2004, the first new citizenship ceremonies were held by registration officers to welcome newcomers and 'help them gain a fuller appreciation of the rights and responsibilities of British citizenship'. They were popular with new citizens. The government prepared a *Living in Britain* handbook for them and planned compulsory citizenship studies and English language lessons.

## Citizens and Aliens

At the same time the process of stripping British citizenship from anyone 'seriously prejudicial to the vital interests of the

UK' was speeded up. This was the Abu Hamza clause – named after the hook-handed Egyptian firebrand who was accused of inciting Muslims to violence in and outside the Finsbury Park mosque. The American government applied for his extradition. Before that claim was processed, he was arraigned before the UK courts for incitement and terrorism-related offences. Yet Labour remained true to human rights clauses which prevented the export of suspects to countries where they might be tortured. A new category of non-person was born: someone too dangerous to be allowed to walk the streets but too rights-laden to be sent away. The answer seemed to be indefinite incarceration.

New citizens had an obligation to 'respect our laws and reject extremism and intolerance', said the Home Office. 'There will be no place for those who incite hatred against the basic values that this country stands for.' Few could disagree – except it opened the door to a woolly new law outlawing 'incitement to religious hatred'. After 9/11 the British National Party (BNP) capitalised on anti-Muslim fears, spreading out to take more council seats. Muslims pointed out that the BNP used anti-Islamic tirades as a legal surrogate for racial abuse; they had been calling for a religious-protection law for years. Blair and Blunkett agreed. They were striving to show their even-handedness: tough on asylum but liberal and progressive on social relationships within the UK. But religion was not race. The National Secular Society and the humanists invoked Voltaire. Religious belief should be subject to the same mockery and treated with the same irreverence as any other set of opinions.

## Asylum

If terror was the genuine threat, sound and fury over rising numbers of people seeking asylum in the UK often felt more politically dangerous to the Blair government. Its polls and focus groups showed this, bundled with migration, was the 'wicked issue', and all the more so in parts of the country where non-white faces were uncommon and new arrivals few.

Tabloid front pages were splashed with pictures of fierce-looking young foreign men with moustaches climbing over the fences at the Eurostar terminal in France, or out of the backs of lorries at UK ports. On Christmas day 2001, with no trains running, 550 asylum seekers stormed the Calais entrance to the tunnel on foot in two great waves. It was one of those images that got etched into national consciousness. It left an impression of a system out of control; it steeled Labour ministers to take and keep on taking hard measures.

They had no choice. Unplanned permeability of borders was unsettling. Why did some people move out of zones of conflict and oppression in Afghanistan (the Taliban still in control) or Iraq (Saddam ditto) or Kosovo, when millions of others did not? Why did people move from West African countries but never come anywhere near the West? Why did the UK attract some, but not others? The British public was rarely told about the large number of asylum seekers in Germany. Cogent answers were lacking. The UK's attractiveness was in some measure related to its prosperity, the English language, the flexibility of labour markets and perhaps – experts differed – the size of its 'grey' or hidden, unofficial economy.

Those Calais scenes occurred after the Tampere summit of European ministers in 1999 had approved creating 'an area of freedom, security and justice' covering visas, asylum and migration across the European Union. The European Commission proposed integrated border management, common border guards, and a common policy on asylum. The government opposed border guards and thought harmonisation of asylum policy had gone far enough – though that did not protect David Blunkett from tabloid charges that he was selling out national interests simply by discussing further cooperation with his European colleagues.

Eurosceptics wanted it both ways. How should migrants be admitted into European Union countries? Asylum seekers could not simply pick the EU country in which they chose to make an application. A common policy was needed. But into the mix had to be thrown the French government, apparently happy to wave illegals through on their way to Britain. Was it entirely coincidence that, from the British point of view, things improved when the Socialist–Communist coalition led by Lionel Jospin fell in May 2002? Some French left ministers had relished the opportunity to embarrass the ideological apostate Blair.

The Red Cross had opened a camp by the tunnel entrance in Sangatte to house asylum seekers while they waited to jump on lorries; 67,000 passed through its doors in the three years it was open. They all expressed determination to get to the UK and most of them did. Finally, the government paid the French £4m to build fences, police the area and install heat-detecting equipment and heartbeat sensors that could find human bodies inside lorries. The French government permitted UK immigration officials to check papers on French soil. Either the measures worked or the forces pushing people towards Calais abated. Numbers fell. Where 400 had entered Britain this way in April 2002, by November there were only seven. The operation not only cut off that route, but arrested 250 of the traffickers who had been transporting people across the continent to the port. Once the Red Cross camp was closed, Calais again found its streets filled with destitute stragglers sleeping rough on park benches. They would be moved on: in 2004, the French government an-nounced a sweeping plan for the revivification of the port town.

Other events contributed to a dual sense of a country besieged and a government struggling to keep control. Riots broke out in detention centres holding people due to be deported. Harmondsworth Immigration Remand Centre descended into chaos after a detainee hanged himself and staff lost control of 441 inmates. Yarlswood, a newly opened £100m centre for 1,000 detainees was burnt to the ground in January 2002: those without hope or incentive for good behaviour were hard to detain. In September 2002 asylum applications soared to over 10,000 a month.

## Labour and Migration

Here was an issue Labour had in no sense chosen. It had bubbled around the edges of the 2001 election but had in itself determined few votes. Some response on asylum and migration would have been required whoever was in power. Just as with 9/11, there was no 'do nothing' option. Ministers were then damned if they did and damned if they did not – which is pretty much what holding public office is all about.

Home Secretary David Blunkett probably failed to get the measure of the issue quickly enough; how competently he was served by the Home Office was a question. The need for successive pieces of legislation showed an absence of strategic thinking. Blunkett's instincts appeared authoritarian but he came eventually to cut a convincing – even reassuring – figure. It was remarkable how quickly asylum faded after it had so gripped political and public attention. Yet what the government was never able to do was face, squarely, the question: if the UK was to be a country of net immigration, what was a reasonable level? In 2003 the Government Actuary's Department predicted annual net immigration of 130,000 – which would cumulate into substantial demographic impact. Enough, too much? Labour's view seemed to be that if there were no adverse headlines, it had no view.

Except at Calais, the government could not physically prevent people arriving and making a claim. Labour never envisaged abrogating treaty obligations to accept asylum claims even though it was broadly accepted that about 50 per cent of claimants were 'economic migrants' and an unknown proportion of arrivals came through the agency of people-smuggling operations and criminal gangs. What it could do, however, was speed up processing, and Labour made progress. More controversially, it sought to make life for claimants harder in the hope a message would get back. Labour MPs, weekly facing the complaints of their constituents about arrivals, backed the tough line. The Nationality, Immigration and Asylum Act 2002 withdrew welfare support from anyone not making an asylum claim 'as soon as practicable' which was interpreted as immediately at their point of entry. Those who did qualify for benefits had to report regularly – a way to ensure they stayed in the part of the country where they had been dispersed.

The National Asylum Support Service was criticised as inadequate. Scattering them around the country was designed to relieve pressures on London and the South East. But that too caused problems, as they were packed into the only available empty housing in most undesirable blocks in desolate depressed areas, with already over-burdened health services and schools. But attempts to place them in the countryside met with such outrage from the village protesters that most of these plans were abandoned. Yet again, the inner cities bore the brunt of large numbers of especially needy people.

As had happened before when Michael Howard was Home Secretary, Labour's asylum law was later overturned by the courts as a breach of human rights. Since its implementation in

January 2003, over 10,000 asylum seekers had been refused benefits and basic food and shelter because they had failed to make an asylum claim as soon as they came into the country. But in June 2004 the courts forced the Home Office to retreat and restore benefit and housing support to all.

## Blair's Big Promise

In February 2003, Tony Blair stepped in to make another of his eye-catching promises. He pledged to halve the number of asylum seekers within six months. No one believed him – except the handful of experts who noted the figures were already on a steep downward trajectory. Did this kind of big promise – on poverty, street crime or asylum – shore up trust in government and its statistics? It often seemed to have the opposite effect, inviting incredulity and a mistrustful sense that politicians can do any kind of conjuring trick with the figures, just-like-that, as Tommy Cooper used to say.

But Blair hit his target. Asylum numbers were cut in half in six months. In fact he outstripped that target, reducing the numbers from their 10,000 a month peak to just 3,000 a month by the spring of 2004, the lowest for ten years. All the figures were good. In 1997 Labour had inherited a backlog of 60,000 cases awaiting adjudication: now it had been cut to 18,000. Speedy decisions were the answer. By 2004 some 80 per cent of new cases were dealt with within two months. The number who succeeded in getting refugee status fell fast too. In 2002 34 per cent were successful, but only 11 per cent by 2004. The UK achieved the biggest fall in asylum claims in any EU country. Asylum applications to France were far higher than to the UK by 2004.

## Appeals

Ever anxious, the government proposed a constitutional innovation which provoked such an uproar it backtracked to the status quo. The Home Office proposed to seal the asylum and immigration tribunals, preventing appeals from them, a first tier of appeals against decisions by officials, to the courts. A second tier of appeals led to delays. But critics said the problem was the quality of initial decisions by immigration officials. The fact so many appeals were upheld showed there was a problem. The judiciary mobilised; ministers retreated.

## Removals

Removing those refused was always the most difficult part of the system. Some countries were deemed just too dangerous to send people back to, other countries refused to take people back. Although the removals figures improved, half of all those refused ended up staying.

So in September 2004 Tony Blair made another of his eye-catching promises: by the end of 2005 the number of failed asylum seekers sent home would exceed the number of new failed applications so the backlog would fall every month. Colnbrook, a new detention centre for the refused, was built at Heathrow, so by 2005 there would be 2,750 places in all for those awaiting deportation.

But even as the asylum figures plummeted no one quite believed it. The sneer was that this target could only have been achieved by letting many more people in as migrants. Indignant, the government asked the National Audit Office to conduct an independent review of the asylum and immigration figures. Naturally, when the bean-counters reported in May 2004, exonerating the government, it made hardly a ripple in the press.

## The Bucharest Connection

The run-up to enlargement of the European Union in 2004 provoked another migration panic. The EU was opening its doors to ten new countries, allowing free movement to all (though not necessarily on day one). No one was much bothered about Malta or Cyprus or the Baltic states. But what would come out of the Transylvanian darkness of middle Europe? The press was filled with horror stories of what sounded like entire peasant or Roma populations on the move – and all of them heading for the UK in time to arrive on 1 May. Television news reporters told of booked coachloads ready to set out. With only a few days to go, Tony Blair ordered that no arrivals from the new EU countries would get benefits: they must work or starve.

Immigration minister Beverley Hughes was forced out. The British consul in the Romanian capital, Bucharest, emailed the Tories claiming immigration scams were being ignored by the government. The suggestion was that Labour wanted to rush through as many East European work permit applications as possible before 1 May, to stop it looking as if the floodgates had opened afterwards. An instant urban legend, the consul told of a one-legged man who put forward a business plan as a roofer, getting a work permit no questions asked.

And as for those coaches setting off at dawn from Bratislava and Bucharest, did the East European hordes (code-name for gypsies) arrive on 1 May? Just 24,000 applied for work permits from all the ten new entrant countries in the first three months after accession. They came as hotel and farm workers, caterers and hospital cleaners. They also came as accountants, nurses and teachers. They were not allowed to apply for council housing or for state benefits and they were, as the government had always said, nothing but a self-supporting economic asset.

## Undocumented Arrivals

David Blunkett kept tightening the screw. The Asylum and Immigration (Treatment of Claimants) Act 2004 made it an imprisonable offence for asylum seekers to arrive without travel documents or to fail to cooperate with re-documentation. There was an issue, but was it another reflection of the desperation of refugees or a ploy by jobseekers? Asylum seekers boarded planes or boats with passports, but 60 per cent arrived with none so it was impossible to know what country they should be returned to. Traffickers who supplied false papers told their clients either to destroy them, or to give them back secretly en route and refuse to divulge their true nationality. Without papers, their home country – if that could be ascertained – refused to take them back.

The 2004 Act also removed welfare rights from those whose applications failed if they were refusing to cooperate. At the last moment, David Blunkett squeezed in yet more punitive measures. Rejected asylum seekers who couldn't be sent home would be forced to do unpaid community work in return for their benefits. Asylum seekers accepted as genuine were also further restricted. The new act denied them a right to council housing unless they stayed in the area to which they had been officially dispersed. Bogus students who were found to have no place at the colleges they had named were to be removed faster. Bogus marriages were to be stamped out.

## Asylum – the Balance

Both the government and its critics failed to answer hard questions. Was the right to asylum unlimited, even if that implied millions of arrivals? On the other hand, why should those claiming a right offered by the UK under treaty obligations be treated as second class? Under Labour it became more difficult for genuine cases to arrive and survive. But motives for moving turned out to be mixed. In a myriad of personal and family circumstances a desire for betterment mingled with a need for protection recognised by international law. Preventing asylum seekers from working – which would have implicitly accepted an economic motivation for moving – forced them to live off benefits.

Out there in the wide world, the UN High Commission for Refugees was trying to cope with millions of displaced persons along the borders of the poorest regions on earth, beside which the UK's asylum problems were negligible. Quietly, with as little publicity as possible, for the first time the Labour government did do the decent thing and agree to accept a very small number – 500 – of these UN refugees. Most other Western nations including the US had been taking their share of them for years. However, by the end of 2004, only sixty-nine had been accepted and resettled, due to the refusal of local authorities to offer them places.

Pity for migrants only showed when they were safely dead. Some fifty-eight young Chinese had suffocated in a lorry coming through Dover; nineteen Chinese cockle-pickers drowned in Morecambe Bay, illegals working under tyrannical gangmasters. Labour moved to regulate such gangs but found it hard to offer the public a lead on migration. Did the UK want incomers? The Health Secretary said yes, for without incomers the NHS could not function.

By 2004, the UN reported a sharp drop in the number of refugees globally: at seventeen million it was the lowest for a decade. The UN ascribed this to the fall of the Taliban, which saw millions of Afghans return home, while the numbers displaced from Sierra Leone, Burundi, Angola and Liberia sharply fell too. Perhaps Labour's measures were less effective than these swings in migratory pressure.

How many people still arrived in the UK unknown and unreported? In autumn 2004 consular officials in Lagos reported 200,000 successful visa applications a year. No record was kept of subsequent comings or goings. Labour had not secured the borders. Blair's illiberalism, if that is what it was, upset few on the backbenches. Labour MPs took from their constituency work a political imperative. The government, they said, had to shout through the megaphone in two directions. First, would-be migrants had to be warned to stay away; perhaps this message did get through. Second, the voters had to be shown that the UK was no soft touch. This didn't work. Despite Labour's success in reducing numbers, 80 per cent of voters still told opinion pollsters at the end of 2004 that the government was 'not tough enough' on immigration.

## Criminal Justice

People had extraordinarily little confidence in criminal justice – that panoply of police, courts and punishments. According to the British Crime Survey (BCS) only a third of the public were confident that the system was effective in cutting crime. Fewer than a quarter thought it dealt promptly with young people accused of crime. The only item on which criminal justice scored well was in 'respecting the rights of people accused of committing a crime'. Small comfort that people thought the system favoured the rights of criminals without preventing crime.

Such findings prompted Home Secretary and Prime Minister to make fierce, almost weekly, speeches on law and order. Blair infuriated penal reformers; 'liberal' his government was not. The Criminal Justice Act 2003 toughened

penalties to be meted out to serious offenders. Life meant life
was the message for convicted killers. But get-tough speeches
maybe only confirmed a perception of society and justice out
of control. By 2004 people were marginally less satisfied with
the system than they were at the 2001 election.

Were they right to despise the administration of law and
order? It was topsy-turvy, so much spent on catching, trying
and punishing so few, compared with the trivial sums spent
on preventing crime. The rate at which the authors of crime
were detected nudged up by 7 per cent from 2002 to 2004.
But it was still only in 23.5 per cent of crimes that an offender
was identified. In only 18.8 per cent of crimes was the
perpetrator punished or cautioned. In four out of five crimes
victims went without justice.

## Crime Rates

Crime was falling, but so it was across the Western world,
and so it had been since the mid-1990s, and no one had given
John Major any credit for that. But to whom should credit
go? Were government or social forces responsible for the 39
per cent fall in crime rates in the decade since 1995? Crime
reduction was not directly linked to public spending on
crime. Jobs probably helped – the passage of over a million
more people into work under Labour's New Deals for the
long-term unemployed had some effect. Or was it prosaic
home security, such as locks? Houses and cars were better
secured and since most crime was done on impulse, fewer
opportunities meant fewer crimes. Materialism played its
paradoxical part. Mobile phone theft dropped as they became ubiquitous and besides they were largely useless once
stolen – a new law made it illegal to re-programme them and
harder to re-register stolen cars. Burglary now paid less well.
The value of electrical goods – DVD players, televisions,

stereos – plummeted below the level where any but the most desperate drug addicts bothered to steal them.

## Street Crime

Sometimes it was possible to make progress. Muggings often consisted of young boys taking mobile phones from other kids, but they were growing in volume. In March 2002, after a spike in the figures for street crime, Blair convened another summit. Ministers, experts and chief constables from the ten police forces with the highest mugging rates met at Number Ten and promised to slash street crime within six months. Eight progress-chasing meetings followed, £261m was spent, and the target was hit. Street crimes dropped by a quarter within half a year, producing an annual fall of around 17 per cent.

A success, but was it cost effective? The blitz did result in over 5,000 fewer recorded street offences, but each arrest had cost £51,500. That sum could have purchased the very best drug treatments and muggings were sometimes frantic acts by drug addicts.

Micromanaging operations from Whitehall caused resentment on the part of local police forces, though they also acknowledged the extra money. Pressure to hit the target did kick-start new joint initiatives between police and other services – which continued. But in the end high-profile, quick-hit, eye-catching initiatives from on high were unlikely to make a lasting difference.

## Violence

Violent crime had been falling, down 24 per cent since 1995, according to the British Crime Survey. But police recorded a rise in violent crime, up 12 per cent in the year to 2004: more people reported violence to the police while fewer were actually victims.

Half the incidents of violent crime involved no physical injury to the victim. Nearly half of those that did involve injury were alcohol-fuelled, as young men with more money in their pockets drank more and hit out. Young men between sixteen and twenty-four were at most risk both as victims and perpetrators. Since the 1995 high-water mark, violent attacks by people unknown to the victim dropped by 5 per cent.

A campaign to encourage more reporting of rape, domestic violence and race-hate attacks showed through in the official figures. A quarter of violent incidents happened in the bosom of the family. Labour determined to direct attention to domestic assaults, provoking headlines in tabloids about the nanny state. New laws offered victims more protection and a register of offenders against whom civil orders had been taken out, so women could discover whether they have been assaulted by a serial attacker of women. Consciousness was shifting and progress made: 'acquaintance violence' and domestic violence fell by 50 per cent over the Blair era from 1997.

Gun crime hit the headlines. Restrictions on handguns after the Dunblane massacre had been followed in 2003 by a ban on air rifles, with five-year mandatory sentences for anyone caught with a gun. A gun amnesty in 2003 yielded 44,000 weapons. The public's low capacity to understand proportions was put to the test in autumn 2004 when a schoolgirl was shot in the streets of Nottingham. Gun crime had indeed been rising, by an alarming 35 per cent between 2002 and 2003, and by 2 per cent the following year. But crimes involving weapons were a tiny fraction of all crime, 0.3 per cent. Despite the improvement in maths scores in school how many people could safely work out 2 per cent of 0.3 per cent and then make an assessment of whether Blair's

Britain was less safe? As for the homicide rate, it rose at the same average 1 per cent as over the last two decades. Serial murders by Dr Harold Shipman caused an upwards blip.

## Property Crime

Theft accounted for 78 per cent of all crime so the improvement in the safety of property that continued during Labour's second term made a big difference. Burglary fell 39 per cent in the decade after 1995. Car crime was down by 31 per cent which made the chance of becoming a victim in this category lower than it has been for twenty years, despite growth in car ownership and in the volume of desirable things that tend to get left on the backseats of cars.

Homes without security locks and alarms were six times more likely to be burgled; Labour put money into home security in poorer areas, which tended to have high crime rates. Some 2.1m homes were made less vulnerable. A new agency was established – making the civil liberties people anxious – to proceed with the confiscation of money and goods from crime. Big brother CCTV cameras now followed citizens day and night, though a full evaluation of their effectiveness in preventing and detecting crime remained to be done.

## Drugs

Addictive drugs were at the heart of crime, fuelling almost half of all offences. Over a generation a sizeable population of drug users had established itself. In 1971 there were only 5,000 registered addicts, but in 2004 estimates of the number of hard drug addicts ranged between 250,000 and 300,000, rising at a steady 7 per cent a year. The government reckoned the total cost of drug addiction, its associated crime, pursuit and punishment of criminals and treatments was £17bn. Each addict on average raised £13,000 a year through crime to fund their habit.

In the second term, ministers faced up to reality. They abandoned the wildly unrealistic target Blair had set in 1998 when a 'drugs czar', the former chief constable Keith Hellawell, was appointed with much fanfare to proclaim that he would cut drug use by 25 per cent by 2003. When David Blunkett, no slouch at grand targetry himself, arrived at the Home Office, he junked the target and replaced it with a general commitment to reduce supply and consumption of Class A drugs.

The evidence was that many addicts could maintain an orderly, crime-free life with jobs and families if they were given a steady and reliable supply of heroin, so did not need to commit crimes to get it. Only fifty doctors were licensed to prescribe heroin and Blunkett set a target to increase this number to 1,500. Two years later, by 2004, only 100 doctors had been licensed. But then the National Treatment Agency (set up in 2001) won permission in 2004 to experiment with seventy-five heroin addicts in three cities for eighteen months, giving them the drug, but insisting it must be injected or smoked in the clinic.

New drug testing and treatment orders proved popular with the courts which issued over 18,000 orders diverting addicts out of the criminal justice system if they would agree to undergo treatment. Waiting times to get into treatment fell by two-thirds since 2001 to an average of four weeks (though far longer in some hard-pressed areas). The amount of time people stayed in programmes rose from fifty-seven days to 203 days and an extra 30,000 addicts were in treatment compared with four years previously – up 40 per cent since 1998. The target was to provide enough places to treat 200,000 people by 2008 with waiting times down to two weeks. Over £500m a year was being spent on all this – still chickenfeed compared to the total cost of addiction.

Success rates varied widely. Only 2,000 places were residential, not nearly enough to meet demand for intensive support. The National Audit Office found that only 28 per cent of offenders completed their drug treatment orders. Four out of five addict offenders committed crime (and were detected) within two years – though those who completed a treatment course did better and only half of them were reconvicted. Even in prison – ideal for intensive treatment programmes in theory – there were only 4,700 prison drug programmes for over 70,000 prisoners (in 2003–04) and many far from intensive or therapeutic. Failure rates were high once they left prison.

Labour moved on soft drugs. In January 2004 cannabis was downgraded from a Class B to a Class C drug. This was surprisingly brave. Mo Mowlam and Clare Short had been among the ministers publicly slapped down in earlier days for even suggesting cannabis policy should be rethought. Some 97,000 people a year were being arrested for cannabis possession and faced widely varying sentences in courts across the country. Instead the police were now expected to confiscate the cannabis or issue an on-the-spot warning. Five months after the re-classification, arrests for possession dropped by a third. The Home Office estimated that 180,000 hours of police time could be saved each year. Did drug use surge? Surveys suggested that cannabis use among teenagers was falling. In 1998 28 per cent of sixteen- to twenty-four-year-olds said they had used it in the previous year, but the 2004 figures showed 25 per cent.

## Drink

Town centres became no-go areas on Friday and Saturday nights as huge new hard-drinking bars tipped out legless young people at closing time. Drinking disorder was visited even on quiet country market towns. Drink was becoming relatively cheaper and young people, like most other people in Blair's Britain, had more to spend on non-essentials.

At least 44 per cent of all violent crimes were committed by people who had been drinking, especially – the phrase came into common usage under Labour – binge drinking. Although it was young men who drank most, young women's consumption was rising sharply, too. Labour had created 'partnerships' between the police and councils and these crime and disorder committees were encouraged to clamp down on rowdy bars, underage drinking and any irresponsible sale of drink leading to alcohol-fuelled violence. A pilot scheme in Manchester involving CCTV surveillance and better late-night transport managed to cut incidents by over 12 per cent in a year.

Government would not (to use one of the favourite clichés of the period) declare war on drink, because the corporate interests involved were strong and, besides, urban economic activity depended on drink, especially in vulnerable areas. Home Secretary David Blunkett raised fines for selling alcohol to children. But what about adults, buying cheap drink in supermarkets as well as Wetherspoon's? The pubs complained that minimum pricing for drinks was unfair when supermarkets discounted like mad.

A new licensing act, passed in 2003 to be implemented in 2005, was criticised for its mixed messages. Councils were given powers to shut down rowdy bars and revoke licences, and the police to confiscate alcohol in public places. But the act would also allow twenty-four-hour drinking, in the hope of creating a civilised all-day European culture of food and drink in bars, without the panic and binge associated with closing time. The chief constable of East Sussex, responding to a proposal from Brighton council to permit all-day drinking, said selling cheap alcohol amounted to transferring a cost into the public domain, picked up by others in degraded environments, noise and disorder. There were doubts about whether deeply ingrained British drinking barbarism could be transformed into quieter wine-imbibing habits.

## Prison

Despite the fall in crime, the prison population kept rising. Labour inherited 60,000 inmates in 1997. By 2004 there were 75,000. The Home Office planned further expansion of jails: its projection to the end of the decade was 109,000 inmates and it was building prisons to cope at huge expense.

Judges and magistrates took their cue from the punitive tone used by Blairite ministers and the newspapers they were trying to impress. Sentence lengths went up. Although the Home Office also developed excellent alternatives to custodial sentences and tried, by means of circular letters to magistrates and crown court judges, to persuade them into diverting more non-violent offenders away from jail, the political talk was all about banging 'em up, especially the young louts. The courts did, for increasing lengths of time.

A first-time burglar was twice as likely to go to prison in 2004 as eight years previously. The average sentence for burglary went up from sixteen to twenty-five months. Seven out of ten prisoners would re-offend. Despite costing £30,000 a year per prisoner, jail failed to rehabilitate. Women were twice as likely to get prison sentences as they were in the early 1990s, for the same offences.

The UK was the prison capital of Europe. Although over 15,000 new prison places had been built since Labour took office, well over half the prisons were severely overcrowded with 16,500 inmates sharing cells built for one person. The pressure meant the prison service failed to provide the minimum of twenty-four hours a week's 'purposeful activity'. In some jails prisoners were locked in for twenty hours a day. Prison suicides rose steeply.

However, prison education figures improved. More prisoners picked up basic skills, though 80 per cent of inmates still had reading and writing skills below the level of an eleven-year-old child. Keeping contact between prisoners and their families was a sign they were less likely to re-offend, but due to overcrowding and prisoners being placed far from the family home, prison visits by partners and close relatives fell by a third in the five years to 2004.

Labour's response was bureaucratic reform. It set up a new National Offender Management Service (NOMS). This combined the prison and probation systems into a single body, which was supposed to manage the handling of each offender throughout, with a coherent programme for outside support while serving a sentence and after. NOMS was instructed to reduce re-offending by 10 per cent by the end of the decade. That would depend on its rehabilitation work, and whether it led to more time for training and therapy. Labour's objective had become less imprisonment, but this U-turn in policy was never admitted in public.

### Dangerous Youth – the Big Target

Irritation about loutishness and disorder rose then fell back. Perhaps this was an example of how speechmaking and grand pronouncements – in which the Home Secretary and Prime Minister specialised – did work. Perhaps successive criminal justice revisions and anti-social behaviour measures did convince people that something was being done.

For Britain had a new public enemy almost as menacing as terrorism and asylum called youth. They were 'louts' and 'yobs'. The tabloids called them 'feral' and they came from 'families from hell'. But anti-social behaviour was not something made up by newspapers. The policy imperative was bottom up rather than top down. It came from backbench Labour MPs who at their weekly surgeries faced the wrath of estate dwellers whose lives were being wrecked. Anti-social adolescence (low-income adolescence that was) was poked and prodded, coerced, chivvied, tagged and bribed. The Home Office established a new Anti-Social Behaviour Unit in 2003 and its head talked of 'charm and menace' as her methods.

The scale of the problem was hard to gauge. These were the young people who did not get GCSEs, who did not stay on after sixteen, who were not modern apprentices. The objectionable behaviour included racing across greens on scooters and in cars, graffiti spraying, noise, littering, petty theft and harassment. It was most evident among council and housing association tenants on the same estates that were being targeted by a raft of Labour initiatives.

## Anti-Social Behaviour Orders

A new kind of restraint was invented, the Anti-Social Behaviour Order, the Asbo. It could even be slapped on young people without taking them to court. Some social workers protested it was the wrong way to deal with the multiple disasters of chaotic families. Asbos could ban people from going into areas where they have caused trouble, ban them from wearing gang uniforms – a golf glove or a balaclava. Identified young people could be banned from meeting more than two others to stop large threatening groups hanging around and intimidating shopkeepers.

Although few Asbos were taken out at first, the new culture was said to encourage vigilantes and bullying of unpopular families. Some young people ended up in jail for breaching their Asbo conditions – imprisonment without having ever been convicted of a crime, the civil liberties lobby complained. But residents often thought Asbos were the first thing that had ever worked in improving life on the estates: 'I'm tired of being lectured on civil liberties by people who live in Surrey,' said a councillor in Manchester, where the local authority took a hard line. It was putting back the social glue and re-creating society, said enthusiasts.

While youth offenders in courts had their anonymity preserved, some councils named and shamed those on Asbos. The faces of children as young as ten were posted in local newspapers and leaflets through local doors, asking people to report them if they were seen breaching their conditions. Yet councils were slow to take up these powers. By September 2004 some 2,500 orders had been taken out.

The Home Office Anti-Social Behaviour Unit had no powers to order local authorities to do anything, but with pressure and money to offer, they started a blitz. Nuisance Neighbours Panels, Operation Scrub-it against graffiti, Operation Scrap-it against abandoned cars, Operation Gate-It to close off back alleys and an anti-begging drive, were backed by a new breed of specialist 'anti-social behaviour prosecutors' within the Crown Prosecution Service. To read the flurry of press releases, Britain was about to become a land with not a blade of grass out of place, nor a citizen less than courteous and neighbourly. It had an effect. Public perceptions improved: the British Crime Survey showed 2002 was a peak year for anxiety about disorder, and it had fallen markedly by 2004.

The emancipation of football from its violent past continued. Arrests connected with the game declined 10 per cent in the year to 2004; court orders banning known trouble-makers increased slightly in number.

## Youth Justice Board

Young people between fourteen and twenty-one were the most likely to offend. A quarter of all crime was committed by those aged seventeen and under – 40 per cent of burglaries, car thefts and street robberies.

As just 3 per cent of them were responsible for a quarter of all youth crime, the idea was to seize hold of that hard core of repeat offenders. Preventing young people from becoming criminals was the centrepiece of second-term strategy. No government had put so much money, research and effort into trying to micromanage the lives of out-of-control young people, hoping to pull them back from the brink before they ended up in prison.

The Youth Justice Board had been set up in Labour's first term with a target to reduce by 10 per cent the number of under-eighteens placed in custody. It oversaw local Youth Offending Teams (YOTs) which pulled together funds and support from health, education, social services, police and probation to make sure families of children in trouble got joined-up treatment rather than a host of separate public agencies crisscrossing their doorsteps. Offenders, both serious and trivial, were sent for punishment and treatment to the local YOTs. Under strict supervision, they had to go to school or train or work. They might get drug treatment, anger management courses, personal mentors or whatever else could help keep them straight.

## Parenting Orders

Their parents might be served with parenting orders, forcing them to attend classes or even, occasionally, residential courses. Parents might be obliged to take their child to school or impose a curfew on them, with a £1,000 fine or prison sentence hanging over them for failing to comply. Parenting orders were more popular with courts than Asbos, and although only about half of them were completed, they cut youth re-offending rates in those families by a third. The surprise was how many reluctant parents ended up pleased with the result on their family.


## Intensive Supervision and Surveillance Programme

Special attention was reserved for those under-eighteens who were more serious offenders. Most of the 4,200 sent by the courts on the new Intensive Supervision and Surveillance Programme (ISSP) had at least nine convictions in the last year – bad enough for jail. This last-chance-saloon sentence specified six months in the community, but they were electronically tagged to see they observed a strict curfew keeping them indoors when they were most likely to commit crimes. The scheme, with several surveillance checks a day, got most of them back into school or college, into restorative justice programmes trying to get them to pay something back, and into programmes on personal relationships, anger management and intensive self-examination in how to break their criminal habits.

This was the great hope for youth justice. These were the toughest cases, the ones long written-off, from relentlessly catastrophic families. Over 15 per cent were using heroin or crack cocaine, 15 per cent had injured themselves or attempted suicide. Only one in five had been to school in the last six months, so they were on average five years behind in literacy. If the programme worked with them, then an adapted model might take in other young people at risk.

It did succeed in getting nearly all into education, training or jobs, at least for a while. It also hit its modest target of reducing re-offending by 5 per cent. Frequency of re-offending fell by 43 per cent, and, just as important, the crimes they did commit were less serious. But still 85 per cent of them were reconvicted within a year of participating in the intensive supervision programme.

Needless to say, this figure was seized on to make gleefully bad news headlines. Yet experts compared these results with what happened to hard core young offenders given custodial sentences. Of those sent to prison 96 per cent re-offend. Intensive supervision cost £12,000 per head, £40,000 cheaper than keeping a youth in custody.

## Youth Inclusion Programme

Youth Offending Teams had also been charged with trying to prevent another group turning to crime: those at risk, but not yet in bad trouble. The Youth Inclusion Programme (YIP) was to seek out the fifty local thirteen- to sixteen-year-olds in most peril, as identified by schools, social services or police. What happened next was purely voluntary, but for at least five hours a week they were encouraged into glorified youth clubs. YIPs provided somewhere safe to go after school, with sport, art and drama, alongside some training, general emotional support and personal mentors. Their target was to cut truancy and school exclusion by a third, arrests by 60 per cent and reduce the crimes attributed to these fifty by a third. In 2003, after three years, YIPs had reduced arrests by 65 per cent among those who were already offenders, and 74 per cent of those who had never committed an offence continued crime-free. As ever, eyebrows were raised over these figures. How could just five hours a week achieve so much? A few of the schemes were feeble youth projects, others well-managed and highly focused. Including non-offenders opened a door to statistical manipulation as a local YIP could make its figures look better by including children who were never at much risk.

Next, younger children, the eight- to thirteen-year-olds, were targeted by Youth Inclusion Support Panels, which picked up young children already in trouble and worked with their families to solve problems. As with YIPs, participation was entirely voluntary.

## Connexions

As a preventative step even further down a chain of social circumstances that might predispose some young people to crime, there was Connexions. Created in Blair's first term, this was an age-specific network of panels and offices for thirteen- to nineteen-year-olds based on the former youth and careers services run by councils. Some 400 Connexions shops were set up, most of them open out of hours, to offer help to disaffected or distressed young people. Personal advisers arranged support for those with drugs, school, emotional, medical or family problems. But Connexions won few friends. It was given a target of cutting by 10 per cent the number of children not in education, employment or training; but that meant neglecting ordinary children's need for careers advice. In 2004 a review found two-thirds of children relied for careers advice on unqualified teachers.

## Success or Failure?

Visitors to the best of these projects were bowled over. There never had been so many schemes, based on evidence of what worked, so many hard targets met or so much money spent. But it was easy for ministers to get carried away with all they had done, and forget all they had left undone. On the ground, there was often confusion. Partners did not work together. Things were not joined up. Social work was under-funded, the government preferring new schemes before it made sure the bedrock services delivered by distrusted local authorities were up to strength. Not enough was too often the cry from health visitors, probation officers, social workers, housing officers and others in the front line of social dysfunction. The press was never short of stories: take the 'terror triplets' of Gillingham, who caused a mini crime wave in their area. In court it emerged they came from a chaotic family with five children, who kept moving on so the children never settled, the parents never in work. No multi-agency team had descended on them with some coherent offer of help and support, neither carrots nor sticks.

Some of the 2,000 worst estates identified by the Office of the Deputy Prime Minister were much improved in their physical fabric, some showing signs of social regeneration too. But progress was patchy. It began to dawn on the ministers who started out so full of hope and determination in 1997 how difficult it was to repair the damage done during generations of deprivation. Certainly it would not be done in the span of a political administration. Perhaps it was a recognition of that which made the Home Office set itself a grimly realistic target for the next five years: all this panoply of effort was expected to reduce re-offending by just 5 per cent.

But success has to be registered, too. The Youth Justice Board was supposed to reduce the numbers of young people in prison by 10 per cent by 2006 from a 2003 base line. Like many of Labour's targets, this was tricky. Numbers sent to prison might not have much to do with crime levels. The Youth Justice Board had no control over the whims of judges and magistrates: it could only persuade them that it could offer better alternative treatments. Still, while the adult prison population was soaring, the number of young people in prison did fall. By the end of 2004 youth in jail was down by 12.5 per cent.

## Conclusion

The public subsisted on stereotypes. Muggers, asylum seekers, terrorists. Some were indeed out there and the government's job was control. Measured by their competence, Blair
and his ministers performed creditably. Policy and external
factors secured a fall in asylum numbers; migration remained
an open question. Terror threatened but – luck or operational
effectiveness – stayed away. Crime fell.

But crime facts were for experts. Attitudes were shaped by
the front pages and the bombardment of horror stories, tales
of useless judges and ineffective policing. Where researchers
gave a group of people an array of evidence in citizens' juries,
say, people's attitudes became more nuanced.

In the absence of a national seminar, Blair and Blunkett ran
with the hue and cry on crime, and maybe became their own
worst enemies, their dramatic announcements themselves
stoking up fear. If people knew nothing of the good work
the Youth Offending Teams were doing or how well some
community sentences were beginning to work, that was
because Labour never quite dared tell them. They always
preferred to score a quick hit with tough-sounding punitive
measures that might or might not actually materialise.

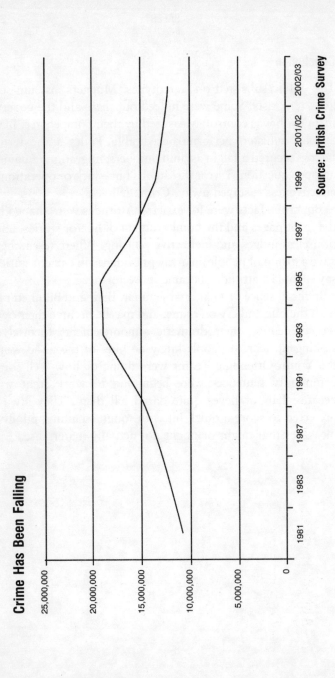

Crime Has Been Falling

25,000,000

20,000,000

15,000,000

10,000,000

5,000,000

0

1981   1983   1987   1991   1995   1997   1999   2001/02   2002/03

Source: British Crime Survey

Asylum Applications from all Source Countries

Source: Home Office

# CHAPTER SEVEN

# Greener?

As he stood by the side of Richard Branson, at the end of platform twelve at Euston Station in September 2004, welcoming the first high-speed arrival from Manchester on the rebuilt West Coast line, Tony Blair might have made this connection. The electricity powering Virgin's new Pendolino train now came from a mix of sources. North Sea gas was one, but two months before the Euston ceremony a supply boundary had been crossed. It was officially acknowledged that, come 2006, for the first time in a generation the UK would become a net importer of natural gas. Since gas generated about 38 per cent of British electricity, this loss of self-sufficiency would be momentous.

Growing anxiety about whether Britain had planned enough growth in its energy supply often turned out to be fuelled by various hidden energy interests, usually nuclear. But however hard the government denied any danger of California-style 'brown-outs', the story kept resurfacing.

Energy couldn't – shouldn't – be kept apart from global warming: now only a handful of maverick scientists were still warming-deniers, though that did nothing to stop broadcasters giving them excessive airtime for a 'balanced' debate on an issue that no longer had two sides. The questions were rather about the coming calamity: how fast, how bad, how soon? Lockstep with the Bush White House, Blair could only occasionally gesture weakly about the American refusal to adopt the Kyoto protocols, but was the British record really so impressive?

When storms blew and unseasonable rain fell, spewing untreated sewage out of overloaded drains into the rivers, people wondered. Insurance claims for storm and flood damage doubled between 1998 and 2003. Yet still climate change was an also-ran in Westminister politics. John Prescott, the Deputy Prime Minister, had striven against the odds but Labour had not gone green. Environmental consciousness was barely greater in 2005 than in 2001 or 1997. Fuel-price protesters had turned out to be a stronger political force than anything the greens could muster.

Even such an obvious and easy adaptation of household behaviour as recycling paper, tins and bottles was slow to spread. The people who might put out a weekly box of newspapers for the council to collect didn't give a second thought to another ultra-cheap Ryanair booking, spewing greenhouse gases across the skies. Labour had no fear of flying. Instead it blithely projected growth in airport capacity over the thirty years to come and allowed work to start on a new runway at Stansted airport, eager to compete for global air-traffic trade.

Nearer the ground, Labour started to accept, halting and cautious, the need for congestion charging on urban streets. Having gleefully expected Ken Livingstone's scheme to fail in London, the government did at least eat humble pie, congratulate him and embrace the policy after it had triumphed. But this was a rearguard action recognising that car ownership and car usage was still going to grow: Labour had long ago abandoned that 1997 early optimism that it could be slowed. The green balance sheet was in the red.

A rational or integrated transport policy still looked a distant dream. Ministers had no coherent explanation for why on a per head or a per kilometre basis the railways deserved so much subsidy, relative to buses or roads. Nor did they choose to confront motorists or lorry drivers with the real, long-run costs of their road use. Perhaps no government could tell such truths: small militant transport lobbies had proved their strength. Perhaps, equally, no government could tell a coherent tale about the costs and claims of town and country, ancient and modern, science and sentimentality. So, in the second term GM crops, foxhunting, rural post offices came and went as issues.

Its own internal contradictions did for the Countryside Alliance, which was exposed as a front for politically dispossessed Tories and property owners who simply resented the dominance of Labour. Meanwhile, all too slowly, the argument about the economic redefinition of the countryside went on. Half-reform of the Common Agricultural Policy was agreed, from 2006. The Ministry of Agriculture, Fisheries and Food gave way to a Department of Farming, Food and Rural Affairs. That marked the beginning of a separation, long overdue, between those responsible for food production and those charged with ensuring its fitness for consumers.

Farming – 1 per cent of the economy – still enjoyed disproportionate weight in policy and subsidy. But Labour did make a decisive shift towards trying to make landowners understand that the countryside would only deserve state support because it enhanced the lives of the 90 per cent of British people who dwell in towns, not for the sake of the tiny minority of rural landowners. Farmers and landowners grumbled that they didn't want to become park-keepers, but that was their destiny.

The real battle of the countryside only just began in Labour's second term, presaging much tougher battles to come, whoever might be in power. This was much more fundamental than fox-hunting. Burgeoning growth meant growing demand for building land. In an expanding economy where home ownership was a near-universal aspiration, space had to be found for dwellings. Radical alternatives existed, such as state-led redevelopment of existing urban areas or some attempt to redirect growth to poorer, emptier regions. But these were not seriously considered. Too much effort by previous Labour governments to relocate industry to places people did not want to go had failed, and risked stalling national growth itself. John Prescott, the prototypical man of the North, accepted Treasury arguments for keeping the overheated South bubbling. He plumped for extending the urban areas in the South along the Thames Gateway to the east of London, and far more controversially, among the angry NIMBYs in Eastern England up through Peterborough, Cambridge and around Milton Keynes.

## Climate

Sir David King, the chief scientist, called global warming the greatest threat we face. He had to retract his clear implication that it was more lethal than international terrorism, which was not quite the Blair party line. We got the point. Science paid renewed attention to the greenhouse slowing of the circulation of water in the North Atlantic, disturbing the climate system.

On the diplomatic level, the UK government continued to play goody two-shoes. Prime Minister and cabinet endorsed the priority to be given the climate, especially during the UK presidency of the European Union in the second half of 2005. In 2004 Russia signed the Kyoto Treaty, finally giving it enough signatories to bring it into official legal existence. Its target was a reduction of 12.5 per cent in the gases deemed responsible for the greenhouse effect, especially carbon dioxide; that was a reduction by 2012 from the levels existing in 1990.

The UK government set itself a higher target, a 20 per cent cut. Taking all the gases together, the UK could claim to be 14.9 per cent below in 2002. But emissions of carbon dioxide were only 8.7 per cent below. Indeed UK emissions of $CO_2$ rose 1.5 per cent between 2002 and 2003, largely as a result of the continuing and relatively high rate of economic growth. More not less coal was burned in power stations in 2003. Carbon emissions rose to where they had been in 1997. Environment Secretary Margaret Beckett was penitent, confessing there was no way the 20 per cent cut would be met.

## Carbon Trading

Off course, off track. The figure of speech abounded. MPs called for a long-term strategy linking transport and domestic energy efficiency. But 2005 was to mark the dawn of a Europe-wide scheme intended to push Kyoto along. Carbon trading would use market forces to give an incentive for large energy-consuming companies to cut their emissions. Some 1,300 large companies in England and Wales were expected to apply for permits to trade. If they wanted to emit more carbon, they would have to buy surplus allowance from some other company. They would have an incentive to emit less, investing in energy-saving devices so they could sell on any surplus allowance at a profit. It was hoped that carbon trading would become so powerful and lucrative that US companies would eventually pressure their government to join the Kyoto scheme.

## Energy – Oil and Gas

Despite the protests of autumn 2000, fuel had not been much of a Labour issue before. It had done a bit for coal in the first term by holding up the construction of yet more gas-fired capacity. The problem was that electricity and gas prices were falling. The Major government had encouraged a switch to gas-fired electricity generation. Capacity had expanded. While prices were low, the relative cost of in-stalling alternative ways of generating power rose. One department, Trade and Industry, stood for competition; another, Environment, Food and Rural Affairs, tried to insist on moving towards non-fossil and sustainable sources of energy. For most of the second term market logic told against renewables.

An energy white paper in February 2003 (*Our Energy Future – Creating a Low-carbon Economy*) recalled La-bour's heroic targets: carbon emissions to be cut by 60 per cent by the middle of the century. It made the startling claim that already the UK had 'decoupled economic growth from energy use and carbon emissions'. This was extraordinary since the UK's energy pattern was 39 per cent gas, 35 per cent oil, 15 per cent coal and 9 per cent nuclear – wind, solar, tide, hydro and biomass making up the tiny fraction remaining. Even more outlandish, it promised the smallest sector of existing electricity generation would grow at the expense of the rest: the future lay with renewables, they claimed.

The white paper was a missed opportunity. Energy sup-plies would certainly have to change. Coal, old coal, still produced a third of electricity, in plants up to thirty years old. But pits were closing; Selby ceased production after barely three decades in October 2004. By 2010 North Sea produc-tion was expected to fall from 3.75m barrels of oil per day or equivalent in gas to 2.45m. Although at the end of this decade, the North Sea would still be firing cookers in Cookham and boilers in Bridlington, keeping the pilots alight would soon increasingly depend on supplies from Malaysia, Algeria and other countries of questionable geopolitical stability. There was a new fear that gas supplies might soon be controlled to our disadvantage by a gas producers' version of OPEC. By 2015 Britain would depend on imports of gas for 75 per cent of its supply.

During 2004, the energy economy turned. Average bills for gas rose by nearly 12 per cent during the year and over 7 per cent for electricity. Gas supply contracts for 2005 were 50 per cent more expensive than in 2003. Oil prices rose by 35 per cent in one year. Instability in Nigeria, in Venezuela, Russia and the Middle East panicked the markets. Saudi pumps did not compensate for mayhem next door in Iraq and was it really sensible to pump billions of dollars into Saudi coffers? Prices looked set to stabilise at a new, higher level. However, thanks to the remaining North Sea supplies, the UK was one of the industrialised countries least damaged by oil price rises. It used a third less oil per unit of production than in 1982.

## Nuclear

About a fifth of UK electricity came from the only significant renewable source – nuclear. Unfortunately nuclear was a little too sustainable; its radioactive waste lasted for millennia. But nuclear power stations were ageing.

Falling prices before 2004 were only the final nail in nuclear's lead-lined coffin. The entity created to run civil nuclear assets had been privatised but – as the National Audit Office pointed out – no thought was given to the taxpayers' exposure to the eventual costs of decommissioning nuclear plants, for which the government would always be ultimately responsible. British Energy made substantial payments to shareholders; its directors thought they might as well follow suit, copy other companies and award themselves large bonuses. Yet the business was failing. As electricity prices fell, British Energy faced bankruptcy and, in 2002, Labour bailed it out with an emergency £410m credit.

The following year it did a deal with the Department of Trade under which the taxpayers (who used to own the whole shooting match) now assumed £1.7bn of its liabilities plus the future costs of decommissioning. In return the state would get 65 per cent of British Energy's cash flow. The European Union, already anxious about illicit state aid to a private company, also wanted to know what was happening to 1.3 tonnes of plutonium stored in a pond at Sellafield. It was an 'international' issue, as the government of the Republic of Ireland was quick to point out. Sellafield was due to be taken over by the new state decommissioning authority in April 2005.

But could the Kyoto targets be hit except by massive expansion of non-carbon emitting nuclear power stations? Some serious climate-change scientists said the threat from nuclear power was damaging but it was on a small scale compared with the calamity of global warming. A nuclear disaster might kill a few hundred thousand: global warming would kill everyone before long. The government stalled. It ordained no new nuclear power stations would be built to replace the old ones fast wearing out, pending a review. The trouble with this uncertainty was that it delayed whole-hearted heavy investment – public and private – in the necessary other renewable energy sources. The merest hint of nuclear revival would kill private sector interest.

Labour did little to make relative costs or structure more transparent. Take the disposal of waste. Just before the 1997 election the Tories had stopped work on underground storage of intermediate level waste. (The Finns and others went ahead.) Labour set up committee after committee. For the time being the Nuclear Decommission Authority would take responsibility for clean-up of sites, but long-run storage remains an open question.

## Renewables

In 2004 the Environment Agency reported that renewable sources generated 2–3 per cent of UK electricity. By 2010, 10 per cent of power (10,000MW) was to be generated by sustainable, non-nuclear sources, wind farms, solar and tidal schemes. The government offered sticks and carrots, with incentives for energy saving. The 2002 Treasury paper *Tax and the Environment: Using Economic Instruments* outlined the strategy. Energy suppliers had an obligation to provide 10 per cent renewable. The Climate Change Levy, enforced in 2001, persuaded some big users to adopt efficiency measures or switch to renewable sources. Lower taxes on low-sulphur fuel also had an effect.

The renewable energy target implied the installation of plant, mainly wind turbines, generating 1,250MW a year, which would need £1bn to £1.5bn of private capital. That investment would only materialise if prices were on an upwards tilt and the relative price of wind-generated electricity was going to fall compared with coal and gas. Price rises in 2004 helped make renewables look a little more economic.

John Prescott backed renewables by demanding that all new homes built in Britain after January 2006 should be designed to receive solar power – to the disgruntlement of the building industry. The Solar Energy Trust aimed to ensure all new homes will be powered in part by solar by the end of

2010. However, only 10 MW of solar was produced in 2003, about the same as a small wind farm and only 1 per cent of Sizewell's nuclear output. The solar industry begged the government to invest. Just as Denmark, with government help, pioneered the market in developing wind turbines with a thriving export market, now Germany was stealing a march in photovoltaic production: in 2003 alone Germany installed 121MW of photovoltaic cells, twelve times the entire UK output.

Germany was now growing its own wind turbine industry, and overtook Denmark in 2004, stealing its markets. The Environment Agency pointed out the huge employment potential of these industries, as global demand was shooting upward. The government made the right noises, but did not invest heavily enough to compete.

## Energy Saving

The Energy Saving Trust, a quango, said the best chance of cutting carbon was to use less energy. Late in the day, at the end of 2004, it launched a £6m climate change advertising campaign, to encourage people to turn out the lights. The trust pumped out information telling people that exchanging one light bulb for an energy-saving bulb had the same benign annual effect as nine trees' absorption of carbon dioxide. The trust was campaigning for a surcharge on ordinary light bulbs: Denmark had a light bulb tax. Or for extra charges on energy inefficient household appliances. But Labour hesitated to penalise poorer people whose cheaper appliances were the least energy efficient.

But, beyond special schemes for insulating the homes of the elderly, other householders did not rush to insulate their roofs or draught proof their doors. The government did bring in a scheme allowing energy companies to give discounts for energy efficiency and more energy efficient appliances were sold; but the number of cavity wall insulation jobs is tiny.

Radical ideas, such as lifting stamp duty for houses which boldly cut energy use, did not find favour. Yet relatively painless increases in energy efficiency could cut carbon emissions by millions of tonnes; households accounted for a third of the total.

## Recycling

Changes in environmental behaviour through taxation were possible. Business still buried half its waste in holes in the ground. From 1999 the tax on landfill (introduced by the Tories to discourage tipping and encourage recycling) went on an escalator, moving up to £15 per tonne by April 2004. Following an EU landfill directive, the squeeze tightened and Brown hiked the 2005 rate to £18 on the way to a 'medium-to-long-run' rate of £35. The Treasury did not gain; the tax was revenue neutral, with proceeds recycled. The proportion of industrial and commercial waste going to landfill was cut. But even so, big gaps remained. It was estimated £5bn worth of new investment in plant and sites was needed to comply with the directive, of which only £1bn had been seen. Landfill tax produced about £600m a year. The government target was to recycle or compost at least a quarter of the waste produced by households. Labour's second term saw no sudden spurt, just a slow, steady increase, about 1 per cent more a year.

## Wind

The UK had the greatest potential for wind, wave and tidal energy generation in Europe but, the Environment Agency said, it 'performs badly'. Still, in Labour's second term wind power became a symbol both of the way forward to sustainability and a warning of the high political price that would have to be paid.

The forces of dissent mobilised. Their networks interlaced with the Countryside Alliance and the fox hunters, with the NIMBYs and that dark island in 'middle England' that wanted no truck with Europe let alone the rest of the world.

Advocates of wind power set down their plans for 1,000 new turbines, with the aid of £100m from the government. In 2004 twenty-two new wind farms began turning, producing 475MW but a much more intensive programme would be needed to meet the 2010 target for wind power generation.

Offshore wind had fewer environmental objectors, but it cost far more to build. The antis geared up under the banner Country Guardian, whose leaders included such progressive thinkers as Sir Bernard Ingham, former press secretary to Margaret Thatcher and former employee of the nuclear energy industry. Television biologist David Bellamy also joined the vociferous anti-wind-farm campaign, which was mostly powered by country-dwellers who lived near proposed sites. These reactionaries should have been reminded that in the seventeenth century the pristine English landscape was covered by some 90,000 turbines, the few remaining now regarded as picturesque windmills, carefully conserved by these same heritage worriers.

In England some 50 per cent of planning applications for turbines were failing. The government tried to help, gingerly, by amending planning guidance to make a presumption in favour of applications for renewable energy sources. The Labour–Liberal Democrat coalition running the Scottish executive showed what could be done, and permissions were easier to get in Scotland where the target for renewable generation was raised to 18 per cent by 2010, but then Scotland already generated 11 per cent of its power from hydro sources. Ministers in England – and Wales, where permissions were strongly resisted – rarely dared go out to argue the case, though opinion polls, even in areas where the farms were planned, consistently showed strong popular support for wind turbines.

Pushing on with green alternatives usually boiled down to grants. The Royal Commission on Environmental Pollution (a standing body) said biomass could produce up to 12 per cent of UK energy by mid-century. (Biomass is renewable coppiced wood such as willow, special crops and waste products.) But subsidies were needed for farmers to grow 'carbon neutral' biomass crops and to build generators.

## So Who was Responsible for 'The Environment'?

On climate or carbon, Labour was no more ambiguous than any conceivable alternative government; public attitudes are riven with contradiction. People could be sentimental about the environment, a mainstay of primary education, and yet drive their children to school in 4 × 4s. None the less, at elementary levels of public action and policy, Labour might have joined up more. Who, after all, was responsible for 'environment' in its broadest sense? The Chancellor, the Transport Secretary, Margaret Beckett, or the Deputy Prime Minister?

Blair's re-engineering of Whitehall to suit John Prescott produced policy gaps. The Office of the Deputy Prime Minister (ODPM), a ragbag of a department, might have offered environmental leadership. Instead, it became a quasi-department for urban growth. Nothing wrong with that, except the ODPM was too marginal in the Blair political power firmament to lead through all the many consequences of growth – in transport, finance and the land that was going to be built on.

The Department for Environment, Food and Rural Affairs was created after the 2001 election along with a set of powerful quangos which did much of its executive work, among them the Environment Agency. It failed to brand a Labour image on environmental policy.

Environment was incoherent partly because Margaret Beckett was a political firefighter whose main strength was to minimise trouble. She gradually dropped from view until, with the hunting demonstrations in 2004, she had disappeared completely, leaving her unfortunate colleague, Alun Michael, to face the flak. Was there a connection to be made between sustainability and the hunting ban? Perhaps not directly, but there surely was a narrative about rural affairs and the custodianship of the countryside that Labour could claim from the fox killers. We never heard it.

Defra created a quality of life barometer, and over the next four years put ticks against woodland birds and land use. Targets were missed (cross in the box) for the proportion of household waste recycled, which fell, and road traffic volume, which rose. Did such an eclectic list mean anything? After all, economic output (good) and poverty reduction through employment growth (good) might be said to decrease sustainability by increasing consumption of land and energy (bad). Was Defra in any position to influence, let alone deliver on policies on which its own environmental success would be judged?

It was the Treasury that controlled tax rates and Gordon Brown did make green gestures. The government reimbursed 80 per cent of the fuel duty on ultra-low sulphur diesel and 100 per cent for newer, cleaner fuels, amounting to £343m in England in 2003–04; but such figures can only be evaluated against rising road use and additional miles driven. MPs concluded in 2004 that environmental taxes were lower than they had been for a long time as a proportion of total tax.

The long-term trends towards improving the quality of the air breathed by British people showed a hiccup in 2003 when the number of days showing poor quality were twice the number of the previous year. But this seemed to be due to the hot sunny weather, with extra ozone. The number of days showing high concentrations of particles continued falling. Some 20 per cent of emissions of carbon dioxide come from road vehicles – an increasing number.

## Transport Objectives

'We will not do nothing and allow gridlock to engulf our roads, nor will we splash down Tarmac over endless fields, villages or town centres in order to keep apace with unrestrained demand,' said Alistair Darling, his double negative highly appropriate for Labour's convoluted objectives. When he launched Labour's revamped transport plan in mid-2004, he captured the Augustinian nature of modern environmental politics: save us from temptation, Oh Lord, but not just yet.

Transport produced 34 per cent of the harmful gases, mainly from cars. (Plane emissions are not counted internationally and hugely inflate this figure.) The policy logic was obvious: cut car use and fly less. While Labour at least stated the ambition to move people out of cars into buses and trains, the collective love affair with planes went unchallenged.

Labour's transport plan A had crashed when a GNER train went off the rails outside Hatfield in October 2000. But the protests against the fuel duty escalator that same year showed how strong was resistance to adjusting relative costs to discourage road users. In the first term Labour had allowed a minority, the tiny 4 per cent of the population who travel daily by train, to dominate with their demands.

But Labour had also dodged forcing the majority who travel by road to confront the true long-run costs and the possible alternatives.

## Flying

Half the UK population was now flying at least once a year. The number of passengers passing through UK airports was projected to rise from 200m in 2003 to between 400 and 600m by 2030, airport capacity permitting. Capacity depended on government decisions. In a white paper in December 2003 the government accepted a growth projection of 470m passengers by 2030 but declared against building a new London airport. Growth would be accommodated by regional hubs such as Birmingham International and Edinburgh, better use of existing terminals and the construction of two new runways in the South East, at Stansted by 2011 and another at Heathrow by 2015. Land would be safeguarded for a second runway at Gatwick 'in case environmental conditions at Heathrow cannot be met'.

Messages were mixed. Instead of an overarching plan this was to be done in bits; specific proposals would be subject to the planning system and the delays that might entail. The government acknowledged the additional capacity could fall short of demand. Yet at the same time – the green sting in the tail – it acknowledged that aviation would be expected to start paying for its environmental costs. Labour 'commits to playing a major role internationally in tackling aviation's share of greenhouse-gas emissions'. But not yet. Meanwhile air-traffic growth had resumed, after the 9/11 hiatus. The National Air Traffic Service, the great example of New Labour privatisation, was no longer in jeopardy because of falling revenues.

## Trains

Labour had effectively renationalised Railtrack, but nothing as straightforward could be admitted. The bankrupt rail infrastructure company gave way to Network Rail, an arm's-length body which was not at first permitted to figure on the public accounts, allowing government spending (dressed up as lending) not to be directly counted. Network Rail was to spend £22bn on operations, maintenance and renewal between 2004–05 and 2008–09. Three years after Railtrack's unlamented disappearance, the running of the railways was further simplified, with the abolition of the Strategic Rail Authority and the absorption of decision making back into the Department of Transport; responsibility for rail safety shifted from the Health and Safety Executive to the Office of Rail Regulation. Meanwhile, on the tracks, there were some visible signs of the investment as new rolling stock was introduced and stations were refurbished. Southwest Trains even took to advertising the merits of its 155 new Desiro trains, with their clean, modern carriages, upgraded toilets, sockets for PCs (in first class) and CCTV cameras in each carriage. They might not run on time, but the delay on the 10.55 from Farnham would be endured in greater comfort.

Reliability did not much improve as measured by trains arriving on time; 90 per cent did when Labour took office in 1997, now it was about 83 per cent. But the railways' safety record was outstanding, though every small incident was pounced on by the press. Train protection warning systems were being installed. Travelling by rail was six times safer than travelling by car and the long-run trend through the Potters Bar crash – which damaged Jarvis, the contracting company involved, without dampening Labour's enthusiasm for outsourcing public services – was further improved.

Significant train accidents per million train miles on all railways in Britain were now at their lowest level on record, said the Health and Safety Executive.

Safety aside, on some sections of the railway performance was getting better. The first section of the rail link to the Channel Tunnel opened, cutting twenty minutes off Eurostar journeys to Paris and Brussels. Some 110 kilometres of track were replaced in 2003. Labour's original target had been to increase rail use by 50 per cent over the decade. Passenger kilometres travelled were up, but not as much as the target implied: at the end of 2003, passenger kilometres were 5.8 per cent up on the base line (and 26 per cent up on 1997). But less freight was being carried by rail. The decision by the Royal Mail to phase out rail from March 2004 was a blow.

The vignette with which we began this chapter, with Blair at Euston with Richard Branson, illustrated both the potential and the pitfalls of rail investment. The London–Manchester journey time would be cut by thirty-five minutes to two hours and six minutes, thanks to the West Coast line upgrade. But it was costing £7.5bn. Virgin Trains, the joint venture between Virgin Group and Stagecoach, had first signed a contract with Railtrack in June 1998 for the upgrade. But the moving block signalling system that would allow the trains to run faster did not work. Projected speeds came down from 140mph to 125mph. 'Our greyhounds have become Labradors', quipped Virgin's Chris Green. Railtrack said the complete West Coast upgrade could cost £13bn. After the Strategic Rail Authority took over in early 2002, estimates cooled: the line to Glasgow should be complete by 2008 at just over half that exaggerated sum.

## Roads

The government's own adviser, Professor David Begg, the chairman of the Commission for Integrated Transport, summed up the record. Labour started out recognising 'we could not build our way out of congestion on the roads, that people needed to be offered real alternatives to the car, that public transport needed to improve and that transport and land use planning needed to be joined up. But it failed to back its intentions with either adequate funding or legislation in the first few years.'

But the revamped 2004 transport plan did produce money and a steadier sense of direction. Investment was nothing like the £250bn over ten years demanded by the Confederation of British Industry which, to its credit, had tried to keep the infrastructure argument going during the years of Tory investment famine. But relative to public investment at large, the amounts committed to transport were substantial. Though the Treasury looked at rising oil prices and postponed the fuel duty increase due in autumn 2004 (so further cutting the cost of motoring in relative terms), the new transport plan talked about charging road users, asserting that up to a fifth of peak-time traffic could be shifted by manipulating the price of travel. A national road pricing scheme would become feasible in the next ten to fifteen years and it had the potential to cut congestion by half.

Gordon Brown's 2002 budget had opened Pandora's box by pledging new charges for lorries. Now local authorities are to be given incentives to bring in road-charging schemes. This was a turnaround. In earlier days, when the Commission for Integrated Transport had advocated nationwide road charging, envisaging a 44 per cent reduction in congestion, the Treasury and transport ministers had greeted it with deafening silence.

Now bells rang for tolls. A new stretch of private-sector motorway looping around the West Midlands to relieve congestion on the M6, instigated by the Major government, was completed in December 2003; it seemed to work. Planners wanted a nationwide scheme for charging lorries, similar to schemes in Switzerland and Germany. The technology needed extensive testing, but suddenly the political will appeared firm, though whether it would last the protests bound to come from hauliers in 2008 or whenever freight charging was introduced, remains to be seen.

Road building went on but traffic growth had been stronger than expected – a result of economic growth. The permanent secretary of the Department of Transport confessed to the Public Accounts Committee that targets for cutting congestion on trunk roads by the decade's end were 'deeply unsatisfactory', which presumably meant would not be met. Lack of information was part of the problem. Geographical positioning by satellite improved things; future targets would be specific to individual roads.

## Road Safety

Travelling by road was becoming safer. Total road deaths and serious injuries fell by nearly a quarter between the mid-1990s and 2005 with a faster rate of decrease in children's deaths and serious injuries. A target was introduced to cut death and injury on the roads by 2010 by 40 per cent; a third of that had been reached by 2002. Two-thirds of the target to cut child deaths by half in the same timespan had been exceeded by 2004; roads were still the biggest killer of twelve- to sixteen-year-olds. The *Daily Mail*, friend of the child killers, campaigned against safety cameras, ignoring the evidence which showed significant reductions in casualties at camera sites and in the wider areas covered by the partnership schemes which allowed the proceeds of fines to be recycled. Cleveland recorded a halving of crashes involving injury on roads where cameras were in use during three years of operation.

Did the government do enough to face down the Safe Speed Road Safety Campaign (ie the campaign for homicidal drivers) and the Association of British Drivers? Perhaps a bit more publicity could have been given the projection that if more urban areas implemented 20mph zones, thousands (especially children) would be saved from death or injury. The government banned driving while using mobile telephones in December 2003. These changes occurred while the number of specialist traffic police was falling – by 12 per cent between 1997 and 2002.

## Car Dumping

Ministers deal with policy at a high level of abstraction but when they returned to their constituencies and held surgeries they found people's pressing concerns were rarely picked up in the national press. One was what happened to cars once drivers got fed up or they became unusable on the roads. Over 800,000 vehicles were abandoned in England and Wales each year, the Local Government Association said, creating eyesores, nuisance and costing £34m to remove. Dumping had grown by nearly a third in the three years since 2001. New environmental rules were blamed for upping the cost of disposal for owners; perhaps it was just that old cars were worthless, no one wanting spare parts. Councils rarely prosecuted because of the cost. Labour legislation, to take effect from 2007, would transfer to manufacturers a duty to dispose of vehicles they had made. Why was its implementation delayed?

## Buses and Trams

Labour avoided making direct cost comparisons between different modes of transport which would have shown how the cost of motoring was falling relative to rail. But the government rejected a proposed extension to Manchester's Metrolink tram. Light rail systems in Leeds and South Hants were also stopped. The romance of trams had blinded some to their relatively high costs. Along with regional rail services, spending on such schemes compared adversely with investment in buses. Use of light rail systems was up by 14 per cent between 2000–01 and 2002–03, but a large part of this was increased travelling on the Docklands Light Railway, due to be extended to London City Airport during 2005. Figures for the Croydon Tramlink were less compelling. But a study in Manchester showed 19 per cent of Tramlink users had previously used their car for the same journey, so the tram saved 3m car journeys a year.

There were other, cheaper ways of getting people out of their cars. Guided bus schemes were launched in Crawley and along a disused railway between Luton and Dunstable. Another ambitious scheme, in the growth zone between Huntingdon and Cambridge, used twenty-three kilometres of disused railway track and seventeen kilometres of bus priority lanes on town streets. This scheme, paid for jointly by the Department of Transport (£65m) and developers, ought to relieve congestion on a road, the A14, where congestion has been growing.

Cost benefit analysis kept pointing to buses but Labour was reluctant to take the hint. Public support for buses was worth about one seventh of Network Rail's budget over the three years from 2005. It was partly the way the Tory years had broken up local bus services and partly the reluctance of local authorities. Labour's phrase was 'quality bus networks', allowing councils more scope to dictate terms to private operators. These got going in Milton Keynes, Northampton and Coventry while councils elsewhere strove to provide better real-time information on bus movements with less randomness about the time buses arrived at stops.

About £1bn a year was allocated to local bus services, but buses still carried too few middle-class, middle Englanders to report the good news about their improvements. In April 2003 men over sixty became entitled to local concessionary fare schemes, the same age as women: this stood to benefit one million between sixty and sixty-four. Improvements were made to the accessibility of buses. Yet bus travel still failed to make that crucial breakthrough into popular consciousness. But the Commission for Integrated Transport tried its best: 'At last the bus has the opportunity to come into its own, put its Cinderella past behind it and to make the car less of an inevitable choice for most journeys.'

## London Leading the Way

It was happening in London. There Labour election strategists – and London MPs – casting round for 'did things get better' examples got on the bus. London, assisted by national subsidies, was a shining example of public transport plans that worked. Bus operational mileage in London was now higher than at any time since the Beatles first topped the charts. Journeys grew by nearly 10 per cent between 2003 and 2004. Old Labourites could point out that a form of transport disproportionately used by women, poorer people and ethnic minorities had expanded mightily, thanks to large public subsidies allowing fares to be held steady or even cut. (They will have to start rising from 2005 if the books are to balance.) New Labourites could exult in a 'public private partnership' that has generated none of the controversy that has dogged the renewal scheme for the London underground.

Red buses served green ends. Satisfaction ratings improved along with evidence that a telling fraction of people using London's buses were 'switchers' from cars – half the extra journeys were made by people who say they did not use buses up to three years ago.

Part of the London lesson was that transport had to be integrated. The success of the buses depended on control of the roads. One element in the package has been better routing for buses along reserved lanes, though only 3 per cent of road space was kept for buses. Another was congestion charging. It did not produce the sums needed to cover the subsidy to buses, but it turned out to be the key to unlocking the roads, allowing the buses to run faster and more reliably.

Cold-shouldered by Labour when he introduced it, Livingstone triumphed. True, the costs of administering the charge were high, earning fat profits for the contractor, the Capita group. The charge had some adverse effects on retailers and questions remain about the balance of charges on incomers and residents, which would get livelier if, as planned, the charging zone is expanded westwards into affluent residential London.

## Sustainable Communities

For John Prescott Labour's main second-term event was the publication in February 2003 of his Sustainable Communities plan. Community had long been a Blairite word, though the vogue enjoyed by communitarianism associated with the American thinkers Amitai Etzioni and Robert Puttnam had been brief. Unremarked by commentators Prescott did two things. One was put growth first. Social cohesion depended on jobs and income, which in turn meant land had to be allocated for new dwellings; green, conservationist ambitions took second place. Second was Prescott's geographical reorientation. This old Northerner accepted the socioeconomic logic of New Labour's 1997 electoral victory. It was the South of England that both powered GDP growth and contained the constituencies which Labour had to win to take power at Westminster. Prescott now signed up to the expansion of the South, locking Labour's electoral fortunes even more tightly to its mastery of the attitudes and aspirations of the relatively affluent.

Behind the ODPM was the Treasury. Gordon Brown and his adviser Ed Balls regretted the gap in productivity between the regions of England but they were not going to constrain the South for the sake of the North. As he contemplated his own future as Labour MP for Normanton in West Yorkshire, Balls chose to emphasise the positive elements in Labour's mapping of the future landscape of England. There would be investment in skills in the poorer regions so they too could join the knowledge economy, but nothing must impede the contribution of the South to growth, as a magnet for foreign or homegrown investors.

ODPM said households in London would grow by 46,000 a year and by 33,000 in the rest of the South East, on the assumption space could be found for them. Such numbers meant more than half of all the additional households likely to be formed in England in the first two decades of the twenty-first century would be in the zone from Southampton to Norwich, London its heart.

## Labour and the South

If Prescott's plan needed intellectual justification, it arrived a year later in Kate Barker's housing report to the Treasury (see chapter four). Although rising interest rates meant London house prices started to come off the boil during 2004, it didn't alter her conclusion that to cool the housing market would need many more houses to be built.

Prescott had understated the deficit. His Communities Plan designated four areas to take 200,000 homes above what had already been planned. The government would ensure permission to build was granted. 'Local barriers' to growth would be beaten down. But the government itself was not going to build; most of the housing would be private. The state would assist with infrastructure, but only up to a point. Would this be enough? Since 1997 Labour has presided over the building of fewer homes – public or private – than at any time since the later 1940s. No wonder the housing market had overheated, with low interest rates and high employment to fuel demand for property.

## Housing – the Price Explosion

As Barker was doing her sums, demolition men were moving into the Lyng estate in Sandwell in the West Midlands to blow up three tower blocks. Demand for social housing in Birmingham was falling. Spending half a million on demolition would, so the 'renewal' plan said, clear the ground for redevelopment: some 230 new dwellings, some of them owner-occupied, some rented, would arise in improved physical surroundings, plus a new medical centre.

The ODPM allocated £500m for schemes across England intended to regenerate not housing but housing markets in struggling places. At Labour's 2004 conference the paradox was exposed. Hazel Blears, a Home Office minister and Salford MP, delighted in the fact that houses on the Manchester fringe were going for over £110,000 when a few years ago, a brace of terraced houses could be had for £15,000.

Was this good news? 'Unaffordable by local residents!' cried
someone in her audience.

Labour stopped short of the logic of its own policy which
surely ought to have been universal owner occupation. Alan
Milburn began to hint at this, perhaps involving subsidies to
encourage tenants into part-ownership, part-rent schemes.
However, policy had moved temporarily in the opposite
direction when Prescott took powers to curtail the 'right
to buy' enjoyed by council and housing association tenants in
certain areas. Wide boys and sharp estate agents were persuading tenants to exercise their right to buy at a fraction of
their real value and securing handsome profits, so in 2003
ODPM suspended the right to buy in certain areas.

## Housing Renewal

It was as if Labour wanted to do as best it could by lower-
income tenants while fearing their tenure was a thing of the
past. Council tenants had once been the very stuff of
Labour electoral success. Now they were a problem group.
But Labour had tied itself to targets for improving their
dwellings along with poorer households in privately rented
or owner-occupied accommodation. By 2006–07, the target
for the proportion of private renters deemed vulnerable
living in 'decent' conditions was upped. The target was
to cut the number of 'non-decent' properties (1.6m in 2001)
by one third by 2004; that was achieved, albeit a few
months late.

The Barker report laid out stark arithmetic: to the hundreds of thousands of new dwellings that should be built each
year to accommodate the growth must be added those needed
to replace housing that was simply worn out. But progress
depended on councils and they wanted money. Labour stuck
with its policy of refusing councils additional support unless

they were willing to get rid of their stock, preferably to tenant organisations or non-profit landlords.

This ball had started rolling under the Tories and since 1988 nearly 200 large-scale transfers had taken place, covering 800,000 dwellings, though the tenants of Birmingham and Camden councils rejected the option of transfer to a 'social landlord', preferring the devil they knew. Some predicted that by the end of this decade these new bodies would predominate and council housing become a rarity.

## Regeneration

But Prescott, wearing his developer's hat, then looked at the array of separate social landlords and railed against their fragmentation. If they pooled resources, or if there were fewer of them, they would be better able to build the new housing needed.

And some of the new housing was to be in the North, after all. A year after Prescott's Communities Plan, the Northern Way was unveiled. This long-term projection for Yorkshire and Humberside, the North West and North East seemed in some ways a reversion to an older way of thinking; it implied central resources would be concentrated on helping these regions cut the gap between their growth rates and those of the South. But regional economic assistance was constrained by European Union rules and Blair showed no sign of revising his belief that private markets knew best, even when it came to depopulation and deindustrialisation. Alongside its regional policy, Labour talked up 'core cities' such as Birmingham and Manchester and provided their councils with powers to create business improvement districts in which special levies might be raised to pay for improvements.

Community continued to be a magic word for Labour. A myriad schemes and initiatives were meant to be coordinated by the Neighbourhood Renewal Unit in Prescott's depart-ment – the £2bn New Deal for Communities putting extra money into thirty-nine neighbourhoods designated as spe-cially deprived and the overlapping Neighbourhood Renewal Fund, another £2bn (over ten years from 2000) for eighty-eight councils. Plus grants for neighbourhood wardens (£90m) to stop littering and anti-social behaviour and neigh-bourhood management pathfinders (£80m) to create neigh-bourhood managers as a single point of contact for residents and better coordinate services in a given area. Once, Labour's intention had been to 'bend' mainstream programmes to benefit these poor areas and there was some evidence, for schools, that focused money produced somewhat better results. But the very fact new initiatives kept being invented, especially on anti-social behaviour, suggested progress was slow. But surveys picked up signs of renewed confidence among residents. Labour cleaved to the idea that deprived people in run-down areas wanted to be active participants in the self-government of their areas in a way that their better-off fellow citizens did not; the evidence was mixed.

## Green and Brown

Labour had green ambitions for housing. The second term saw an expansion of the total acreage of land designated as green belt, where no building was allowed. Labour hit its target of building 60 per cent of new housing on 'brown' or previously developed land. But that had social consequences, including people living closer together in cities. The average density for new developments outside London was rising to thirty dwellings against twenty-seven in 2002. In London, it was fifty dwellings. New Labour, new proximity.

One theme of this book is the disarticulation of policy in Labour's second term. Despite their accumulating experience, ministers could not get their heads around the gap between their pronouncements and what happened on the ground. Take the anomalous quango called English Partnerships, a mystifying title for a body concerned with digging holes and pouring concrete – 'concerned with', but not itself doing the digging. English Partnerships, a quango 'owned' by John Prescott's department was one of the deliverers of the Communities Plan. Its reports talked ambitiously about linking housing, transport and employment but the administrative reality was a host of different bodies, sometimes fighting over the same piece of ground.

## The New Geography of Blair's Britain

The principal area designated for expansion was to be the Thames Gateway, Kent, the London to Cambridge corridor and a region no one had ever heard of before called the south Midlands – actually Milton Keynes north to Corby in Northamptonshire. Once, governments used to commission great overarching schemes leading to the new towns and a deliberate effort to 'decongest' the capital. Now the aim was to bolster London by finding space for private growth in adjacent areas.

On paper, the plan for the Thames Gateway integrated jobs, homes and means of getting about. By 2016, it would accommodate 128,000 extra homes. Some 150,000 of the jobs for their inhabitants would be in London, 82,000 in Kent and Essex. To get to them, the plan said, the east and south east of London would have new rail links, such as Crossrail. A start was made. Crossrail secured the Treasury's conditional approval, provided private money was forthcoming.

The government created two new development corporations to speed up the acquisition and development of land. But money was doled out in packets. A new bridge, the

Thames Gateway Bridge, would get £200m, but only in the form of credits for a privately financed deal. Ministers approved £327m to prepare sites and begin development in Thurrock, North Kent and Barking Reach.

## Countryside

Labour allowed farmers to retain their favoured status in Whitehall, though successive reports from Sir Donald Curry and Labour peer Lord Haskins announced a new understanding of the economics of rural life. Farmers needed to enhance the value they added and find other use for their land than the production of subsidised food. A package of reforms to the Common Agricultural Policy, necessitated by the enlargement of the European Union, simplified payments from January 2005, freeing farmers from incentives based on particular crops and no longer rewarding them for intensifying unnecessary production. At least one hectare out of ten used to produce food could come out of production by 2006.

Blair said consistently UK fields would be open to the commercial cultivation of GM crops. But there was no immediate prospect, even for GM maize, which was grown extensively in other countries. An EU-wide moratorium on new GM food, feed and crops was lifted, but establishing a regime for 'co-existence' between GM, non-GM and organic crops proved difficult. MPs concluded that because there was no great appetite among consumers for GM products, there was no great pressure for speedy resolution.

The extent to which farming interests had been allowed to make artificial headlines was exposed in the late summer of 2004. The farming lobby predicted that the downpours during the harvest in August would cost more than the entire foot and mouth episode of 2000–01, which had caused such an outcry at the end of Labour's first term. The farmers made a plea of poverty to the Agricultural Wages Board – the one remaining wages council not swept away by Mrs Thatcher – and got 2005's wage rise for labourers fixed at 5 per cent, when the minimum wage rose by 7 per cent (and many farm workers got little more).

Strangely, by October the National Union of Farmers reported that fine September weather had saved the day and there was, after all, a good harvest, higher than the year before. By then the workers' wages had been set. One of the less wholesome faces of the countryside was shown after the death of Chinese cockle-pickers in Morecambe Bay in 2004. Illegal or shadowy agricultural gangs were not new; but the scandal made action more urgent. Defra established a licensing authority (from April 2005) to regulate temporary and casual labour for agriculture and shellfish collection.

A rural development programme tried to encourage farmers to accommodate walkers and tourists, to take up organic farming, growing trees and 'stewarding' the land. Labour continued to subsidise the rural life so envied by townies: they extended to 2008 the £150m subsidy paid since 2003 to keep rural post offices afloat. Of the 8,100 rural post offices only one in ten was profitable, the smallest 800 attracting fewer than twenty customers a week.

## Hunting

Labour could have made its wish to ban hunting foxes with dogs part of a wider scheme to 'modernise' the countryside, by making it a fit place for enjoyment by the townspeople who were, one way or another, paying for it. Instead, hunting paraded Old Labour atavism, Blair's ambiguities and the government's failure to complete its reform of the House of Lords. The economic facts of life had been laid out by Terry Burns, the former servant of Thatcherism as permanent secretary in the Treasury, now elevated to the Lords and recruited as Blairite rapporteur. Hunting accounted for a tiny fraction of rural employment. There were many alternatives, principally offering visitors from the towns a warmer welcome and greater comfort. Only bloodlust prevented fox hunters jumping over fences and following dogs on drag hunts. After parliamentary pingpong, the ban was enacted on a shorter timetable for implementation than the government had wished. The menacing reaction of the Countryside Alliance was revealing and a mistake. In 2005 hunting became a law-and-order issue.

## Right to Roam

As deep-dyed in Labour tradition as anti-hunting was the old passion for a townies' 'right to roam'. Legislation passed in the first term, the Countryside and Rights of Way Act 2000, came into force in September 2004. Its symbolism can be overdone. Over eighteen months it would extend a legal right to walk to about 3,200 square miles of open countryside, mainly in the North. Woodlands and riverbanks were not covered, nor was ploughed land and that peculiar acreage of 'green' known as golf courses (though some golf clubs allowed it). The stimulus given walking by the right to roam was worth hugely more in rural jobs and money than hunting ever was: walking is worth some £6bn a year in accommodation, travel and associated revenues, providing employment for a quarter of a million people.

## Water

As sewage plants were modernised and expanded and water quality raised, English water companies projected a £22bn investment programme to the end of the decade to replace pipes. Ministers condoned the price increases necessary to stop male fish growing female reproductive organs (because they had been ingesting endocrine disruptors, an ingredient in plastics, packaging and shampoos).

So in Labour's second term water bills started to rise. Thames Water wanted to increase its basic charge by nearly 40 per cent by 2008, while Anglia wanted a 16 per cent rise. These were not large sums but a report for the OECD noted that poorer households pay three times more than the average household for water and sewerage, expressed as a fraction of their total income. The government said the price rises needed for the sake of fish and to reduce discoloration in water supplies would add £1 to the average annual bill for a household (£249 in 2004) on top of the £34 increase condoned by the water regulator to pay for other investments.

Some 95 per cent of England's rivers and 82 per cent of lakes would fail to meet emerging EU standards for 'diffuse pollution'. Pollution from specific sources, such as chemicals factories, had been controlled. The problem was discharges from the land and transport, especially that caused by farmers. Lavatories continued to flush untreated effluent into the sea at Margate and Broadstairs while along the coast some progress was made with sewage treatment at Dover, Folkestone and Eastbourne. Bathers beware.

## Birds, Trees and other Biota

Defra claimed credit for overseeing a small increase in the population of wood birds but a number of farmland species continued to decline. The government's stated aim was to recover 'biodiversity'. One tool was to designate small parcels where the wildlife population could be protected. Some 4,000 such sites of special scientific interest were registered, covering a million hectares.

The government (the ODPM in fact) pushed tree planting,

for example in the Forest of Marston Vale between Bedford and Milton Keynes. This was a charitable community forest, one of a dozen created across England in an initiative led by the Countryside Agency and the Forestry Commission. With government support the charity Groundwork improved 780 hectares of green and open spaces during 2003. Planning adjustments added 25,000 hectares of designated green belt since Blair first took office. Were hedges safe in Blair's hands, however? The Anti-Social Behaviour Act 2003 empowered local authorities to take strimmers to high hedges, behind which nuisance teenagers might lurk.

## Animal Rights

BSE had provoked near panic during the first Blair term. But as the epidemic died away and the number of cases fell from 445 in 2002 to 200 in 2003, apparently related cases of variant CJD mercifully proved to be rare. Epidemiologists kept a watching brief over a disease whose gestation was possibly of great length; but the hysteria died away.

Self-promoting defenders of animals plagued researchers. A new police unit, the National Extremism Tactical Coordination Unit, took on the case. The government, somewhat passive, watched while the University of Cambridge abandoned a primate laboratory under threat from 'activists', despite Cambridgeshire police spending £1m and consuming up to 3,000 officer days a year protecting Huntingdon Life Sciences. Oxford University had to look for a new builder after one company pulled out, in the face of intimidation. Ministers were rightly embarrassed at a leak which showed the eminent biologist Colin Blakemore, now chief executive of the Medical Research Council, being blackballed for a knighthood because of his work involving animals. (He was subsequently honoured.)

In fact the number of experiments on live animals had been falling over the decades. The increase by 2.2 per cent between 2002 and 2003 when some 2.79m experiments were carried out was explained, Blakemore said, by the increased use of genetically engineered mice. Some of the mice died to boost the profits of pharmaceuticals companies, it is true, but biotechnology and its applications to medicine remained a British strong point and source of employment as well as profit. Labour did a reasonable job in balancing competing claims and interests. Much the same could be said about its handling of genetic research and 'cloning', where the UK remained a beacon of rationality, compared to the United States and some other European countries.

## Conclusion

Most green things got a bit better. But the one issue that towers above all others in this book has been given a dangerously low priority. Labour never had the nerve to spell out the brutal facts of global warming, let alone to prepare people for the necessary sacrifices and changes in lifestyle that will be needed to combat it. Terrorists may succeed in killing many thousands, but climate change is here already and risks suffocating all of human life.

The House of Commons Environmental Audit Committee delivered a punishing verdict in 2004: 'The government's Climate Change Strategy is seriously off course and current policies have yet to make a significant impact on UK carbon emissions. We are sceptical of the figures quoted for emissions savings. Politicians have failed to make the case for the environmental benefits of taxing fuel, and despite recent oil price rises, petrol is still at least 10 per cent cheaper than four years ago in real terms.'

# CHAPTER EIGHT

# Better Governed?

Lack of trust in public institutions spread like an epidemic across the advanced world. On Blair's watch a sour spirit of disengagement and cynicism pervaded the air, suggesting citizens were bored with democracy itself. The phenomenon was as apparent in Graz and Grenoble, but in parochial Britain it got redefined as peculiarly Blair's problem. His government's response was to carry on, rather half-heartedly, with aspects of modernisation begun in the first term.

But reform of the House of Lords foundered, elections to create new regional assemblies were cancelled and what could anyone say about the town that rejected other candidates for mayor and elected a man in a monkey suit? Reinvigoration of elected local government receded. Self-government in Scotland and Wales became ordinary, though permanent. Handfuls of patients and citizens voted for foundation-hospital governors. Proportional representation to breathe new life into moribund local democracy, let alone for Westminster, vanished off the radar.

Once, when Roy Jenkins was his mentor, Blair had seen fair elections to the House of Commons as the acme of his project for a progressive twenty-first century. Now he had given up on the chance to break with a tribal politics; gone was the chance to give voters a wider range of choices than the three traditional parties that engaged so little enthusiasm in the polls these days. Only 24 per cent of voters actually

chose Labour in 2001, yet still 'choice' – the new Blair mantra
– did not extend to the ballot box.

Yet, slowly, with no theory or coherence, and certainly no
heart-stopping rhetoric to be carved in tablets of stone, a new
constitution for the UK was being written.

## Better Government?

Sometimes Labour was centralist, commanding national
programmes (at least for England) micromanaged from
Whitehall – cancer czars, Sure Start, anti-social behaviour.
But sometimes, worried about the lack of political engagement, Labour swung the other way: these were years when a
rhetoric of 'new localism' was heard. Councils to be freed one
day; the next curious alternatives to local authorities were
proposed, such as elected police authorities.

The first-term charge of control freakery was still levelled
at Labour. Did it stick? Here is a vignette. In 2004 an inquiry
found serious failings in police handling of Ian Huntley,
convicted for the murder of two Soham schoolgirls. Home
Secretary David Blunkett demanded the head of the chief
constable of Humberside. But he refused to stand down and
his police authority, a hybrid committee of councillors and
Home Office appointees, backed him, later to back down
when the government threatened court action.

High-handed? But Labour repeatedly handed over to
genuinely independent inquiries, royal commissions in all
but name. The very fate of the Blair government was relin-
quished to Lord Hutton and then again to Lord Butler over
the Iraq war. Cynics denied their independence. A growing
band of media pundits had decided the government was
congenitally dishonest while they, of course, were unstained.
Yes, it turned out that judges and former civil servants
conducting the inquiries were 'responsible', and showed

no inclination to bring down the government. Nevertheless, Labour got little credit for opening up the processes of government in a bid to regain trust.

A vocal and persistent body of opinion thought Blair's ministers were enemies of liberty. The leitmotif of the years after 2001 was, they said, oppression: police powers, imprisonment, control and the rejection of checks and balances on executive power. Some linked these with Blair's political dominance over his cabinet, party and parliament: the Committee on Standards in Public Life called for the numbers of special advisers to be curbed. Lord Butler, the former Cabinet Secretary, used a Tory magazine to level the charge of 'insufficient debate'. Others were unhappy at changes to the way judges were appointed; others bemoaned the diminution of councils' discretionary power; a botched experiment with all-postal voting constituted an assault on democracy (even though it increased turnout).

A number of these arguments came from the left, which was surprising since they were essentially conservative complaints against change by those who valued process and venerated the way things used to be done. But Labour was surely right to say that we had constantly to review the constitution. 'Constitutional reform matters since it is a driver of change beyond the reform itself.'

## The Making of a New Constitution

Labour – without ever stating this as a purpose – was giving the UK something that looked more and more like a written constitution. Labour's first-term constitutional changes had been upfront, bold and brassy: everyone could understand them. Scottish and Welsh devolution had been open acts of the Westminster parliament subsequently endorsed (grudgingly in Wales) by the people in ballot booths. The 1998

Human Rights Act had long been signalled and was widely discussed, though in the second term it began to dawn on Labour ministers how the individualist, anti-state version of human rights they found themselves implementing often ran counter to collectivist social democratic ideas. It risked turning citizens into individualist consumers.

New large steps were still being taken towards codifying power relationships, between the executive and the legislature, between the executive and its permanent staff, between them and judges and between Westminster and the devolved administrations. Vernon Bogdanor, the Oxford professor of politics, saw it as 'a process unique in the democratic world', converting an uncodified constitution into a codified one. It was an empiricist exercise, done piecemeal, without agreement either on founding principles or on the final destination.

One element in Labour's scheme was the plebiscite – consulting people directly. Ministers now reached for referenda. Councils were given powers to call them. Ad hoc votes were called for boards of hospitals and English regional assemblies; UK-wide votes were promised on the new constitution for the European Union and, a long-standing pledge, entry into the Eurozone.

Power seeped from parliament. Labour had now inculcated the idea that Westminster was no longer supreme. Human rights were now a law above parliamentary proceeding. Devolution was now a practical fact. Rhodri Morgan, first minister in the Welsh Assembly Government, was Labour but his policies had a Welsh inflection: no league tables for schools and hospitals, for example. Commentators noted that Blair and his cabinet accepted that their writ, especially in social policy, really did only run in England.

The constitutional highlight of Blair's second term was the creation of the Department for Constitutional Affairs in June 2003 and its first legislation, the Constitutional Reform Bill.

As if to emphasise how cautious Blair had been in altering the landscape of the state, the landmark bill was introduced into an upper house of parliament which, only half-reformed, was itself a constitutional abomination to most observers.

## House of Lords

Labour suffered during its second term for dithering over what to do with the upper house of parliament. Finally, like a grumpy navvy walking away from the building site, it simply abandoned further reform. This proved a bad mistake since the Tory-dominated peers took on a new lease of legislative life and blocked government measures left, right and centre. The convention that the unelected lords gave way to MPs broke down and in autumn 2003 the government suffered a rare defeat over a motion stemming from the Queen's Speech, the government's official legislative programme.

The original deal struck in the first term between Labour and Lord Cranborne, the Tory leader in the Lords, had left ninety-two hereditary peers in place together with an appointments commission, the first product of which in April 2001 was to select several new 'people's peers', who looked much more like the existing lords than they looked like the 'people'. One of them was Elspeth Howe, married to a knight, who himself was elevated to the Lords . . . once, twice, three times a lady.

The peers created in 2004 were political nominees plus some independents. A director of Enron and paid apologist for the press, John Wakeham, had been asked to report on the options in the first term. Given to obeying directions, he duly produced what Blair and Derry Irvine, the Lord Chancellor, had required – a report in favour of an essentially appointed upper chamber. 'Tony never wanted any elected members of the House of Lords,' according to Robin Cook's recollection of a conversation with Derry Irvine.

Wakeham's options included elections, though only up to a maximum of 35 per cent. Much argy-bargy followed. Re-elected, Labour produced a white paper in November 2001, followed by a long sequence of reports. In February 2003, thanks to Blair's lack of enthusiasm for doing anything much and bungling mismanagement of the bill in the Commons, MPs were presented with a confusing series of options. Most favoured a large elected element and a proposal for an 80 per cent elected chamber failed by only three votes. Another consultation paper was followed by the announcement of the Lords Reform bill. This proposed to remove the hereditaries, but instead of some peers being democratically elected, all were to be appointed. The white paper in September 2003 took several paces back, proposing an appointments com-mission that would appoint peers for life with a party component proportional to the previous general election results.

All this confusion sprang from the failure to begin with a set of principles. Labour, after all, believed in strong govern-ment: Conservatives wanted to weaken and diminish it. One approach pointed to a strong revising second chamber, the other away. Blair preferred the status quo. In March 2004, the government decided not to proceed. The reform bill was dumped before it was published. 'They will not pass,' said Charlie Falconer, meaning the hereditaries and their allies would not permit his reform. Watch out for the manifesto, he promised, half-heartedly. 'It is important to decide what the Lords is for, and what it should contribute to the parliamen-tary process before turning to the issue of composition.' It was a bit late in the day for that inspiration.

As a result, Labour left the sweepings of the aristocracy to disrupt its business in the Lords with its large Tory majority:

the so-called cross-benchers mostly voted with the Tories. But most bizarre of all were the weird and wonderful 'by-elections' to replace the old aristos when they died to keep their numbers up to the agreed ninety-two. Hereditary Lord Milner of Leeds died in 2003, but he was Labour and the constituency which voted to replace him comprised three people, the only Labour hereditaries.

## House of Commons

In the debate about the Lords, few made a connection with the way the House of Commons was elected. If coalition government (the probable result of proportional representation) became more normal, would there be any need for a second chamber to check the first? Anomalies grew. If proportional representation was good for Scotland (which employed four different fair voting schemes in its various elections) and good for the government of London, why not for Westminster?

The question was not put. After flirting with Paddy Ashdown, proportional representation and Roy Jenkins in his first term, Blair said the affair was over and nobody much demurred. The balance of power in the debate over electoral reform had shifted to the antis, the Constitution Unit opined in 2001. It stayed there.

The Commons, as a legislative chamber separate from the executive, flexed its muscles. There were specific Commons votes on the Iraq war and Blair had to win MPs' support in set-piece debates in February 2003. It would be difficult for any future government ever to go to war again without following that new precedent.

Early on Labour's mighty majority was stopped in its tracks from bulldozing through the Commons. Labour MPs rebelled over the chairmanship of the Commons select committees when Downing Street tried to exclude two crusty backbenchers, Gwyneth Dunwoody and Donald Anderson. They had to be reinstated, though the whips got their revenge later by defeating a plan to take nominations to committees out of the executive's control. Plainly, the choosing of the chairs of the House's own committees should be a matter for the House itself, many MPs said, but not enough of them to make it happen. Still, the select committees seemed to be sharper, more willing to tackle and challenge. Elements of an alternative career structure for bright MPs on the committees were put in place when it was agreed to pay the chairs a supplement of £12,500 a year on top of their MPs' pay.

A sign of the growing power of select committees was Blair's agreement in his second term to appear at fixed regular intervals before the liaison committee, which was made up of all the chairs of the select committees. These long and gruelling sessions were televised live and any questions could be thrown at him. Never before had prime ministers subjected themselves to such open scrutiny. Nor had any previous prime minister called a monthly televised press conference, often lasting an hour and a half. The novelty of both these remarkable acts of openness wore off quickly, perhaps because Blair was so adept at fielding questions.

Modernisation came gently. A package of reforms passed in October 2002 stipulated more bills should appear first in draft form giving time for discussion, and speeches should be shorter, allowing more people in. The parliamentary year became more rational, with September sittings of the Commons and hours of work more normal, thanks to pressure from Labour women MPs. Robin Cook, Leader of the Commons till he resigned over Iraq, noted that thanks to the rule change the big votes happened at 7pm, in prime time, perhaps giving the public more sense that parliament mattered. However, a groundswell of old sweats was making headway with an effort to reverse the change and bring back late-night voting and drinking by MPs who never saw their families.

The Commons Modernisation Committee had no sooner recommended more 'outreach', better tours of the Palace of Westminster, a new visitors' centre and all, when an invasion of the chamber by foxhunting Hooray Henrys provoked tighter security. The men in tights with swords who failed to skewer the intruders faced redundancy.

## The Courts

In July 2004 Lord Woolf, the Lord Chief Justice, announced that the fears that had led him to wonder whether Britain needed a written constitution had been 'largely allayed'. This was ironic since, no thanks to the senior judges, a written constitution was what was being crafted. After a row, a concordat had been agreed between government and judges to protect judicial independence; it would be written into statute law.

Labour stuck by its pledge to winkle the law lords out of the House of Lords into a new supreme court. Similarly, it intended to carry through, after a delay, the abolition of the anomaly in britches that was the Lord Chancellor, simultaneously a partisan cabinet minister, head of the otherwise independent judiciary and de facto speaker of the House of Lords.

The head of the courts would instead be a judge, the Lord Chief Justice. Responsible for the training, guidance and deployment of judges he would represent the views of the judiciary of England and Wales to ministers. This was tremendous progress but it hardly stirred the blood of the citizenry. Labour reaped less recognition than it deserved, partly because it so bungled the way it sprung the plan without working out the details first.

The supreme court would do the jobs of the appellate

committee of the House of Lords and the judicial committee of the Privy Council. The anomaly of senior judges sitting as a committee of the House of Lords – which even the Victorians had tried to do away with – was finally to end. It happened despite the antique preference of a majority of the law lords themselves, whose conservatism on this issue cast the up-to-dateness of their jurisprudence in a dark light.

Lord Bingham, master of the rolls, was more far-sighted than his colleagues, saying 'the functional separation of the judiciary at all levels from the legislature and the executive [is] a cardinal feature of a modern, liberal, democratic state'. The court would have its own staff and, eventually, its own building. Creating a proper 'final' court was modernisation, as was trying to make the bench a little more reflective of the country. Dame Brenda Hale became the first woman law lord from January 2004.

Labour insisted its proposals would secure the appoint-ment of judges on merit while retaining accountability through the political system to the voters. Judges were public officials, paid for from public funds. But they enjoyed and would be allowed to continue to enjoy great privileges of self-regulation, which might explain why only 15 per cent of them were women and only 3.4 per cent came from ethnic minorities. Ministers were specifically barred from trying to influence judicial decisions and, it turned out, from control-ling judges' effulgent pension provisions.

The existing Commission on Judicial Appointments (CJA), a complaints body, did not like the reforms but its reasons were confused. The charge of political interference was a peculiar one. It was barely decades since judges were, to a man, Tories. Here was Labour opening up appointments and, in an accusatory climate, laying itself open to vehement attack if a minister got anywhere near expressing a quite legitimate preference among two equally qualified candidates. In future it was conceivable one could be a woman, of whom only two sat among thirty-five appeal judges and only nine among nearly 100 high court judges.

Before the bill could get under way Labour had to concede that judicial appeals were a matter for judges rather than ministers. This came to a head over the politically hot issue of asylum. Had the administration worked better and made quick decisions on asylum applications, judges would have been less involved. But they were hearing many cases and appeals and the government came to see them as agents of delay.

A cooler government might have demanded a thorough review of administrative law, linking the need for reform of asylum appeals with that of tribunals. Penetrating questions might have been asked about the competence of divisional courts in sorting out the machinery of government.

But instead of that coolness, and without any softening up of opinion, the government announced it would end the right to appeal outside the asylum system. It looked like a government grasping for headlines, creating controversial change on the hoof. If there was a good efficiency reason, it merely looked capricious. It was, after all, Labour in its first term that embedded the Human Rights Act 1998 in UK law. In its second term, they seemed to regret it, stubbing their toes frequently.

Labour modernised the courts. Magistrates got computers as they were placed under another of New Labour's inspectorates to audit performance. The trawl for lay justices was widened and the gender and ethnic balance slowly improved.

A white paper proposed tidying up the tribunals through which each year a million plaintiffs sought money or apologies from employers or public agencies. Employment tribunals faced coping with new cases based on religion and sexual orientation and, from 2006, age discrimination. In its reform, based on a report by Sir Andrew Leggatt, the government went halfway, bringing together ten of the biggest tribunal systems and separating them from Whitehall departments, with a unified tribunals agency from April 2006.

Labour stopped well short of performing a makeover on the jungle of organisations meant to provide citizens and customers with satisfaction, with all the various ombudsmen, audit and inspection bodies. The government said it was looking at the system from the users' viewpoint. What they wanted to achieve was the better resolving of disputes at source, before they got into the legal system.

## Democracy – Getting the Vote Out

In a few local authority pilots online voting was given its first trial. Labour was looking for ways to persuade people to vote, and there were plenty of elections, with referenda for mayors, votes for new public authorities and hospitals, new tenants' boards and community organisations.

The independent Electoral Commission had been established prior to the general election, so the June 2001 contest was the first to be overseen, and what it saw was turnout fall to a shocking 59 per cent. As a result polling firms grew fat on contracts to find ways to stimulate voting. They met little success as people complained simultaneously about not being consulted enough and having to vote too often.

Indeed the evidence on turnout went two ways. People tended not to vote if they were broadly satisfied and if they thought a result was a foregone conclusion; but lower levels of participation, which were also being recorded in other countries, were perhaps also a sign of the prevalent sense of alienation and disaffection picked up on in polling. However, the Electoral Commission, supposedly a guarantor of fairness, did not seem to think its job was to counter the belief fomented by newspapers and broadcasters that all politicians were crooks and liars. The commission might usefully have made the case that UK politics at all levels were remarkably clean and free of graft and under intense scrutiny, probably cleaner than ever before.

Labour had set up another quango, the Standards Board, to receive and investigate complaints against councillors. The Local Government Act 2003 let councils mount all kinds of polls and referenda, but signs of revitalised local democracy were hard to spot. Councils consulted widely on the new executive arrangements Labour required them to set up, with 'cabinets' and scrutiny panels. Executive mayors had, for a while, been favoured by the Prime Minister as a way of creating a local hero to put life into local politics. It was not a success.

The first referendum on whether to have a mayor was held in Watford in July 2001 and attracted a turnout of just 24.5 per cent. The number of spoilt ballots was double the majority in favour. Elected executive mayors were too few and too idiosyncratic to provide a model outside their areas. Councillors had seen off this potential threat to their dominion. But there was a growing feeling that councils had too many members without enough to do at the same time as their elected members were ageing and not representative in gender, work status or ethnic origin.

Allowed to vote online in some local council elections in 2003, more people had participated – in pilot areas the average turnout was over 37 per cent. But less than a third of those who could did choose electronic means of recording a preference. In the same elections thirty-three councils tried all-postal ballots. The average turnout was higher, doubling the voters in most areas.

The government was enthused. Elections were planned for 10 June 2004, combining the European Parliament with local elections in England. Testing the evidence, the Electoral Commission said two regions should try all-postal ballots, the North East and East Midlands. The government wanted four trials, adding Yorkshire and Humberside and the North West. But the House of Lords demurred, claiming (against the evidence) postal voting was more open to fraud. The legislation was delayed, forcing electoral registration officials into a last-minute scramble. In the event turnout did rise but the experiment was unpopular.

Labour decided, after consultations, to keep the minimum voting age for voting at eighteen. Young people themselves did not seem keen on reducing it to sixteen, but then they were not keen on much to do with the public realm. The minimum age at which someone could stand as a candidate was reduced to eighteen.

## Freedom of Information

In Labour's second term, the state gave and the state took away information. Public bodies had been given nearly five years to prepare as finally the Freedom of Information Act came into effect, giving citizens a right to be told more or less whatever the state knew.

The state needed to know more. After prevarications and drawn-out consultations, Home Secretary Blunkett announced a national identity card in November 2003.

Part of the rationale was easier access to public services; the card would establish entitlement. A card might pull together personal data already in the system. The promise of a (compulsory) scheme was security, disrupting crime and terrorism. Work went on to develop biometric identifiers to be fed into a national database when passport and driving licences were renewed. The Americans were insisting that from October 2005 the only countries that could qualify for its visa waiver programme were those which embedded biometric data on passports. The Home Office said it wanted to roll out identity cards – voluntary not compulsory – in 2007; they would have a chip containing an iris scan or facial details. MPs said, 'the security and reliability of biometrics are central to the government's proposals'.

Later (no earlier than the end of the decade) people would have to register. The government believed that 80 per cent of the economically active population would have an ID card by 2013. Some saw this as a sensible pragmatic step but for others it was a touchstone, threatening liberty. For others too it looked like a huge sum – many billions probably – on something that would make a marginal impact. The record of this (and other) governments – and the private sector – in big IT projects did not indicate Big Brother would be around for a while.

## Devolution

It was instructive how in early autumn 2004, the (English) press could not muster much enthusiasm for the story about the cost of the Scottish Parliament. The building, originally commissioned for £40m, ended up costing £400m. One reason was the growing sense among the residents of Scotland that, inefficiently procured as it was, this was their legislature. Another was the sheer indifference to devolution. Those in power at Westminster, many of them, including the Prime Minister and Chancellor Scottish by birth, and the English political class, just did not want to be bothered by the geographical periphery. This worked to Scotland's advantage as Gordon Brown continued to condone public spending levels in Scotland both remarkably higher than in England but also higher than in England's poorest regions.

Curiously, Labour kept on separate ministries for Scotland, Wales and Northern Ireland, despite devolution, but titles were doubled up. Alistair Darling was first of all Transport Secretary with some UK and some England-only functions, then Secretary of State for Scotland, at best a glorified postman.

Most people were content to live with anomaly. On the contentious bill establishing foundation hospitals the government defeated an amendment against them by seventeen votes on 19 November 2003. Labour's majority included forty-four of its MPs from Scotland and twenty-four from Wales who supported the government. What were these Celtic fringe members doing voting on a controversial bill whose clauses on foundation trusts applied only to England? The Tories said that if only MPs representing English constituencies had voted the government would have lost. But this West Lothian question never really caught fire, beyond the think-tanks and lawyers' conclaves.

## Scotland

With the elections in 2003 the Scottish Parliament entered its second term. The Labour–Liberal Democrat coalition held while commentators fretted about calibre and cost as ministers came and went. Frank McAveety was sacked as minister for culture, sport and tourism in October 2004 after he had turned up late for question time pleading that he had been delayed by important business. He was later discovered to have been having a meal of pie, beans and roast potatoes in the parliament canteen.

The parliament's power to alter income tax rates by plus or minus three pence in the pound was not used, but policies did begin to differ markedly. First minister Jack McConnell – mindful of greying Scottish demographics and shrinking population – said his country was open to immigrants without checking with the Home Office. The Scottish NHS began to look different, both more expensive and less subject to targets. From 2007 Scottish local authorities will be elected on a single transferable vote. Westminster constituencies were decoupled from electoral boundaries for the Scottish Parliament. Scottish seats will be cut from seventy-two to fifty-nine, in line with population ratios elsewhere.

## Wales

Welsh schools and hospitals were also spared the targets regime, but that was why waiting lists in Wales were so much higher, said Welsh Labour MPs at Westminster, who became no more enamoured of the assembly in Cardiff. They claimed too that Wales' insistence on no league tables was what caused Welsh schools to improve more slowly. Its administration stabilised under the leadership of Rhodri Morgan. As with Ken Livingstone in London, Blair learned to live with a popular sub-national leader he had once made the error of scorning.

Lord Richard of Ammanford (formerly Labour MP for Fulham) was appointed by the assembly in July 2002 to look at its powers. He said it should, like the Scottish Parliament, be able to make law in those areas where administration had already been devolved such as agriculture, education and health. This would require Westminster to pass a fresh Government of Wales Act and – Morgan said – a fresh referendum vote. Westminster was unenthusiastic, but a strong demand for more from Welsh Labour would probably be satisfied. Welsh public opinion shared Westminster's lack of enthusiasm.

Morgan, a former civil servant, began to reshape the state in Wales, promoting common training for all public servants and abolishing (from 2006) quangos he thought had become too big and grand, including the Welsh Development Agency and the Wales Tourist Board. Their functions would be absorbed into the executive.

## Northern Ireland

Blair tried vainly to move Northern Ireland back to the promising days of the power-sharing executive. The hoped-for next stage of normalisation would be when Sinn Fein stopped being the wing of an armed gang and the protestant parties realised the Irish Republic could prove a reliable guarantor of their identities and maybe their incomes. Even in the midst of Iraq, Blair was willing to find time for the futile pursuit of bringing the sides together. He chose to ignore the finding of the Independent Monitoring Commission that paramilitary organisations were entrenching themselves and remained well connected with political parties. Sinn Fein would, it implied, have to be excluded from government, if the devolved executive were functioning. Blair chose to ignore a parallel implication that Sinn Fein members and officers should be deprived of public money.

But Northern Ireland was mostly at peace. Troop and police numbers were scaled back. The new Police Service of Northern Ireland had replaced the Royal Ulster Constabulary in November 2001. Incomes were rising as elsewhere in the UK and in the Irish Republic. But this was a deeply dependent province still. Some 62 per cent of Northern Ireland GDP came from public spending and a third of those in work were government employees. One definition of normality might be when Northern Ireland's tourist sector (2 per cent of GDP) was the same as the Republic's at 7 per cent.

However, direct rule was proving effective. Ministers were able to take decisions local politicians flinched at, closing hospitals and introducing water rates. No wonder two-thirds of protestants told pollsters they were indifferent to the restoration of self-rule. With house prices rising and hospital waiting lists falling, Professor Paul Bew of Queen's University asked if Ulster people really wanted to make a compromise with someone they did not like?

The power-sharing executive had been suspended in February 2002 then reinstated, but both the executive and the assembly were suspended again in October 2002 after political cooperation was made impossible by the discovery of an IRA spy ring in government offices in Belfast, never explained by Sinn Fein. Elections due in May 2003 were deferred and when they were finally held in November that year the moderates (David Trimble's Ulster Unionist Party and the Social and Democratic Labour Party) lost while the hardliners in Sinn Fein and Ian Paisley's Democratic Unionist Party made gains. The DUP said it would not form a government with Sinn Fein as long as the IRA retained arms. The centre-right Irish government, led by Bertie Ahern, proved unable or unwilling to deliver movement from the Republicans. An 'historic' summit at Leeds Castle in Kent in September 2004 gave way in December to renewed negotiations over decommissioning. Small but hugely symbolic points stalled agreement. The 108 unemployed members of the assembly continued to be paid half their salaries.

## England: Regional Assemblies – or Not?

Enthusiasts for regional government wanted England to have a taste of that invigorating sense of local identity that seemed – at least from afar – to be doing Scotland and Wales good. But English regional sentiment was not to be imposed.

Labour, anxious to do something for its core vote and heartland areas, said regeneration would start with the creation of an extra level of government. The Tories had created new government offices in the nine English regions. In its first term Labour had extended their remit (they 'influenced' some £9bn of spending in 2002–03) and created development agencies in parallel, state-funded but led by people with business backgrounds.

On the side, police, fire and emergency planning were becoming more regional in their outlook and Prescott pushed housing and land planning in the same direction. The coping stone on the new regional edifice was to be elected assemblies which would not necessarily take over these functions but would keep an eye on them; at no point did the government envisage a transfer of financial decision making to the English regions.

But assemblies filled neither the Prime Minister nor most Labour MPs with wild enthusiasm, although they were an Old Labour commitment and the cabinet's statutory northerner, John Prescott, was keen. MORI found few people even knew which region they were in. But the ODPM listened to the wind (50,000 people were said to have been consulted) and felt there was enough interest in three regions. A referendum on whether to proceed with assemblies was scheduled for November 2004.

Prescott's 2002 white paper was called *Your Region, Your Choice* but it turned out that the functions of the new regional assembly people were asked to vote on mainly concerned such things as the running of fire and rescue services, important but hardly likely to inflame electoral passion. Rationalisation and efficiency was one reason put forward for regional government: for example it cost councils in England and Wales £4bn to administer the buying of goods and services worth £40bn, so shouldn't they band together regionally? Others wondered why regional consortia couldn't get together without all the paraphernalia of a new tier of government.

When Labour did badly in the June 2004 local and

European Parliamentary elections, with the Tories gaining the most MEPs, Prescott's harmless regional adventure suddenly looked like it would give the voters yet another free hit at an unpopular government. MPs queued up to tell Prescott he was on a hiding to nothing. So the government summarily cancelled the referenda in the North West and Yorkshire and Humberside, leaving only the North East, where a positive vote looked most likely. The Electoral Commission conceded an all-postal ballot there, although in general it said postal voting should be a matter of choice. The voters of the North East, or at least 47.8 per cent of them, took the chance to state their view. Over three-quarters said no thanks.

## English Local Authorities – and The New Localism

If trust was Blair's big problem Labour hunted for an antidote in the 'new localism' to reconnect with the people. Labour believed in the existence of natural communities – on estates, in wards, in 'partnership' zones. Somehow these hard-pressed people in the most dysfunctional places were supposed to want more control of decision making than those in better-off areas.

David Blunkett speculated about directly elected judges. Other ministers floated new ideas for ways to connect the people directly to the institutions that ran their lives. But since low turnout was the problem, creating a cat's cradle of yet more complex voting was a bit like dosing the patient with more of the same poison. If they wouldn't vote for local councils, why would they flock to vote for a police authority or a hospital board?

Another reason for seeking out exotic new democratic bases was to cut out local councils. Blair did nothing to resolve a profound and probably permanent tension between elected councils in England and the centre. Services such as

Labour's new children's trusts were ordained by Westminster and more or less paid for in grants. Councils were to make the service work locally and pick up residual costs. Over the years some services have effectively become more centralised – schools and lately social services. Room for local choice shrank and the low turnout at council elections made the legitimacy of any choices questionable. The party balance on councils shifted. Labour suffered big losses in elections and in 2004 the Tories took over the Local Government Association, banging the drum for freedom, just as rebellious Labour councils had under Mrs Thatcher.

In response to this cry for freedom Labour did two things. One was to make vague, rhetorical promises of future emancipation from the thralldom of Whitehall – minister Nick Raynsford specialised in this. The other was to reward good boys and girls. Councils were given room for man-oeuvre on capital spending, provided they were 'prudent' and could convince auditors future repayments of interest were underpinned by identifiable revenue streams.

Starting with county and unitary councils in December 2002, the Audit Commission introduced 'comprehensive assessment' of councils, which was meant to look at their operations in the round rather than focusing on value for money in specific services. It reported 'overall improvement'. Those doing especially well were to be rewarded with fewer inspections and freedom to keep some of the money they took in, for example from fixed penalty motoring fines. For the other councils, a tight regime of inspection and performance audit would have to remain in place.

## Council Tax

The government worried about council tax: increases for 2003–04 shot up to an average 12.9 per cent. Pensioners –

at least those living in higher-value properties – came out in protest. The Treasury put some more money in the next year while John Prescott threatened to use the capping powers he had been bequeathed by the Tories. Council tax rises fell to an average 5.9 per cent in 2004–05. A further sweetener, worth £600m., was proffered by Gordon Brown to mitigate 2005's tax.

Eager beaver minister Raynsford talked of re-establishing councils on a new local tax and conducted long inquiries. No sooner had one review finished than another began: every reform has losers who make more noise than winners and Labour well remembered the damage council financing had done Mrs Thatcher. The second review, by Sir Michael Lyons, former chief executive of the City of Birmingham, was to be carried out with no report until safely after the general election. He had just completed a study concluding that 20,000 civil servant jobs could be shifted out of London, provoking mouth-watering expectations on the part of civic leaders in Manchester and Newcastle. For now, there would be no change in the fraught council tax regime.

## London Government

The one elected regional government in England that Labour had got up and running was London's. In Blair's second term he was obliged to bring Ken Livingstone in from the cold and back into the Labour Party, or face the humiliation of having another official Labour candidate mangled again in the 2004 second mayoral election.

London remained a mess of ad hoc and elected bodies, with its own government office and too many boroughs, but Livingstone navigated the muddle he was given as best he could, maximising his few powers and becoming a political leader better known and liked nationally than most cabinet ministers.

Tony Travers of the London School of Economics concluded on the eve of the election that London still desperately needed someone to sort out its railways, roads, housing, schools and hospitals. The culprit was not Livingstone but the centre's refusal to think through how this conurbation, site of the creation of a fifth of the UK's GDP, should be taxed and governed. One day the logic would be to give more power to the Mayor and assembly, but not yet.

## Public Services

It was all very well criticising efficiency at local levels, but Whitehall departments were no paragons. We knew that because Gordon Brown said so in no uncertain terms in July 2004.

Like penitents under the Soviet regime, permanent secretaries stood and confessed they had been running at bloated levels and signed up to cuts in their staff. So 'efficiency' became one of Blair's second-term war cries, along with 'choice'.

The Marconi executive Sir Peter Gershon reported that the public sector could cut 2.5 per cent off its operating costs over the three years to 2008, a productivity increase larger than the 2.25 per cent the Treasury itself was forecasting for the economy at large.

It would be accomplished – a typical Blairite assumption – by applying information technology to government. But slowly it dawned that people mattered as much as software and computers. Putting patients' records online – a magnificent aim for any health system – would only work if new relationships were forged between surgeries, hospitals and patients; the IT, even where it worked, could not substitute for the organisational re-engineering.

In a succession of set-piece speeches after the end of the invasion of Iraq, Blair sought to re-establish his domestic political authority by promising more reform of public services. Partly this was camouflage. When Brown announced his great efficiency drive, his reform rhetoric was intended to distract: he wanted headlines for his plan to cut 104,000 civil service jobs not for the employment consequences of his spending plans – at least 250,000 new public sector jobs and many thousands more for private sector and non-profit bodies dependent on the flow of public money.

Reform, for Blair, was a flag to wave at middle-class and marginal voters. Taxation (which was rising slightly) for public spending could be justified if public services were constantly presented in a state of reformation. This was nothing new and had been acknowledged as an aim even before Labour took power in 1997. Reform embraced the use of private finance schemes, the importation of personnel from the private sector and what was coming to be called outsourcing – public service bought from private suppliers.

The Treasury, deliberately, failed to keep aggregate scores. No calculation was ever made, say, of how many private companies depended on the state for more than 75 per cent of their turnover.

## Whitehall Remodelled

After the 2001 election Blair ordained a Delivery Unit, which succeeded in focusing attention on a small array of health and education targets, a Strategy Unit, which produced interesting and largely ineffectual reports, and an Office of Public Services Reform, which was never heard from again. Health, social security and education swapped functions and a new Department of Work and Pensions was created. John Prescott's former Department of Environment, Transport and Regions was dismembered; the Department for Environment, Food and Rural Affairs picked up some pieces, the Department of Transport, Local Government and Regions under Stephen Byers the rest. The Office of the Deputy Prime Minister was, at first, just a suite of offices tucked inside the Cabinet Office to give a political big beast but no great administrator, John Prescott, a berth. Byers resigned in May 2002 at the end of a chain of linked events made fatal by the operations of the political press and by his own lack of political support.

A Blairite, he was well-liked but had no constituency nor a long, shared past to give him roots when the winds blew. The storm broke when a civil servant leaked a memo from Jo Moore, his special adviser, saying September 11 2001 was a good day to bury bad news. Moore was retained when she should have gone; she made the same mistake twice by suggesting the death of Princess Margaret was another occasion for obsequies for official news.

Byers' resignation led directly to a scrambled restructuring, the overnight expansion of the ODPM and the re-re-creation of a separate transport department. Indirectly Byers led to a review of government communications, which itself was bound up with the fate of the Prime Minister's press adviser, Alastair Campbell, and to a long-winded and inconsequential debate about special advisers, or 'spin doctors' as the press erroneously called them.

## Special Advisers

Special advisers became a lightning conductor, attracting bolts which failed to touch Olympian Blair. Their numbers had risen, but there were still not that many spread across busy ministries. The Major government had thirty-eight. Now there were seventy-four; but more than half of these were concentrated in the Treasury and at Number Ten. Special advisers in other departments had increased by only twelve.

One issue was Campbell and Blair's ascendancy. Blair's arrangements at Number Ten were no different in principle from his predecessors' except that his chief of staff, Jonathan Powell, was a special adviser who by a special dispensation had limited command of civil servants, not including the cabinet secretary or substantive heads of departments.

Any occupant of Campbell's position would have excited disproportionate and usually negative press coverage since he was their daily feed. What was more anomalous, Campbell's efforts to manipulate a hostile press, or the existence of a government PR function which tried, unsuccessfully, to present neutral information to journalists who if not politically biased were usually after a slant? After a review conducted by Sir Bob Phillis, chief executive of the Guardian Media Group, the communications function was given new management and Campbell's departure removed a target.

## Committee on Standards in Public Life

Worrying about special advisers was rife. The Committee on Standards in Public Life, chaired by Sir Nigel Wicks until Sir Alastair Graham took over in summer 2004, tried to set a limit on their number. Those honorifics are significant. The committee might more profitably have looked at the potentially corrupting effect of an honours system which disproportionately awarded top officials in Whitehall and a certain class of business executive.

Wicks said the civil service was the property of government, not the property of the government of the day. Labour, it was implied, had upset some convention about how civil servants should be treated. But the charge of 'politicisation' was unfounded. Privately, ministers were bitterly critical of the capacity of the officials they were given by a machine that had largely escaped the reforms applied elsewhere in the public service. Part of the problem was the increasingly anomalous nature of this elite group, 'the civil service', taking responsibility for services delivered by council and health service officials still regarded as below the salt.

The Commons' Public Administration Committee wanted civil service duties and responsibilities laid out in a statute, taking them out of the 'prerogative' powers enjoyed by the executive. The government reluctantly published a draft bill, but Blair chose not to use the opportunity to recast the public service as a whole. The problem with Whitehall was talent and capacity. This much was recognised by cabinet secretary Sir Andrew Turnbull when he proposed a half-reform of its professional services.

What proportion of senior civil servants' time should be spent managing services, what proportion advising on policy and managing the essential processes of government? Slowly, the civil service started to produce answers. Sir Andrew Turnbull announced that officials would be expected to show they had specific skills in finance, policy advice and other fields. If parts of the constitution were being written out for all to see how power was distributed in the state, even Whitehall was joining in.

## Hutton

One of the law lords who declared against Labour's modernisation plans, creating a proper supreme court outside parliament, was Brian Hutton. Still it was to him the government turned to conduct an inquiry into the circumstances surrounding the death of Ministry of Defence specialist David Kelly. The press, during months of maximum hostility towards the government, would have been happy to give space to conspiracy theory but virtually no one suggested Hutton was anything but a stolid lawyer who would examine the evidence in front of him dispassionately. His inquiry, with full panoply of barristers and witnesses, concluded that the Prime Minister's staff had not 'sexed up' the dossier of evidence on Saddam and weapons presented to the public in September 2002. Therefore, the report by Andrew Gilligan on BBC Radio Four was wrong; the BBC should have apologised. Inability to accept this core finding led to the resignation of the BBC's chairman and, shortly after, the director-general Greg Dyke, who promptly set up shop as Blair's nemesis.

It was striking, for all the talk about declining trust, how much confidence was placed, by all sides, in the Hutton *processes*. Law lords gave impartial rulings. And the BBC should – could again – report reasonably impartially. It was remarkable, after the event, how quickly normal relations between government and broadcasters were restored. There were issues: a spreading culture of denigration of elected politicians, most evident in such programmes as *Today*. But the appointment of Michael Grade as chairman and the arrival of a new director-general, Mark Thompson, with none of Dyke's flamboyance but more common sense, restored the 'constitutional' status quo ante bellum.

## The BBC

The BBC's charter had to be renewed in 2006 but, even before Hutton reported, it was clear there was no government animus against the BBC as such. That anomalous tax, the broadcast licence fee, was in no danger of abolition; the government even turned against the apparent rationalisation of putting the BBC under its new regulator, the Office of Communications or Ofcom. Its online presence, its new digital stations, had to be reviewed. But the BBC as a broadcaster of news was in no danger.

## Conclusion

A constitutional midwife might listen through a stethoscope and conclude that, thanks to Blair, a more open, decentralised and more democratic polity was struggling to be born. She might have to listen hard. Was, for example, the plethora of big inquiries under Blair a sign of more plural, open government or mere desperation? The press complained about control freaks, excessive concentration of power at the centre, the withering of checks and balances (of which of course journalists working for malevolent, destructive foreign proprietors were supposed to be one).

Some of the charges had merit. The constitutional changes during Labour's second term were half-baked. The Freedom of Information Act came into effect in January 2005. Citizens could potentially learn much more about their government (and trust it more?). Yet at the same time, the prerogative powers of the executive – things ministers could do off their own bat, without reference to the House of Commons – were wielded with abandon. Announcing the abolition of the Lord Chancellorship in a press release one day then rescinding the decision the next was not clever, though it was quite extraordinary to see purported radicals streaming to the defence of a man in silken tights and horsehair wig. But were such actions dangerous? Did they threaten some fundamental principle on which there was deep unanimity, without compensation in terms of public security or all-round justice? We should not take at face value the claims made by lawyers (a professional interest group doggedly determined to maintain their privileges) or members of the House of Lords (ditto).

## CHAPTER NINE

# Future Britain?

It suits ministers and those who report on their doings to exaggerate their effect. Academics have graphs for spending and policy in which changes of government are impossible to spot, often making scant difference. Some of the things that happened during Blair's second term would have happened anyway, regardless of who was in power. Fate-tempting Richard Branson would probably have announced his plan for space tourism whoever had been in Downing Street. Yet governments also, by accident or design, create moods and contexts as well as spend money.

Take one example: in recent years incidents of arson have been falling but nobody quite knows why. Fires logged as deliberate were on a long-run upward trend to 2002 but dropped since. Labour had a target (of course), to cut deliberate fires to 55,000 by 2008–09, which is half 2003's total. But ministers had no formula, nor fire chiefs either. It's a complicated mixture of intensely local circumstances, campaigns in schools, preventative work by the fire service, anti-social behaviour orders and so on. Jobs and training for young people probably help too.

It would be stupid to say government policies have no effect on behaviour just as it would be self-deluding for ministers to claim their decisions necessarily have a straightforward or measurable impact. Governments can, however, nudge things along in a progressive direction.

For instance, we know the health of the UK population has been improving, with less disease and longer lives fairly steadily over the long haul. It was happening when Margaret Thatcher was in power and did not stop when Tony Blair succeeded in 1997. But things do seem lately to have got even better. Over the past nine years, according to actuarial calculations based on actual versus 'expected' deaths in each age group, British men have enjoyed the biggest single gain in life expectancy since data were first collected in the 1920s, but there are huge regional variations.

With occasional hiccups we have been getting more afflu-ent. But under Blair and Brown there were no hiccups. As measured by jobs and income things got better in Labour's first term and even better second time round. That meant more money to spend, more holidays, more drinking and so on. Go to Castle Donington or Dyce, not just to Stansted or Birmingham International, and see in the jammed car parks and the jet-engine plumes the statistical fact that half the UK population now flies at least once a year.

A puzzle for Europhiles was that easy access to Madrid or Forli or Carcassonne appears to have done nothing for positive attitudes towards either the euro or the European Union. What about vice versa? More foreigners visited the UK in the first three months of 2004 than in any first quarter for the past twenty-five years – some 5.5m visitors, a rise of 11 per cent on the same period in 2003. Visitor spending in 2003 had already been 4 per cent up on the previous year. If, some said, this Britain was less safe or less attractive, these extra visitors disagreed.

## What was Happening Abroad?

Despite the visitors, isolationist Britain is exceptionally bad at comparing itself with its neighbours, always imagining it alone faces problems or opportunities that are in reality common to many others. Were things better abroad?

In these years France was experiencing a bout of anguished introspection. It was partly France's place in an encroaching Anglophone world and in an enlarged Europe where the badly brought-up children of the East (that was more or less Jacques Chirac's phrase) showed themselves reluctant to be tutored by Paris. Chirac himself had written in 1995 of a people that had lost confidence, whose confusion was producing a sense of resignation. A decade later he was in the Elysée, a socialist government had come and gone and yet the diagnosis still applied. Newspapers pronounced French hospitals in crisis; public service workers took to the streets; a generation faced retirement with no guarantees their children would shoulder the cost of their pensions. France agonised over the standing of its ethnic minorities. Hijabs that headteachers in Britain were happy to accommodate became a defining issue in secular France.

Across the Rhine, Chancellor Schröder struggled to pass labour law and welfare reforms, straining the loyalty of his party, opening his flank in the West to the Christian Democrats and in the East to the former Communists and rightwing extremists. When push came to shove, principled foreign policy stances were irrelevant; jobs were. Germany agonised over its present and future population mix. Pundits predicted for Blair the fate of the centre-right Spanish popular party headed by José-María Aznar, who had supported the Iraq war. They failed to notice that the successful socialists, led by José Luis Rodríquez Zapatero, promptly enacted a set of programmes that looked remarkably similar to Blair's – market-friendly and fiscally conservative with liberal initiatives on, for example, domestic violence which were radical in still macho Spain but a lot less radical than New Labour's. European politics had shifted slightly to the right during

Blair's second term, but that surely made his commanding hold on power in Britain the more remarkable.

## Tankers and Synchrotrons

Governments do things which don't hit the headlines but directly affect the life chances – and the chances of dying – of small groups. Under Labour a timetable was pushed out for phasing out tankers liable to spill their contents.

Try another element. In December 2003, the largely British Beagle II lander successfully separated from the European Space Agency's Mars Express but contact with the lander was then lost, conjuring images of a Union Jack bedecked craft trundling forlornly across the Martian plains. Nine months after Beagle got lost, science minister Lord Sainsbury pledged £5m to the European Space Agency's next Mars mission, codenamed Aurora. It was nothing to do with prestige, he said, everything to do with scientific interest and potential commercial spin-offs, from the robotics, software and miniaturisation it would require.

Labour's commitment to long-haul science was real. The government committed £120m on top of £235m announced in 2000 to the Diamond synchrotron, in collaboration with the Wellcome Trust. This produces beams, allowing close study of complex molecules. The first experiments at the Diamond complex, adjacent to the Rutherford Appleton Laboratory in Oxfordshire, are due in January 2007. As with space, Sainsbury said pure knowledge would advance along with opportunities for industrial and medical applications.

## Eating and Drinking

Blair's Britain got fatter, despite the expansion of health clubs. For a small number of patients doctors began prescribing gym membership on the NHS. The Food Standards Agency said twenty-six million people in Blair's Britain ate more than the recommended daily intake of 6g of salt. Three-quarters of that came from processed foods, only 10–15 per cent shaken over chips or added at table. It was a sign of the times that the Health Development Agency started talking about the diseases of affluence, notably diabetes and other consequences of obesity. One half of all potatoes consumed are processed. One in five children eats chips every day of the week in Northern Ireland, to take one part of the UK. In the Manchester area dental caries is so bad that every year some 1,200 children undergo general anaesthesia to have teeth extracted.

Blair's Britain drank more. Increased alcohol consumption was part of the reason the city centres of Newcastle and Manchester had returned to life. It was also a cause of violence and anti-social behaviour, which the spreading CCTV cameras captured but could not prevent. Deaths on the roads caused by alcohol or drugs rose.

## Fun and Games

There was similar ambiguity on gambling. Blair played Vegas. He backed a gambling bill – a 'managed relaxation of outdated restrictions', said the government. Observers noted the intense lobbying of ministers by American gaming interests. Casinos were presented as a means of regenerating Manchester, Sheffield and Glasgow. Blackpool wanted to transform itself into a (wetter) version of Nevada – a measure of its desperation: the Fylde Coast would need a lot more than slots to restore its attractiveness. What were the government's real intentions? Tessa Jowell, secretary of state for culture, media and sport, wrote a pamphlet extolling the 'power of culture'. Was gambling culture? Labour seemed intent on making its most abiding cultural memento gambling and drinking. What would Labour's non-conformist founders have made of it?

In 2001, the Treasury had swapped a new tax on the betting industry's gross profit for the betting duty and turnover tax. Within three years, betting-shop turnover had leapt, increasing five times to £40bn a year (six times the annual overseas aid budget). It was partly that tax take had dropped, partly the introduction of fixed-odds betting terminals. Warwick Bartlett, lead partner at Global Betting and Gaming Consultants, pronounced, 'The UK is already regarded as having the best odds-making skills and regulation in the world, as well as a system of taxation that has been copied by some and envied by others.' Online betting was booming. One company, Betfair, had 300,000 registered customers and processed about one million bets a day. The Treasury decided to privatise the Tote, but by transferring it to a trust owned by the racing industry rather than outright sale.

The National Lottery, ten years old in November 2004, had turned around during the second term, too, after the agitation over its contractual renewal. It took in £2.35bn in the six months to September 2004. The profits of Camelot increased and the next big thing – lottery gambling via mobile phone text messages – hove into sight. Nobody much noticed how Labour made permanent its appropriation of a chunk of lottery earnings for government rather than charitable purposes. The principle of 'additionality' was being eroded. Lottery money was not supposed to be used for straightforward public spending; the Treasury's lottery tax gave the state a double hit. A new good cause was invented, London's bid for the 2012 Olympics, but MPs feared it could drain as much as £1.5bn from voluntary sector beneficiaries.

## Sport

An unspecified 'cultural Olympiad' was to go with the
Olympic games. What this might be exactly, after the em-
barrassing cultural vacuity of the Dome, no one dared hazard
a guess.

After much delay and confusion, eventually the National
Audit Office said the government's stake in the renewal of
Wembley Stadium – due to open to hold the 2006 FA Cup
Final – had been risky but well-managed. But sport threw up
a confusing mix of public, non-profit and private interests.
Take the FA – a non-profit regulator increasingly dominated
by the Premiership, which itself was dominated by a cartel of
companies locked in an embrace with Rupert Murdoch. The
state, in the shape of UK Sport, a quango, conducted 7,240
drugs tests in 2003 and found 1.38 per cent positive for
banned substances – the world testing average was said to be
2 per cent. The UK regime for drugs testing was commended
as highly effective.

## Bikes, Coal, Quieter Roads

British values went in divergent directions. If there was an
appetite for blackjack in Blair's Britain, there was also one for
bikes. Labour's transport plan showed councils promising to
lay 5,500 kilometres of new or improved cycle tracks. They
put down 1,350 kilometres in 2003, a few more than in the
previous year. Labour did not offer any serious disincentive
to parents driving their children to schools, but it did publish
a good practice guide, which recommended walking or
cycling.

An aggregate assessment of a government requires balancing one area's benefits and losses against another's. So
transparent in many ways, modern society also contains

shielded pockets, forgotten or ignored. Imported coal continued to be an essential fuel. Scargill, King Coal and the coal industry of old had long died. However, Labour tried hard to sweep up the physical and social remains.

During 2003 some 320 hectares of used land was reclaimed under the national coalfield programme and the government said it had created nearly 3,000 jobs at a rate of nearly five jobs a day. A new fund, in existence from April 2004, provided venture capital for businesses starting up in coalfield areas. When Selby – a new pit – was closed, an existing scheme swung into action seeking to retrain miners for careers in the building trade.

Among the work on offer: resurfacing highways with new noise-resistant materials. The Department of Transport claimed 15 per cent of the major roads network had been treated this way.

## Social Stability?

This Britain talked to itself more and more. By 2004 mobile phone subscriptions totalled fifty million out of a population of fifty-eight million, with about three-quarters of the adult population regularly using one. If people were talking to each other more, did that dispel fears of atomisation, alienation and anomie?

Sociologists noted how in some communities contact with kin and association with neighbours had not changed much since the 1950s, but those communities tended to be low-income and lacking educational qualifications or the chance to move. They were the communities most at risk as industrial and manufacturing employment shrank. But elsewhere, in 'middle England', the social decay that the Savonarolas of the press loved to spy was hard to detect. Studies showed three-quarters of households had a non-resident relative visit in any given week. Half of all households had close kin living nearby. Half of all households had daily or weekly contact with a maternal grandmother.

## Women

Grandmothers were not the only powerful women. Not because of anything the government did, the earnings of women managers grew perceptibly; they now formed about a third of all managers, up from 2 per cent in 1974. The Chartered Management Institute found 13 per cent of companies had women directors, compared with less than 10 per cent in 1999. Women heads of department were found to be earning more than male counterparts, too. But FTSE 100 companies had among them only a single female chief executive.

An anguished debate sprang up about work–life balance but it was largely and typically deaf to trends abroad. Professor Peter Taylor-Gooby of the University of Kent, no particular friend of Blair, compared the UK with other European Union countries and concluded the UK was leading the way in facing new needs arising from changing work–life balance and from much greater insecurity in employment. It helped that the skilful behind-the-scenes operator, Patricia Hewitt, was both minister for women, and running round the table to argue with herself as secretary for trade and industry. On her watch family-friendly policies got a high profile: she moved the issue centre stage so for the first time it was talked about by male ministers too. A coherent pattern of policies began to be laid out on good quality, affordable childcare, family-friendly employment, better access to work and support for low wages.

But in British homes, women were still being beaten up, with two deaths a week, greatly inflating the violence figures. A study calculated that time off work because of injuries caused by domestic violence cost British employers £3bn. In addition domestic violence cost the courts and police £1bn, the NHS £1.2bn, social services £250m and housing £160m and that was before there was any attempt to put a number on the cost of emotional suffering. Harriet Harman jolted her officials in a legal backwater by turning her previously invisible post as Attorney General into a powerful campaigning platform for battered and trafficked women. Laws were changed, and above all existing laws were enforced better. Over-lenient sentences for domestic murderers, pleading their wife's infidelity as a justification, were sent back to the courts.

Domestic strain manifested itself under Labour in an increase in the number of divorces. In England and Wales they exceeded 150,000 in 2003, the highest figure for seven years. The overall divorce rate stood at 13.9 per 1,000 married people. What was the significance, if any, of a slight growth in the duration of marriages prior to divorce? Some 22 per cent of those divorcing had children aged under five.

## Fathers

A peculiar phenomenon in Labour's second term was the appearance of fathers dressed as Superman and Spiderman demonstrating on high buildings. It was hard to make out whether there had been any numerical increase in 'problem' separations in which fathers were left with a grievance. There was certainly a rhetorical push to give fathers more recognition. As women's minister, Patricia Hewitt said fathers deserved the chance to continue with childcare if they separate or divorce since they were already doing a third of all childcare in the family.

Perhaps it was just a particular maverick group of men with a yen for publicity and stunts. These included climbing cranes and Buckingham Palace and throwing flour from the

gallery of the House of Commons. In fact, both the law and
the conduct of judges in separation cases had been under
review for some time, though 90 per cent of separating
couples came to their own arrangements over children.
The resulting green paper focused on an old ambition,
diverting couples towards conciliation, away from expensive
court hearings. Not very convincingly it explored options for
the courts in cases where one parent (usually the mother) did
flout court orders on access to children.

But Labour, to its credit, was having no truck with the
more impossible claims of Fathers for Justice, Bob Geldof and
other militant groups. No 50–50 splits, said constitutional
affairs secretary Charles Falconer: children were not like CD
collections, their interests were paramount and that demanded case by case judgement. The government was willing
to be proactive in trying to manage divorce better, pushing
couples into agreeing contact arrangements for their children,
both during court proceedings and beyond.

But, unlike previous Tory governments, Labour never
thought it could affect the state of marriage. Blair, the
moralist in foreign affairs, had shown no signs of trying to
apply moral doctrine to divorce or indeed to sex. He had little
choice, given the conduct of his Home Secretary, David
Blunkett.

## Children

Blunkett aside, it wasn't that Labour *discovered* children in
its second term. The pioneering Sure Start programme got
going earlier and primary school improvement had been New
Labour's first focus. There had been a host of initiatives
showered on to children and young people along with the
free fruit in schools. (In its official list of achievements Labour
put free school milk for five- to seven-year-olds in Wales,

without explaining why this benefit should not have been offered English children.)

But in its second term, Labour put children at the heart of all its social justice hopes. Children were not just the future, they would be Labour's historic epitaph. No government ever tried harder to rescue children from failure and give them new opportunities: if its plans didn't work, it would mark the end of an expensive social experiment for many years to come.

The need to join together policies for children was realised and symbolised in the creation of the post of first children's minister, Margaret Hodge, who took office in June 2003. In addition, early years education and childcare took off as mainstream policies. Spending had risen in real terms from £2bn in 1997 to £3.6bn in 2003. If the nineteenth century instigated primary schools and the twentieth century brought in universal secondary education, the early twenty-first 'should be marked by the introduction of pre-school provision for the under-fives and childcare available to all', said Gordon Brown.

In this most unequal of European societies, improving the life chances of adults was near impossible: but starting with the youngest poor children, even before they were born, there was hope of change.

In the first term there were special projects which showed what could be done. One hundred 'Early Excellence' centres opened, new nurseries and 500 Sure Start projects began, though they took longer to establish than planned. In designated wards, usually under the auspices of councils but paid for by Whitehall, Sure Start units set up to monitor mothers from before they had their children, using health visitors. They were offered classes of all kinds – in how to give up smoking, get training, combat post-natal depression or in parenting itself. Some Sure Starts became vital centres of neighbourhood life, becoming crèches and stimulating play centres for local children. Councils were bribed or cajoled into creating childcare places too by enlisting childminders, sponsoring after-school clubs and the like. They were popular and admired but as they were still few and far between, unknown to the wider citizenry.

It was in the second term that Labour's ambition broadened into plans for extending out-of-home care to more low-income parents. The target was 650,000 places by 2005–06 with the dual benefit of letting many more women take paid work if they wanted to and exposing children (with some debate about the starting age) to language, creative play and teaching before full-time education began. The target to get 70 per cent of lone parents into paid work by the end of the decade was a long way off: childcare was the main obstacle.

The breakthrough came when ministers were allowed to utter the word 'universal' and a picture was painted (perhaps not to be realised for another decade) of children's centres in every neighbourhood, richer and poor, where parents could leave their children in safe and stimulating hands for part of the day. The dream was of a children's centre for all mothers that would be the hub of local family life, offering baby clinics, a place to find help and support of every kind, advice, friendship, mother and toddler groups, medical care and affordable childcare. There would be classes for parents too, with training for mothers wanting to seek work.

By 2005 some 300 such centres existed, with a further 2,200 planned by 2008. To be truly universal would require 10,000 children's centres. Although the 2008 target represented a steep acceleration, these would still only be enough to cover areas designated in the top 30 per cent of a list of the most disadvantaged wards.

But, as the Daycare Trust and other charities pointed out, half of all poor children did not live in these 'poor areas' and they would have to wait. And the same councils which had been squeezed out of their previous responsibilities for schools were reinstated. It was their job to find space and set up the new centres. An obvious place was in or adjacent to an existing school, which was already likely to be a focus of parents' lives. But didn't this conflict with Blair's determination to free schools from local bureaucracy while refocusing them on pupil attainment rather than 'welfare'? The National Audit Office observed 'schools are well placed to meet unmet demand for childcare [but] many schools have been reluctant to provide'. Efforts were made to think of children in the round but the NHS national service framework for children did not obviously link with children's policy elsewhere.

Evaluations of local schemes were starting to come in. They tended to be positive. At age seven, children who had nursery education did far better than those without. Children acquired language sooner; the quality of mother–child interaction improved. But some of the over-precise numerical targets set for Sure Start schemes on cutting smoking and getting parents into jobs fell by the wayside. They were inherently unmeasurable in areas where large numbers of people came and went, leaving only a small unusable base line of residents there since the start of the scheme.

The number of children was falling but the amount of state support to families with children was rising. Since 1999 money paid only to them (child contingent support) increased by 52 per cent in real terms. Labour extended to three-year-olds the right (available to all parents, rich and poor) to a free nursery place for half a day Monday to Friday. That was another of the unheralded Blairite donations to private business, since private and voluntary nurseries provided three-fifths of all places. Despite the attempt by some media to whip up a moral panic about their safety, children in such nurseries were generally well looked after. In 2003 the Office of Standards in Education received 6,000 complaints against nurseries and childminders but took action in only 400 cases and cancelled the licences of forty-nine. Private nurseries were twice as likely as the usually better state-provided nurseries to fail Ofsted inspections.

Paying for care and additional nursery education outside the free hours, or for younger children, stretched family budgets. Lobbying groups claimed many hundreds of thousands of women wanted to work but could not afford the cost of care. Tax credits helped some 300,000 families (at January 2004) with childcare costs; auditors worried that unless supply of places grew, the subsidy (which met only a fraction of total childcare costs) would have the perverse effect of pushing up prices. Gordon Brown's 2004 budget exempted the first £50 of weekly payments to nannies and childminders from tax and National Insurance, restricted to couples earning not more than £43,000 a year.

Children acquired a political godfather in Brown, though some of his initiatives were too clever by half. A £450m children's fund was meant to stimulate local voluntary groups to do better things, for example for children with disabilities. But distribution was bureaucratic and ended up creating jobs for adults who expected the funds to flow continually, when the government's idea had been that voluntary donations would start to kick in.

Labour also sought to expand supply of childminders at the same time as it became more difficult to work with children. After initial confusion, registration of childminders became more straightforward. Criminal-record checks became better managed. Ofsted was encouraged to inspect less where circumstances and history said childminding worked, but more elsewhere. It had to run the balance between erecting obstacles to registration and ensuring childminders looked after children properly, but the turnover rate among childminders remained high in many areas.

Then came backlash. Certain commentators seized on ambiguous (American) studies following young children looked after in centres and compared them with those at home. Shouldn't policy shift towards giving mothers financial incentives to stay at home? The most reliable conclusion was that the quality of care had most impact on subsequent development – which implied well-trained, well-supervised and reasonably well-paid staff were a prerequisite. In reality childcare staff were very badly paid – the average salary for annual paid staff in 2003 was £6,100; for their managers £11,800. There was some distance to go until working with children was 'an attractive and highly skilled career'. In Sweden, half of all staff in day care centres have child development degrees.

Over the second term hung the shadow of Victoria Climbié, a north London child murdered by relatives. Her home circumstances were exceptional. Sent from a Francophone country with no tradition of migration to the UK, she had come to the attention of social services and other agencies but then fell through the net of the state's attention. The green paper published after an exhaustive inquiry was entitled *Every Child Matters*. As a statement of intent it tried to devise a system where every child would be tracked, every cause for concern flagged, even in the difficult circumstances of urban areas where families were both mobile and fragmented.

The child's death occasioned a disproportionate moral panic and, arguably, took attention away from the development of a common framework for children's services under a new understanding of the rights of children. These rights (when it came to the 2004 Children Act) did not include protection against smacking by parents. But the rights debate was far from over. Children's commissioners had been created for Wales and Scotland, to oversee services for children and agitate as necessary. The act established this pioneering office for England, too. Kathleen Marshall, Scotland's Children's Commissioner employed her £1.5m first-year budget not pursuing individual cases but developing new policies and looking at how children's services were delivered.

## Rising Cost of Caring for the Elderly

Blair's Britain was ageing. The number of people aged sixty-five plus would nearly double over the next two decades. The pensions debate was renewed, but the highly coloured predictions of the 1980s about demographic collapse were wrong. The National Statistician said it would take thirty years before deaths exceeded births – a demographic threshold that the Italians and Germans had now passed. The UK population would remain fairly stable, with two big provisos.

The ratio of workers to those dependent on distributions (through the tax system or profits) from work would change. But how? Gloomy prognosticators of the previous century imagined a sharp deterioration. They assumed once chronologically old, productive life also ended. But the old were rejuvenating. Saga advertising became a joke: you qualified for its schemes at fifty when for upcoming generations fifty was still prime time.

The other big unknown was how, within a stable population, its composition would change. The only other European country like the UK in sending and receiving large numbers of migrants was Estonia. How far was this churn part of the explanation for the UK's relative economic success? Both sides in the debate about immigration seized on inconclusive evidence.

What was certain was the gradual greying of Britain. In medicine, it meant more spending on stroke units. It also meant coming to terms with the inequalities of earlier times. The English Longitudinal Study of Ageing traced conclusive links between illness, competence and death rates among today's aged back to differences in youth in income and education. Whoever succeeds Blair, policy will have to contend with a choice: focusing money and effort on ameliorating early lives now (in order to fend off ill effects among the elderly a generation hence) versus doing more to address the inequalities in condition among today's elderly.

One bright spot was the 'discovery' of just how extensive informal networks of care still were, even in a more fragmented and individualist society. One in ten people had some claim to be informal carers, and of them one in five were themselves older than sixty-five. It was the case that more elderly people were cared for in institutions in 1900 than now.

# Conclusion

The war in Iraq, with its long lead-in and its bloody, open-ended aftermath is just one chapter here. For some it discoloured everything else. For some – a vocal minority – it made voting for Blair impossible ever again.

Yet however much Iraq preoccupied the makers and destroyers of political reputations at Westminster and in the press, however important Iraq was as a moral touchstone, did it change policy at home? There are two kinds of answer. Look at schools, social security, even asylum and there are no direct effects as, for better or worse, ministers got on with their jobs. That is too narrow an assessment, some will say: listen to the effect Iraq had on deeper strains in our national life. Look how it damaged trust between people and their government.

Already the low turnout in 2001 had caused much heart-searching about how to reconnect with the people. The war, the row over Blair's inflated claims about Saddam's threat, the subsequent inquiries, regime change at the BBC – didn't these rub salt into Labour's already weakest spot, its reputation for spin, exaggeration, fiddling figures and over-claiming?

Iraq did distract attention at the top and it did reinforce disbelief in other aspects of the government's progress. Public service delivery figures were starting to turn Labour's way, as they should after the abundance of spending, but too few people believed it. Labour might be securely ahead in the polls, with the Tories lost in space, yet truculence was the prevailing mood.

Turn back to page 1 and remember the mood was already sourish in 2001, before the al-Qaeda attacks and long before the invasion of Iraq. Before she resigned over Iraq, Clare Short said perceptively that the Blair government's trouble was that it was 'creating a Labour country without telling the story'. Instead of extolling its achievements, the message had been defensive. Yet she went on to acknowledge that 'politics is in a grumpy, grouchy mood all over the world'. How come Gerhard Schröder's approval ratings went through the floor when his policy on Iraq had been diametrically opposite to Blair's?

With growing frustration ministers urged people to open their eyes. Look at their local primary and secondary school, their GP clinic and hospital. Count the police and support officers pounding the streets. Look at the jobs almost everywhere or the colleges and universities beckoning people in. Feel their own wallets. If they didn't believe the official figures, why not believe the evidence of their own eyes?

Ministers were right. As we record, a start had been made on long-delayed reconstruction of the British public space, both literal and metaphorical. Decades of physical decay were slowly being reversed, and it was plainly visible. That Scottish Parliament building, so expensive, but so inspiring. Secondary schools and sports halls, surgeries, children's centres, jobcentres where claimants were treated as if they had a right to respect. Of course there was so much still to be done. The public sector had more computers and more staff but sometimes they did not mesh, sometimes staff failed to supply elementary levels of courtesy and service. NHS waiting lists were falling so fast that private medicine was being put out of business, yet people's experience of hospital was still too often dirty toilets and indifferent care.

Besides, anyone waiting five months for a hip now was not waiting for one eight years ago when the list might have been eighteen months long. Anyone with a primary school child now didn't have one in Conservative days, so what use is the comparison to them? The public is congenitally ungrateful; memories are short and expectations gallop on ahead. Labour's eight years was a long time in politics and most people don't read graphs.

But if you have thumbed through the facts in this book, they make pretty impressive reading. As we dug through the mountains of reports, we surprised ourselves at the volume of programmes, schemes and endeavours. Many barely see the light of day in regular media reporting. We were struck too by the transparency with which they are evaluated. To New Labour the spin tag stuck, but it equally deserved to be known as the most scrupulously self-monitoring government ever. Targets do deliver and where they don't the public (or journalists on their behalf, with half an eye) can pinpoint where and why not.

Turn to the Social Exclusion Unit's 2004 survey of Labour's first seven years, *Breaking the Cycle – Taking Stock of Progress and Priorities for the Future*, or the sixth annual report *Opportunity for All* from the Department of Work and Pensions. They cover everything from poverty to teen pregnancy, infant mortality, rough sleepers, adults without NVQ Level 2 (good functioning literacy and numeracy) – forty-two targets in all. The bad news is not hidden away in small print. Turn to the at-a-glance checklist in the DWP document and it's all too easy to see at-a-glance that while most have a tick beside them, some do not and yet others are either no better or worse than before 1997. No government ever evaluated itself so well or so publicly. It would be a severe blow to freedom of information if any future government scurried back into the untargeted dark. And the Freedom of Information Act, delayed in implementation, but now functioning, was another Labour law.

Credit should be given too to a Prime Minister who makes himself more publicly accountable by means of a monthly televised press conference where he is aggressively questioned for well over an hour, and for his regular grilling in front of the well-informed MPs of the House of Commons Liaison Committee, also televised live. No future prime minister would dare step back from these now.

Yet the story as told was often about secrecy, crooked ways and always and ever Iraq. Blair had reasons, cogent reasons which he laid before his cabinet colleagues and several times before the House of Commons. No one could call the war clandestine and certainly not populist. The merit of his arguments is something else, for at the heart of them lay an economy with the truth. The reasons Blair gave for going to war did not include preservation of Britain's self-deluding 'special relationship' at all costs. Nor did it include what Blair knew to be Bush's prime reason – getting rid of Saddam for the sake of it, weapons or no weapons, consequences be damned.

There would be no personalities in this book, we said in the introduction, but it would be impossible not to mention one neural dysfunction in the Labour brain, warping and disorienting its limbs. Try as you might, it was impossible not to stub your toe on the relationship between Tony Blair and Gordon Brown. The division between them got far worse, so that every policy had to be viewed through a Blair or Brown perspective. Those who are not for me are against me, Brown's advisers said; Blair's too, though perhaps with less Calvinism. When you spoke to ministers or advisers it took no more than a few minutes before the accusations flew about the other side being up to something nefarious.

The rivalry and suspicion between Number Ten and

Number Eleven was not invented by the press but it suited journalists to make trouble and tittle-tattle when they could. Blairites complained that the Treasury was running a secretive parallel government; they were not paranoid to feel there existed a perfectly formed alternative government-in-waiting next door. When Tony Blair was at his weakest and bleakest in the early summer of 2004, Brown advisers thought they would be moving offices within weeks.

Chancellors are usually players. The Treasury, controller of the purse strings, has in-built powers over Whitehall departments. For generations, the centre of the British state has been messily divided between prime minister and chancellor, with, occasionally a walk-on role for a foreign secretary. To the institutional tensions were added differences of direction. Whatever Blairites proposed, Brownites instinctively opposed, and vice versa. Blairites mocked tax credits as cumbersome, typical Gordon, over-obsession with complexity no one understood. The Brownites accused the Blairites of not really caring about the poverty agenda: they just wanted quick, bright, eye-catching gimmicks.

Policies were badly presented because of this internal combustion: foundation hospitals and top-up fees might have arrived in parliament properly hammered out, instead of half-digested. Blairites complained that Brown hampered everything they wanted to do. They in turn bounced policies on Brown to avoid his scrutiny. Results were often bad, for Brown stood closer to Labour MPs on many subjects. Except Iraq, on which, in private as in public, Brown deviated not one inch from the Prime Minister's line when he had the power to scupper it.

The Blair–Brown rift helps explain Labour's lack of a defining legend for its second term. We searched in vain for such a thread, red or even pale-pink. Policies zigzagged here and there. If the public lacked a vision of what Labour was, that was Blair's trick – avoiding labels, ducking and weaving when you tried to place him on the political spectrum. If he announced a fair deal for the contracted-out workforce one week, you could bet he would be promising bosses some great pull back of the 'regulatory state' the next. Like Ruby Tuesday, no one hung a name on him.

It was a good tactic for seizing power in 1997, but in office it failed to cement abiding support. The majority always detested Mrs Thatcher but she never lacked a solid phalanx of devotees. Tony Blair might get enough votes, but admirers were getting exceedingly scarce by 2005. His sinuousness contributed to public misunderstanding – blindness – about what his government had achieved. Even his own party had not got defining messages, for example about increased cash for families with children. They had never heard the word because the preacher never gave the sermon, even in his own church. But the veritable son of the manse, Gordon Brown, played the same game: the social justice encyclicals were deposited with the faithful, never read out loud from the pulpit in places that needed to hear them, such as the City or the CBI.

Those eighteen years in exile and the struggle up the cliff face back to power had moulded the Labour leadership. In the second term things had moved on, the old Tory enemy was moribund, times had changed. The need now was for a galvanising, rallying progressive message that would make sense of what Labour was actually doing – taxing and spending, redistributing, investing in the NHS, schools and children as never before. Why did so few ever hear it?

It was partly because ideological boundaries were shifting. If residents in the worst estates told MPs local youths were making their life hell, Labour would impose strict discipline, with no liberal qualms about boys who were certainly victims as well as perpetrators. Right. To grow the universities, they

would make students who were the future well-heeled contribute more from their future earnings. Left – though not
accepted as such. Blair's doppelgänger Alan Milburn would
apparently let the private sector provide all health services,
leaving the NHS as a commissioner. But then the wiser
Health Secretary John Reid said an appropriate public–
private ratio in health provision would be just 15 per cent.
Where was the red line to be drawn?

But wasn't it the leader's job to paint some persuasive
picture, putting the prime elements in their place? Was there
no progressive vision in which Blair felt at home? If not, he
should have followed his original instinct to break once and
for all with tribal politics. Once, he had seen proportional
representation as the way to ensure pluralist, coalition government that would better capture the shifting sentiments of
twenty-first-century Britain. PR would have been a permanent bulwark against a return either of Thatcherism or the
left-wing mania New Labour had put down. But, it seemed,
winning parties rarely feel the need to share power voluntarily. In their state of hubris, it risked being too late by the time
Labour would see the need for it.

However, this over-cautious Prime Minister paraded
super-convictions on global affairs. His clarity of vision
seemed to grow with geographic distance from complicating
detail. Blair had been derided in the first term as plastic,
bending before every breeze; now he was denounced as
inflexible, too much the man of principle. Far from lacking
conviction, Roy Jenkins observed with knowing dryness that
Blair was 'a little too Manichean for my perhaps now jaded
taste, seeing matters in stark terms of good and evil, black
and white'.

Iraq put paid to Blair's hope that the UK in Europe would
be his passport to the pantheon. In retrospect he had missed
his European chance in the first flush of 1997's victory; every

year that passed the Channel grew wider. Here was the UK's most pro-European government since Edward Heath allowing Britain to drift into the geopolitical shallows. The polls showed British people to be more antagonistic to the European Union than ever. The United Kingdom Independence Party won its victories by stealing votes from the Tories, but its very presence tilted the balance of opinion. Without leadership, even the most passionate Europhiles despaired of winning public support, silently putting away their campaign plans in a bottom drawer.

One reason for Blair's European caution was well founded. The warped nature of the British press (unique in Europe in its configuration) is, together with a strong, remarkably unselfreflective journalistic culture, too often relegated to a footnote when political and public affairs are discussed. British journalism is wearily regarded as if it were a force of nature rather than a perverted product of patterns of ownership and a remediable absence of professional training and pride. Some 75 per cent of the circulation of the daily national newspaper press was owned by maverick right-wingers, all passionate Europe-haters, all inclined to see off any Labour government. Look what Blair had to contend with, and what any future Labour prime minister will always have to face.

British journalists are notoriously easy to bore and, tedious in their tedium, become – Spiro Agnew's old phrase – nattering nabobs of negativism. Long before Iraq a deep cynicism had set in with a disproportionate contempt for Labour. Why did no one believe the facts or the improvements in front of their noses? The press in the second term became considerably more hostile. Good news rarely penetrated, bad news was often manufactured. Time and again we were struck in writing this book at how little people have the chance to know about what goes on, how narrow is the news agenda, how few the topics that stir the reporters hunkered down in the Palace of Westminster. How did the Countryside Alliance come to such prominence, when so few people actually lived in the country and most of those actually favoured a ban on hunting? Strange fevers blew up fanned by press campaigns, such as the effort to remove the speed cameras that had been proven to save the lives of motorists and pedestrians alike.

Perception and reality – the government struggled hard to marry the two. What it lacked was sociological insight. Blair's own Strategy Unit had started exploring what made people happiest. It wasn't income – GDP and average per capita money in the pocket had doubled over the last three decades and yet no one had become a jot happier. Research showed that it is how people feel about where they stand in a pecking order that affects their happiness. In other words, it was inequality that made people unhappy. Surveys showed that the only countries that got happier as they got richer were the ones that distributed the extra income more fairly. Education is a determinant of happiness: a degree would bring far more life satisfaction than the financial rewards the government promised in the tuition fees debate, so Labour should have sold top-up fees because 'a degree makes you happier'. Joining groups, participating, volunteering and going to the theatre all scored high on the happiness scale. Trust in others came with all these things.

Research by MORI concluded that government should seek to dampen down the pressure of consumerism and work. Perhaps targets for public services had the perverse effect of raising expectations that would always tend to expand beyond what could be delivered and help create a state of continual dissatisfaction. Some Labour strategists looked to Canada where all public services were given just one target – to raise public *satisfaction* by 10 per cent. And they did, by focusing on what people appreciate most – politeness, promptness, never being passed from one official to another. Waiting times for hospital appointments mattered less than being treated fast and well once they got there.

Shifting public service targets to 'satisfaction' would be relatively easy. The hard task would be changing beliefs about money. Evidence piles up that as Britain gets richer it gets no better at realising Jeremy Bentham's injunction to seek the greatest happiness for the greatest number. Gross inequality of income is doubly dysfunctional: it gives only a little extra pleasure to the richest while creating deep dismay for the majority. It channels too much money into private hands and not enough into state coffers that deliver the things that really satisfy, such as universal high-quality education from the cradle or safe and beautiful neighbourhoods. Economists say happiness depends on long hours, high productivity and high growth. Not so, said David Halpern of the Strategy Unit, it is the other way round: 'Satisfied nations are the most successful. This is about high human capital economics.' The happiest countries – the Nordics and Canada – combine wealth, growth, shorter hours, higher taxes and greater contentment.

Such ideas take time to drip into the body politic. Labour was a hotbed of think-tanks but such visionary thoughts never permeated the government, whose economic treadmill was still powered by a large, underpaid workforce – imported or state subsidised as necessary – working harder and for less than elsewhere in the EU.

## Our Verdict

By 2005 Britain was a richer and fairer society than in 1997. It was healthier, safer and in many respects better governed. It could not be said to be any greener as long as carbon emissions continued at their world-destroying rate. If Britain was not exactly wiser, it was better educated.

Many fewer people – children and pensioners especially – lived in dire hardship. Most people felt the warm glow of growing income and wealth. Cranes on every city horizon attested to growth, both public and private. Crime kept falling, schools and hospitals improving, work was plentiful. Many comparisons with European neighbours were positive and pleasing (for the first time in many cases). A social revolution was in progress as the new generation of children's centres started to reshape opportunity and offer a chance to escape social class destiny. Blair's era was a better time to be British than for many decades.

If Labour was unloved, it was partly its own fault for joining George Bush's war and failing to offer an inspiring progressive legend. The second term started with a weak manifesto, but it delivered more than it promised. But would Labour, if elected again, look back on a dozen or so years in power with regret? Its ambitions had been too low, its achievements unknit into some compelling or convincing story of a country on a journey towards somewhere. We can only restate our conclusion on Labour's first term: good, but not good enough, with still time on the clock to do better in a third term.

# Labour's Legislation 2001–05

## 2001 (after June)

*Special Educational Needs and Disability Act 2001*
New duties on schools under the Disability Rights Commission

*Human Reproductive Cloning Act 2001*
Bans human reproductive cloning; criminal offence to place in the womb of a woman a human embryo that has been created other than by fertilisation

*Anti-Terrorism, Crime and Security Act 2001*
Post-9/11 police powers: arrest and detention and 'streamlining immigration procedures'

## 2002

*International Development Act 2002*
Disaster and development aid – requires spending be used to reduce poverty and improve the welfare of the poor

*Sex Discrimination (Election Candidates) Act 2002*
Permits party selection based on a single gender, such as all-women shortlists for Labour

*European Communities (Amendment) Act 2002*
Ratifies the Treaty of Nice, signed February 2001

*Travel Concessions (Eligibility) Act 2002*
Equalises age at which men and women become entitled to travel concessions

*Homelessness Act 2002*
Councils to adopt homelessness strategies and do more for those homeless through no fault of their own

*British Overseas Territories Act 2002*
Full British citizenship to 200,000 inhabitants of fourteen British Overseas Territories

*Land Registration Act 2002*
Conveyancing can be done electronically

*Office of Communications Act 2002*
Establishes new regulatory body, Office of Communications Ofcom

*Commonhold and Leasehold Reform Act 2002*
Easier to convert long-term residential leasehold into free-hold through 'commonhold' tenures

*State Pension Credit Act 2002*
Guarantees minimum income for people aged over sixty on low incomes

*National Health Service Reform and Health Care Professions Act 2002*
Shifts the balance of power within the NHS – securing delivery and involving patients and the public in health care

*National Insurance Contributions Act 2002*
Brown's budget plan to use extra National Insurance contributions for NHS spending

*Industrial and Provident Societies Act 2002*
Gives more flexibility to non-profit companies

*Tax Credits Act 2002*
Brown's two new credits – the Child Tax Credit for families with children and the Working Tax Credit for working households facing low income

*Employment Act 2002*
Extends rights to paternity, maternity and adoption leave and pay

*Copyright and Trade Marks (Offences and Enforcement) Act 2002*
Rationalises law on intellectual property and unauthorised copying

*Export Control Act 2002*
New controls on arms and technology exports, especially 'dual-use' items with civil and potential military application

*Proceeds of Crime Act 2002*
Creates Assets Recovery Agency for confiscating proceeds of crime

*Police Reform Act 2002*
Establishes community support officers and reorganised national intelligence gathering

*Mobile Telephones (Re-Programming) Act 2002*
To stop tampering with mobile phones' identification numbers

*Education Act 2002*
Reforms school governors' performance, teachers' pay, role of councils, etc

*Tobacco Advertising and Promotion Act 2002*
Further restrictions on tobacco adverts, but not immediately

*Private Hire Vehicles (Carriage of Guide Dogs) Act 2002*
Bans charges for guide dogs in mini cabs

*Adoption and Children Act 2002*
Enables unmarried couples to apply to adopt and speeds up adoption procedures

*Commonwealth Act 2002*
Admits Cameroon and Mozambique to the Commonwealth

*Enterprise Act 2002*
Reform of bankruptcy, sets up stronger Office of Fair Trading, plus measures to protect consumers

*Nationality, Immigration and Asylum Act 2002*
New citizenship ceremonies and test of knowledge; accommodation centres for asylum seekers; immigration appeals, work permits

*Animal Health Act 2002*
New measures to clear up Foot and Mouth Disease and transmissible spongiform encephalopathies (TSEs) in sheep

## 2003

*Northern Ireland Assembly Elections Act 2003*
Postpones assembly elections in the (vain) hope of finding a way forward between the parties

*Community Care (Delayed Discharges) Act 2003*
Allows NHS to recoup costs from councils if discharge from hospital delayed by lack of 'community care'. A largely abortive attempt to get Peter to pay Paul

*Police (Northern Ireland) Act 2003*
Further enactment of the Patten report of September 1999, 'normalising' police administration in the province and protecting whistle-blowers

*European Parliament (Representation) Act 2003*
Adjusts representation after enlargement of European Union and bundles Gibraltar voters in with the South West of England

*National Minimum Wage (Enforcement Notices) Act 2003*
Tightens enforcement

*Electricity (Miscellaneous Provisions) Act 2003*
After bankruptcy of British Energy the privatised nuclear generator transfers clean-up costs to the state

*Regional Assemblies' (Preparations) Act 2003*
Voters who choose assemblies will also have to choose ways
of simplifying county and district councils

*Northern Ireland Assembly (Elections and Periods of Suspension) Act 2003*
Further postponement of elections to the assembly

*Co-operatives and Community Benefit Societies Act 2003*
Tidies up the law on public benefit companies

*Marine Safety Act 2003*
Improves safety and pollution controls

*Licensing Act 2003*
Changes rules allowing more flexibility on late-night opening
but also restates one of the purposes of licensing as control of
anti-social behaviour

*Railways and Transport Safety Act 2003*
Transfers safety from Health and Safety Executive to new
Rail Accident Investigation Branch in response to recommendations by Lord Cullen in September 2001, following the
Ladbroke Grove crash. Also applies drink-driving tests to
flight and ships' crews; new transport police authority

*Communications Act 2003*
Changes regulatory regime for telecoms and sets up a public
interest test for media mergers including accurate presentation of news and sufficient plurality of views

*Fireworks Act 2003*
New regulations for supply and use of fireworks

*National Lottery (Funding of Endowments) Act 2003*
Lottery money can be put into funds

*Human Fertilisation and Embryology (Deceased Fathers) Act 2003*
Allows a man to be registered as the father of a child

conceived after his death using his sperm or using an embryo created with his sperm before his death

*Northern Ireland (Monitoring Commission) Act 2003*
Cuts the pay of assembly members while it is in abeyance and backs the independent commission looking – unsuccessfully – for signs of an end to paramilitarism

*Local Government Act 2003*
Changes date of 2004 elections and allows councils to borrow more easily if they are 'prudent'

*Dealing in Cultural Objects (Offences) Act 2003*
Toughens controls on import and export of material illegally removed from archaeological sites or buildings anywhere in the world

*Legal Deposit Libraries Act 2003*
Extends to non-print materials requirement to deposit new publications at British Library and other national collections

*Household Waste Recycling Act 2003*
Encourages recycling

*Sustainable Energy Act 2003*
Promotes 'low carbon' economy in line with 2003 energy white paper

*Female Genital Mutilation Act 2003*
Extends the offence of procuring or assisting in mutilation to acts carried out by UK nationals or residents abroad

*Waste and Emissions Trading Act 2003*
Cuts waste sent to landfill and sets up a new regime for trading emissions quotas

*Arms Control and Disarmament (Inspections) Act 2003*
Updates 1990 agreement on conventional armed forces in Europe

*European Union (Accessions) Act 2003*
Makes the accession treaty part of UK law and gives nationals of the candidate countries the same rights to work in the UK from 1 May 2004 as nationals of the states in the European Economic Area

*Fire Services Act 2003*
Picks up on ending of fire dispute to allow the government to fix conditions for fire brigades

*Water Act 2003*
Promotes water conservation and changes competition rules in the industry

*Anti-Social Behaviour Act 2003*
Increases police and council powers to deal with crack dens, air and imitation guns, illegal raves and unauthorised encampments. Social landlords get powers to discipline unruly tenants

*Courts Act 2003*
Changes criminal procedure, the management structure for magistrates' courts and establishes a new courts' inspectorate

*Ragwort Control Act 2003*
Extends the Weeds Act 1959 to ragwort (but not in Scotland)

*Extradition Act 2003*
Makes it easier to extradite

*Sexual Offences Act 2003*
Targets paedophiles

*Health and Social Care (Community Health and Standards) Act 2003*
Establishes foundation hospitals with their own regulator

*Criminal Justice Act 2003*
Cuts the number of cases going from magistrates' to crown courts, toughens bail conditions and sentences and tries to speed up proceedings

## 2004

*European Parliamentary and Local Elections (Pilots) Act 2004*
All-postal voting in certain regions at the 2004 European Parliamentary and combined local elections

*National Insurance Contributions and Statutory Payments Act 2004*
Extends NI to certain unearned income and tightens up administration

*Justice (Northern Ireland) Act 2004*
Sets up a judicial appointments body to secure judges 'as reflective of Northern Ireland society as can be'

*Planning and Compulsory Purchase Act 2004*
Speeds up planning, including big infrastructure projects

*Child Trust Funds Act 2004*
All children born after September 2002 to get an endowment – baby bond – worth £250 plus £250 for children from poor homes to be invested in long-term accounts cashable at age eighteen

*Gender Recognition Act 2004*
A new quango will certify applicants wanting to change gender so that, for the first time, for example a male to female transsexual will be legally recognised as a woman

*Higher Education Act 2004*
Permits top-up fees, sets up a new Humanities Research Council and new student complaints system

*Age-Related Payments Act 2004*
Extra payments to pensioners aged seventy-plus

*Gangmasters (Licensing) Act 2004*
New regulation of workers in agriculture and fishing through a Gangmasters Licensing Authority

*Scottish Parliament (Constituencies) Act 2004*
Decouples Scottish Parliament constituencies from Westminster's boundaries, allowing the number of House of Commons seats in Scotland to be cut

*Carers (Equal Opportunities) Act 2004*
Councils to help and assess carers

*Patents Act 2004*
Brings UK patents in line with European conventions and tightens enforcement of patents

*Health Protection Agency Act 2004*
To tackle infectious diseases along with other hazards, including the UK's response to chemical, biological, radiological and nuclear terrorism

*Traffic Management Act 2004*
Updates enforcement of traffic regulations

*Asylum and Immigration (Treatment of Claimants) Act 2004*
Tougher line on immigration and asylum appeals, marriages of convenience, asylum seekers' housing and benefits. Third asylum act since Labour took office in 1997

*Energy Act 2004*
Establishes nuclear decommissioning authority, restructures British Nuclear Fuels, changes electricity and gas marketing

*Fire and Rescue Services Act 2004*
Further roll out of reforms, moving to more preventative approach by fire services

*Sustainable and Secure Buildings Act 2004*
Insists on use of greener building materials and new rules on demolition

*Employment Relations Act 2004*
Extends statutory recognition of unions and strengthens the law forbidding intimidation of union members

*Constitutional Reform Act 2004*
Abolishes office of Lord Chancellor, creates supreme court

*Domestic Violence, Crime and Victims Act 2004*
Tightens restraints on perpetrators, makes common assault an arrestable offence

*Civil Contingencies Act 2004*
Updates emergency legislation, councils and other bodies to cooperate and plan

*Civil Partnership Act 2004*
Gives legal recognition to same-sex couples; a new status similar to marriage for property, finance, tenancy, pensions etc

*Children Act 2004*
Creates a children's commissioner for England; better cooperation between councils and health bodies; restricts smacking

*Hunting Act 2004*
Bans hunting wild mammals with dogs

*Planning and Compulsory Purchase Act 2004*
Establishes new regional spatial strategy

*Human Tissue Act 2004*
Establishes tissue authority

*Horserace Betting and Olympic Lottery Act 2004*
Sells Tote

# Index